Assimilation

AMERICAN CROSSROADS

Edited by Earl Lewis, George Lipsitz, George Sánchez,
Dana Takagi, Laura Briggs, and Nikhil Pal Singh

Assimilation

An Alternative History

Catherine S. Ramírez

UNIVERSITY OF CALIFORNIA PRESS

University of California Press
Oakland, California

Library of Congress Cataloging-in-Publication Data

Names: Ramírez, Catherine Sue, 1969– author.
Title: Assimilation : an alternative history / Catherine S. Ramirez.
Other titles: American crossroads ; 58.
Description: Oakland, California : University of California Press, [2020] | Series: American crossroads; 58 | Includes bibliographical references and index.
Identifiers: LCCN 2020014494 (print) | LCCN 2020014495 (ebook) | ISBN 9780520300699 (cloth) | ISBN 9780520300712 (paperback) | ISBN 9780520971967 (epub)
Subjects: LCSH: Assimilation (Sociology)—United States--History. | Immigrants—Race identity—United States—History.
Classification: LCC JV6342 .R36 2020 (print) | LCC JV6342 (ebook) | DDC 305.800973—dc23
LC record available at https://lccn.loc.gov/2020014494
LC ebook record available at https://lccn.loc.gov/2020014495

29 28 27 26 25 24 23 22 21 20
10 9 8 7 6 5 4 3 2 1

For Eric, Carmen, and Omar

CONTENTS

Epilogue: Notes from the Interregnum

ILLUSTRATIONS

ACKNOWLEDGMENTS

This book is a product of the unique, interdisciplinary spaces I have been fortunate to inhabit—in particular, the Ethnic Studies Department at UC Berkeley, my alma mater, and the Latin American and Latino Studies (LALS) Department at UC Santa Cruz, my current institution. I landed in LALS after my first department at UC Santa Cruz, American Studies, folded. I thank my colleagues in LALS—in particular, Lorato Anderson, Gabi Arredondo, Lily Ballofet, Jeff Erbig, Sylvanna Falcón, Adrián Félix, Johnny Fox, Rosa-Linda Fregoso, Shannon Gleeson, Fernando Leiva, Christina Navarro, Ursula Oberg, Justin Pérez, Patricia Pinho, Cecilia Rivas, Marianna Santana, Jessica Taft, and Pat Zavella. Many have read and responded to my work. All allowed me to become the scholar I am today by welcoming me and giving me the opportunity to focus on my research and writing. George and Megan Bunch, Vilashini Cooppan, Nathaniel Deutsch, Peggy Estrada, Carla Freccero, Jennifer González, Debbie Gould, Herman Gray, Jody Greene, Miriam Greenberg, Kirsten Silva Gruesz, Dan and Adriana Guevara, Amy Keys, L. S. Kim, Kim Lau, Amy Lonetree, Annette Marines, Steve McKay, Teresa Mora, Judit Moschkovich, Dard Neuman, Marcia Ochoa, Matt O'Hara, Laurie Palmer, Micah Perks, Juan Poblete, Irena Polic, Craig Reinarman, Seema Rizvi, Warren Sack,

Helen Shapiro, Shelley Stamp, Dana Takagi, Veronica Terriquez, Lew Watts, and Alice Yang provided me with sound guidance and sustaining pep talks, often over good food and drink. UC Santa Cruz's former executive vice chancellor, Marlene Tromp, brought Stacy Kamehiro, Felicity Amaya Schaeffer, Megan Thomas, and me together via the EVC Fellows Academy. I am grateful to EVC Tromp for establishing the EVC Fellows Academy and to Stacy, Felicity, and Megan for their careful readings of my work and companionship. Hunter Bivens, former director of UC Santa Cruz's Center for Cultural Studies, gave me the opportunity to share an early draft of chapter 2 at a colloquium in 2015. Jackie Powell provided vital staff support when I directed UC Santa Cruz's Chicano Latino Research Center (now the Research Center for the Americas), while Candy Martinez assisted with research. Other students—namely, Ruben Espinoza, Cesar Estrella, Alina Fernandez, Vicente Lovelace, Mauricio Ramírez, Gaby Segura, Alma Villa, Jimi Valiente-Neighbours, and Aimee Villarreal—helped motivate me with their own scholarly undertakings. Katharyne Mitchell, dean of the Social Sciences Division at UC Santa Cruz, and her predecessor, Dean Emeritus Sheldon Kamieniecki, were steadfast in their support.

Having spent several years developing this book project, I encountered new interlocutors and was delighted to find I could still count on old ones. Jesse Alemán, Alicia Schmidt Camacho, Sylvia Chan-Malik, Nick De Genova, David Eng, Jill Gurvey, David Manuel Hernández, Robert Irwin, Sara Johnson, Josh Kun, Laz Lima, Anthony Macías, Rhacel Parreñas, Birgit Rasmussen, Melina Vizcaíno-Alemán and Matt Wray helped move this project along with their smart questions, helpful suggestions, and friendship. Alicia Laz, Frederick Aldama, José Aranda, Veronica Acevedo Avila, Mati Córdoba Azcarate, Lindsey Berfond, Wilson Chen, Elizabeth Chin, Sean Donahue, Rhonda M. Gonzales, Carmen Flys Junquera, Marián Martínez Martínez, Steve Pitti, and Rachel Valinsky gave me the opportunity to share work in progress at their institutions. "Illegality Regimes," a conference in 2013 organized by Juan Amaya Castro and Bas Schotel at Vrije Universiteit

Amsterdam, and "Studying Race Relationally," a workshop organized by Ramón Gutiérrez and Natalia Molina at the University of Chicago in 2016, were especially generative. I am grateful to Ramón and Natalia in particular for providing me with the feedback and encouragement I needed to get this project off the ground.

This book would not exist without the resolute support of Niels Hooper, my editor at UC Press. I am grateful for the constructive reports he coaxed from the anonymous readers. Special thanks go to Rachel Ida Buff, George Lipstiz, and Rebecca Schreiber for their astute observations and to Ramón, Natalia, and Michael Omi for endorsing my book. Robin Manley and Jon Dertien helped turn this book into a tangible reality.

I thank Jörg Brüggemann, Alberto Ledesma, and Julio Salgado for permitting me to reproduce their works of art in my book. Dario Canul and Cosijoesa Cernas of Tlacolulokos approved the use of the photos I took of their murals at the Los Angeles Public Library. I am grateful to all of these artists for their vision and inspiration. I owe a debt of gratitude to Alberto for coming to Santa Cruz to speak to my students in my Immigrant Storytelling seminar in the spring of 2019. His generosity, wit, and talent continue to hearten me.

Support from the University of California Institute for Mexico and the United States and UC Santa Cruz's Committee on Research allowed me to conduct essential research for this book.

I finished writing *Assimilation* as a fellow at the Center for Advanced Study in the Behavioral Sciences (CASBS) at Stanford University over 2019–20. I am grateful to the CASBS leadership and staff for welcoming me and providing me with the logistical support and intellectual community that I needed to expand this project and bring it to completion. I learned from and enjoyed the company of the other members of my cohort—in particular, Rene Almeling, Brian Arthur, Nina Bandlej, Giulia Baroni, Kathleen Belew, Mario Biagioli, Marco Casari, David Ciepley, Anita Hardon, Mai Hassan, Paula Moya, Noah Nathan, Camilo Pérez-Bustillo, Bruno Perreau, Laura Richman, Ramón Saldívar, Ellie

Shermer, Mark Warren, and Su-Ling Yeh. Carole Hessler provided me with a peaceful home to return to after a long, productive day at work. COVID-19 separated us sooner and more abruptly than any of us ever expected, so I cherish the relationships that I forged at and because of CASBS that much more.

I thank my family for putting up with me as I wrote this book and for reminding me that there is life beyond it. Between trips to archives, writing retreats, and presentations, I lost my Aunts Mawe, Mary, and Arlene and my father-in-law, Scip. I have no doubt they would have taken great pride in seeing me wrap this project up.

Finally, I thank Eric Porter, my friend, colleague, and partner in life. For the past twenty-five years he has listened to my half-baked ideas, read many an inchoate draft, and witnessed more than a couple meltdowns. I am grateful for his patience, insight, candor, company, and generous support. He and our curious, compassionate, and increasingly conscious children motivate, distract, anchor, and buoy me.

CHAPTER ONE

The Paradox of Assimilation

There is a limit to our powers of assimilation, and when
it is exceeded, the country suffers from something like
indigestion.

   —*New York Times*, May 15, 1880[1]

My culture is a very dominant culture, and it's imposing and
causing problems. If you don't do something about it, you're
going to have taco trucks on every corner.

   —Marco Gutierrez, founder of Latinos for Trump,
   September 1, 2016[2]

ASSIMILATION'S PREHISTORY

Dr. Pierce's Golden Medical Discovery and Pleasant Pellets were pat-
ent medicines manufactured in the late nineteenth and early twentieth
centuries at the World's Dispensary Medical Association in Buffalo,
New York. Made with queen's root, bloodroot, mandrake root, and
other ostensibly mystical ingredients, they were advertised as elixirs
of "simple herbs" that could improve "nutritional assimilation," thereby
remedying loss of appetite, fatigue, nervousness, and other maladies.[3]
In a newspaper advertisement for these products from 1898, a Native
American man wearing a loincloth and a long, feathered headdress is
depicted hurling a tomahawk into the air (see figure 1). "Before he was
debauched by modern civilization," the ad proclaims, "the American

In J. Fenimore Cooper's Leather Stocking Tales, we read stories of the wonderful agility, physical endurance and the unerring accuracy of the eye of the American Indian when he reigned supreme over this continent. Before he was debauched by modern civilization, he was a magnificent specimen of physical manhood. He lived entirely in the open air, and knew no medicine, save the simple herbs gathered by his squaws.

Civilized man leads an unnatural and an unhealthy life. Unlike the Indian if he would maintain his physical and mental health, he must take reasonable precautions to combat disease. Nearly all diseases have their inception in disorders of the digestion, torpidity of the liver and impurity of the blood. Dr. Pierce's Golden Medical Discovery is made of simple herbs. It restores the lost appetite, makes digestion and assimilation perfect, invigorates the liver, purifies the blood and promotes the natural processes of excretion and secretion. It sends the rich, red, life-giving blood bounding through the arteries and corrects all circulatory disturbances. It dispels all headaches, nervousness, drowsiness, lassitude, and drives out all impurities and disease germs. It cures 98 per cent. of all cases of consumption, bronchitis, asthma and diseases of the air-passages. It gives sound and refreshing sleep, drives away all bodily and mental fatigue and imparts vigor and health to every organ of the body. Medicine dealers sell it, and have nothing else, "just as good."

"A few of my symptoms," writes Charles Book, of Climax, Kalamazoo Co., Mich., "were heart-burn, fullness after eating, pain in my bowels, bad taste in my mouth, and occasional fever and hot flushes. Dr. Pierce's Golden Medical Discovery cured all these and I am perfectly well."

Dr. Pierce's Pleasant Pellets are sure, speedy and permanent cure for constipation. One little "Pellet" is a gentle laxative and two a mild cathartic. They never gripe. Found at all medicine stores.

Figure 1. Advertisement for Dr. Pierce's Golden Medical Discovery and Pleasant Pellets. *The Rural New-Yorker,* November 5, 1898. Used with permission from American Agriculturalist. Copyright Informa.

Indian ... was a magnificent specimen of physical manhood. He lived entirely in the open air, and knew no medicine, save the simple herbs gathered by his squaws."[4] A "real" Indian, Dr. Pierce's American Indian is unspoiled and unassimilated.[5]

The ad for Dr. Pierce's Golden Medical Discovery and Pleasant Pellets sheds light on assimilation's multiple meanings. It also presages the ongoing contest over this term's significance. In addition to referring to a process of becoming more alike, *assimilation,* in its most general sense, refers to a process of absorbing. For example, as early as the seventeenth century it could mean digestion, the "absorption of nutriment into the system."[6] However, over time assimilation took on new, politically charged meaning in the United States as social groups moved through space and came into contact with one another—for instance, as the nation-cum-empire stretched across and beyond the

North American continent; as the US government and its agents broke up tribal lands and removed Native Americans from their homes and communities; as African Americans relocated from the rural South to the urban North; and as immigrants from all parts of the globe arrived at the nation's ports of entry.

By the start of the twentieth century, assimilation referred not only to a biological or physiological process but also to a social and cultural one. In 1894 economist Richmond Mayo-Smith defined assimilation as the "mixture of nationalities" that resulted from immigration to the United States.[7] Signaling that the concept had indeed moved beyond the natural and biological sciences, sociologist Sarah E. Simons observed in 1901 that "[w]riters on historical and social science" were "just beginning to turn their attention to the large subject of assimilation."[8] "[I]n the future treatises on assimilation will form vast libraries," she predicted.[9] Thirteen years later, Robert Ezra Park, considered by many scholars to be "one of the giants of early American sociology,"[10] connected assimilation's old and new meanings.[10] "By a process of nutrition, somewhat similar to the physiological one," he wrote, "we may conceive alien peoples to be incorporated with, and made part of the community or state."[11]

As these early social scientific definitions underscore, assimilation has been associated with immigration in the United States since the late nineteenth century. Yet the ad for Dr. Pierce's products offers a glimpse of what I call assimilation's prehistory, of some of the term's meanings before it was connected to immigrants and immigration. In addition to referring to a physiological and biological process, assimilation was used synonymously with "civilization" through the early twentieth century. As the opposite of savagery and barbarism, as an "achieved social order or way of life," and as a "modern social process" whose "effects [are] reckoned as good, bad or mixed," civilization is a conceptual precursor of assimilation as social and cultural process.[12]

Along with African Americans, Native Americans once played a salient role in conversations about assimilation. Examining the connection between civilization and assimilation brings that role into relief. In the Civilization Fund Act of 1819, the US Congress charged "capable persons of good moral character" with imparting "the habits and arts of civilization" to Native Americans.[13] Sixty years later, on the cusp of what is known in federal Indian history as the allotment and assimilation era (1887–1943), Richard Henry Pratt set out to civilize and, as he put it, to "citizenize" indigenous youth when he founded the Carlisle Indian Industrial School, the first federally funded, coeducational, off-reservation boarding school in the United States.[14] As I discuss in chapter 2, Carlisle was one in a long line of colonial educational institutions that sought to "civilize" nonwhite peoples in and beyond the continental United States by subordinating them. Pratt modeled Carlisle after the Hampton Normal and Agricultural Institute, a school for African Americans and one of the first historically black colleges and universities. He upheld the deracination of African slaves and their US-born descendants as a model for civilizing Native Americans. In other words, he believed that Native Americans could be assimilated if they, too, were plucked from their homes and forced to live with white Americans. He described the process of civilizing so-called backward races as "assimilation under duress."[15]

While "backward" races were seen as in need of civilizing, they were formally excluded from the polity. That is, they could be civilized, but they could not be citizens, at least not until 1868, when the Fourteenth Amendment granted US citizenship to "[a]ll persons born or naturalized in the United States, and subject to the jurisdiction thereof."[16] The first statute to codify naturalization law in the United States, the Naturalization Act of 1790, restricted US citizenship to free white persons. The Fourteenth Amendment transformed African Americans into US citizens, at least in name, but it did not apply to Native Americans. In 1924 the Indian Citizenship Act (also known as the Snyder Act) extended US citizenship to them.

Yet before the Snyder Act was passed, Native Americans had to prove that they were worthy of US citizenship. For instance, the Dawes Act of 1887 and the Burke Act of 1906 held out the promise of US citizenship to Native Americans, but only after a probationary period of twenty-five years. During that probation, Native Americans who aspired to be US citizens had to live "separate and apart from any tribe of Indians."[17] What is more, they had to demonstrate that they had "adopted the habits of civilized life" and were "competent and capable of managing [their] affairs."[18] In short, assimilation was a transactional trial. As Pratt's motto, "Kill the Indian . . . and save the man," stressed, the price for civilization and citizenship was the Indian's very Indianness.[19]

ASSIMILATION THEORY: ETHNICITY AND RACE

As the meanings of civilization and assimilation diverged over the course of the twentieth century, assimilation came to be associated more with people recognized as immigrants and less with Native Americans and African Americans. Assimilation and immigration were conjoined via such concepts as *Americanization*, the metamorphosis from non-American to American; *Anglo-conformity*, the dissolution of the immigrant or minority group's culture by an Anglo-Protestant mainstream; *acculturation*, adaptation to a different culture, often the dominant one; *incorporation*, the union of two or more things into one body (and sometimes, a synonym for naturalization); and *integration*, the inclusion of different cultures or groups in society, often or presumably as equals (and the opposite of segregation). Like civilization, some of these terms—in particular, Americanization and Anglo-conformity—connote the imposition and presumed superiority of one way of life, the American and Anglo-American, over another.

Theories and models of assimilation say just as much about how society and the nation are perceived—however idealized—as they do about the putative processes by which people are absorbed into or adapt to that society and nation. For example, assimilation as Anglo-conformity assumes that the majority of Americans are "chiefly of Anglo-Saxon extraction," "Caucasian racial stock," and "the Protestant faith." Assimilation into the white Anglo-Protestant "dominant culture group" is unidirectional.[20] This framework tends to be associated with "[e]arly assimilation scholars."[21] It is widely perceived to have been abandoned "[w]hen the notion of an Anglo-American core collapsed amid the turmoil of the 1960s" and to have been eclipsed by multiculturalism, a late twentieth-century offshoot of cultural pluralism.[22] However, political scientist Samuel P. Huntington resurrected Anglo-conformity in 2004 when he warned that immigration from Latin America threatened to destroy the "core Anglo-Protestant culture" of the United States.[23]

Unlike Anglo-conformity, cultural pluralism valorizes cultural diversity, albeit of a limited sort. When philosopher Horace M. Kallen conceived of cultural pluralism in the early twentieth century, he sought to show the compatibility of "continental" (southern, central, and eastern European) immigrants with American democracy.[24] As a child, he emigrated with his family in 1887 from what is now Poland as part of the Great Wave: the arrival of some twenty million immigrants to the United States between 1880 and 1924.[25] During this period, immigrants hailing from southern, central, and eastern Europe were called "new" immigrants. As I discuss in chapter 3, some self-proclaimed "old stock" (Protestant, of northwestern European descent) Americans looked down on the "new" immigrants, doubted their ability to assimilate, and effectively blocked any more from immigrating via restrictive legislation, such as the Immigration and Nationality Act of 1924 (also known as the Johnson-Reed Act). Against a backdrop of growing xenophobia and anti-Semitism, cultural pluralism challenged biological racism and "the grey conformism of the melting-pot."[26] All the while, it upheld "American civilization" as "the perfection of the cooperative harmonies of 'European civilization.'"[27]

Its Eurocentrism notwithstanding, cultural pluralism posits that the United States is a "diverse and dynamic" host society and receiving country.[28] The United States not only shapes immigrants; it is also shaped by them. Cultural pluralism informs assimilation theory in sociology, the academic discipline that has contributed the most to theorizations of assimilation, in at least two ways. First, cultural pluralism helped lay the groundwork for the ethnicity paradigm, "the mainstream of the modern sociology of race," according to sociologists Michael Omi and Howard Winant.[29] Second, cultural pluralism is the foundation of "the pluralist perspective" on ethnicity.[30]

In theorizing assimilation, scholars have distinguished ethnicity from race. There are many definitions of ethnicity; among them are a basic group identity; real or fictive common ancestry; a means of mobilizing a certain population as an interest group; "a process of construction or invention which incorporates, adapts, and amplifies preexisting communal solidarities, cultural attributes, and historical memories"; and "a social boundary . . . embedded in a variety of social and cultural differences between groups."[31] Since the second half of the twentieth century, definitions of ethnicity have emphasized the social and cultural.

Race, meanwhile, is understood as "a concept that signifies and symbolizes social conflicts and interests referring to different types of bodies."[32] Put another way, race is a construct that merges the social and somatic. That said, things that do not necessarily have a clear or direct link to the physical or visual—for example, names, words, languages, and accents—may nonetheless come to be associated with race. The process whereby racial categories are produced and understood as part of a social hierarchy is known as racialization.

Where the assimilationist perspective maintains that ethnic differences dissolve in the melting pot that is the United States, the pluralist perspective holds that ethnicity endures, even if only in symbolic form (e.g., holidays).[33] In the assimilationist model, immigrants disappear into an Anglo-Protestant core. In the pluralist one, they find their place in a society of hyphenated Americans. Differences notwithstanding, both perspectives assume "a unilinear process"—however smooth or bumpy—"of integration into the host society."[34] Whether that society is homogenous or heterogeneous, assimilation occurs. Those who do not assimilate are merely slow to do so, or they are anomalies, failures, or outsiders.

Scholars at the University of Chicago, chief among them Park, are widely credited with developing assimilation theory during the first half of the twentieth century. According to some early iterations of that theory (sometimes called the classical model of assimilation or assimilationism), assimilation is a linear and inexorable process.[35] Immigrants arrive and never look back. They change their names, learn English, acquire capital, and participate in mainstream institutions and culture. Within a couple of generations, their descendants blend in. For Park, assimilation was "a function of visibility."[36] He observed that by the second generation, erstwhile white ethnics, like Polish-, Lithuanian-, and Norwegian-Americans, could not be distinguished from "the older American stock." *Racial* minorities—namely Asians and blacks—continued to stand out. Irrespective of how long before their forebears had landed in the United States (or the United States had gone to their forebears), a "distinctive racial mark" prevented those groups from disappearing into the mainstream.[37]

For Park and other early scholars of assimilation, the twentieth-century city was the ideal milieu in which to study assimilation and relations among groups, immigrants and US-born African Americans alike.[38] In his first article on assimilation, "Racial Assimilation in Secondary Groups with Particular Reference to the Negro" (published in the *American Journal of Sociology* in 1914), Park approached race as a barrier to assimilation. By the 1980s, African Americans would by and large be bracketed out of theories of assimilation and cast as unassimilable.[39] Instead of viewing African Americans' relationship to the mainstream through the lens of assimilation, scholars and policy makers have framed their status as outsiders-on-the-inside via such concepts as segregation, alienation, subpopulation, and underclass.[40] At the same time, assimilation qua absorption by the mainstream has been defined *against* race.[41]

Scholars in critical whiteness studies have approached whiteness as a racial formation, "the sociohistorical process by which racial identities are created, lived out, transformed, and destroyed."[42] To make the shift from immigrant, to hyphenated American, to American plain and simple, white ethnics (e.g., the Irish in the nineteenth century and Italian-Americans in the twentieth century) actively distanced themselves from African Americans and other groups branded "colored."[43] "The struggles of white ethnics were not only with the groups above them, who were seeking to keep the newer arrivals in a subordinate position," sociologists Richard Alba and Victor Nee remark, "but also with non-European groups, African Americans above all."[44] In exchange for the status of (white) American, European immigrants and their ethnic offspring all but relinquished their ties to the Old World. The same did not hold true for non-European groups, even if they, too, gave up the languages, nationalities, names, dress, and religious beliefs and practices of their or their forebears' homelands. Distinguishing ethnicity from race and drawing attention to the relationship of both to assimilation, Omi and Winant conclude that while "[b]eing 'ethnic' turns out to be about whether and how much an individual or group can assimilate into or hybridize with whiteness[,] [b]eing 'racial' is about how much difference there is between an individual or a group and their white counterparts."[45] In a pluralist United States, ethnicity is the path to assimilation. In contrast, race—specifically, nonwhiteness—is an obstacle.

The failure of assimilation theory to account for the trajectories of people of color and "its implicit assumption that most immigrants and their descendants are anxious"—and here, I would add, able— "to shed their social and cultural heritage" prompted some scholars to claim that assimilation had "fallen into disrepute" during the last decades of the twentieth century.[46] Sociologist Nathan Glazer went so far as to ask if assimilation had died.[47] In fact, it never died, but it was reborn. As sociologist Moon-Kie Jung observes, "[I]n the mid-1980s, the long dominant assimilation paradigm ... was theoretically reinvigorated. Through periodic challenges (e.g., pluralism, Marxism, transnationalism) and exaggerated reports of demise ... assimilation theories adapted and remained the primary framework within, as well as against, which to analyze the lives of migrants and their offspring in the United States."[48]

Jung identifies two theoretical frameworks that have revitalized assimilation theory: neoclassical assimilation and segmented assimilation. The former avoids some of the classical model's oversights by taking into account the non-European groups that have immigrated to the United States since the Immigration Act of 1965 removed the national origins quotas of the early twentieth century. Still, the neoclassical model continues to uphold assimilation as the "master trend" for immigrants and their descendants.[49]

Segmented assimilation complicates that trend by examining the multiple ways in which immigrants and their descendants adapt to a racially stratified society. After all, "how one assimilates into American society depends in large part on one's racial status," as sociologist Tanya Golash-Boza points out.[50] Using census data and case studies involving various immigrant groups, sociologists Alejandro Portes, Rubén G. Rumbaut, and Min Zhou argue that since immigrant groups and society itself are heterogeneous, there is no single mode of incorporation. While some immigrants and their offspring acculturate and integrate into the white middle class, others advance economically precisely by remaining in their immigrant communities. Still, others for whom "ethnicity [is] neither a matter of choice nor a source of progress but a mark of subordination . . . are at risk of joining the masses of the dispossessed."[51] Portes and Zhou conclude, "Children of nonwhite immigrants may not even have the opportunity of gaining access to middle-class white society, no matter how acculturated they become. Joining those native circles to which they do have access may prove a ticket to permanent subordination and disadvantage."[52]

Irrespective of the differences among the various theories and models of assimilation, the prediction made by Simons in 1901 has come to fruition. By the start of the twenty-first century, assimilation was declared "an indispensable concept" in "the social scientific study of immigration and intergroup relations" in the United States.[53] As a theory, it remains an organizing rubric in US ethnic and immigration history, the social sciences, and public policy. And despite assertions that multiculturalism had killed or would kill it, assimilation endures as an object of scrutiny in academia and the mainstream media, especially in debates about the so-called Hispanic and Islamic challenges (the contention that Latinxs in the United States and Muslims in North America and Europe are unable or unwilling to integrate fully).

Assimilation is not only the master narrative of American immigration. As a tool for delineating the "boundaries between 'us' and 'not us,'" it is above all a pillar of the US nation-making project and a relationship of power.[54] "The story of how a foreign minority comes to terms with its new social surroundings and is eventually absorbed into the mainstream of the host society is the cloth from which numerous sociological and economic theories have been fashioned," Portes and Rumbaut have noted. "For the most part, this story has been told in optimistic tones and with an emphasis on the eventual integration of the newcomers."[55] The story of assimilation is not merely optimistic; it is also triumphalist, prescriptive, and normative.

That story's cast of characters, however, is limited, for the evolution from immigrant, to hyphenated American, to bona fide American has not been open to all. Some people never lose the hyphen, even if they bear significant signs of acculturation—for example, they speak English without an accent—and hold US citizenship. Signifiers of racial difference and immigration laws and policies prevent them from blending in or formalizing their membership in the polity. Tellingly, some group labels—for example, Puerto Rican and Latinx—are never hyphenated.[56] Some people are not and never were immigrants—for example, Native Americans, African slaves, and their US-born descendants. Others—namely, nonimmigrants, a label I unpack below—are not recognized as immigrants and therefore are precluded from ever becoming hyphenated or unhyphenated Americans. And still others—for example, Oaxacalifornixs, a group I discuss in chapter 5—do away with the hyphen in favor of a portmanteau that articulates the indigenous, the regional, and the transnational.

DECOUPLING IMMIGRATION AND ASSIMILATION
AND PROBING THE GAP BETWEEN CITIZENSHIP
AND ASSIMILATION

This book builds on studies of assimilation that focus on what migration scholars call context of reception—that is, "the political-economic context in which immigrants arrive."[57] Not limiting my scope to immigrants, but still maintaining a focus on whether or how people are received, I begin by decoupling immigration and assimilation. While many rigorous and insightful studies of assimilation focus on immigrants and their descendants, I ask: *How are people who are not immigrants or who are not considered real or legitimate immigrants, but who are still present in and part of the United States, received? What do those people and their context of reception tell us about assimilation and Americanness?* By disentangling immigration and assimilation, I call attention to a key assumption about both: assimilation is supposed to be an outcome of immigration. Depending on one's point of view, assimilation is the price or reward of Americanization and the American dream. Furthermore, immigrants and their descendants are expected to assimilate. Those who do not assimilate, who are deemed unassimilable, or for whom assimilation is not even an option, are outsiders or "failed citizens."

The failed citizen, a construct I borrow from sociologist Bridget Anderson, is the nominal citizen who is imagined as incapable of living up to the ideals of "the local community and/or the nation."[58] Poor people, criminals, and welfare recipients are groups that are dismissed as failed citizens. Often the failed citizen is depicted as or perceived to be nonwhite—specifically, African American and Latinx. The failed citizen is compared unfavorably with the model minority and the hardworking and self-reliant immigrant—for example, the Dreamer, the would-be beneficiary of the abortive Development, Relief, and Education for Alien Minors (DREAM) Act.[59] Contrasted with the bad citizen, the model minority and Dreamer are good citizens (even though the state does not recognize the Dreamer as a citizen per se). Along with the figure of the failed citizen, the figures of the model minority and Dreamer constitute strategies and tactics in struggles over rights, resources, and recognition in the United States.[60]

Historian Mae M. Ngai's concept of alien citizenship, like that of the failed citizen, sheds light on the gap between race and US citizenship. According to Ngai, the alien citizen is a US citizen "by virtue of . . . birth in the United States" but is not perceived to be or treated as a citizen "on account of the racialized identity of . . . immigrant ancestry."[61] For example, the US government rendered Japanese Americans alien citizens when it rounded them up and incarcerated them in internment camps during World War II.

In contrast, Dreamers are not US citizens. They are undocumented immigrants. Yet despite not having the right papers, the iconic Dreamer is depicted as the average American. For example, she speaks fluent English and knows the United States as her only home, having arrived in this country at an early age. Her reference group is made up of US citizens, to use one measure of assimilation. In other words, she sees herself as one of them and shares their outlook—in particular, their education, values, and expectations.[62]

At the same time, the iconic Dreamer is exceptional. Young, bright, and hardworking, she already has or promises to make a valuable contribution to her adopted homeland. Like Africans and African Americans before emancipation and Native Americans who pursued US citizenship in the wake of the Dawes and Burke Acts, Dreamers are probationary citizens, outsiders who must show that they merit inclusion in society. Yet irrespective of their assimilation and accomplishments, Dreamers remain denizens, people who are present in the space of the nation-state but are neither bona fide foreigners nor citizens.

Occupying an intermediary position between citizen and foreigner, denizens dwell in the territory of the nation-state but lack formal citizenship. They are, to use economist Guy Standing's words, "partial insider[s]," sometimes with limited rights.[63] In some cases, they are barred from becoming citizens. Yet despite lacking formal citizenship, denizens do not lack political or social subjectivity or agency, as denizens themselves have demonstrated and scholars such as Rachel Ida Buff, Susan Bibler Coutin, and Cecilia Menjívar remind us.[64] In fact, "denizens have constantly challenged the boundaries of citizenship, in many cases expanding them, and in other cases, forcing the state to publicly articulate its justification for their ongoing exclusion."[65]

In addition to decoupling immigration and assimilation, this book probes the gap between assimilation and citizenship by foregrounding the stories and experiences of people who have been or are deemed denizens, probationary citizens, alien citizens, and failed citizens. The individuals and groups I study include indigenous peoples, African Americans, Puerto Ricans, Japanese Americans, and undocumented immigrants. These groups have been or remain noncitizens, "aliens" ineligible for citizenship, would-be citizens, and/or citizens in name only. I put these social actors at the center of the history of the concept of assimilation in the United States, but I do not equate them with the "new," decidedly European immigrant of the Great Wave. Doing so would reproduce that immigrant as normative, as the yardstick against which all other groups are measured.[66] Instead, I include the putatively unassimilable and partially assimilable in conversations about assimilation in order to show that assimilation is not so much a matter of absorption and becoming more alike as of power and inequality. Bridging and expanding the assimilation and racialization paradigms, I offer a theory of assimilation that reckons with racialization by looking to legacies of settler colonialism, slavery, and an immigration apparatus that ranks and excludes certain people. By showing how indigenous peoples, African Americans, Puerto Ricans, Japanese Americans, and undocumented immigrants have been and are incorporated into a stratified society founded on indigenous dispossession, white supremacy, slavery, imperial pursuits, and capitalist expansion, I argue that racialization and the gap between citizenship and assimilation are constitutive of, not antithetical to, the assimilation process in the United States. I also expose what I call the "paradox of assimilation."

THE PARADOX OF ASSIMILATION
AND DIFFERENTIAL INCLUSION

Drawing from theories of assimilation as the negotiation of a boundary and historian Natalia Molina's work on relational notions of race, I define assimilation as a relational process whereby the boundary between unequal groups and between inside and outside blurs, disappears, or, paradoxically, is reinforced.[67] Some boundaries are hard and bright, while others are porous and ambiguous.[68] In some instances, boundaries blur or disappear. In others, they are reinforced and the dominant group absorbs a minority or minoritized (in other words, disempowered) group as its distinct, constitutive, and subordinate other.

I refer to the incorporation of members of social groups as subordinate and abject subjects as the paradox of assimilation. I take the concept of the abject from feminist philosopher, literary critic, and semiotician Julia Kristeva: "something rejected from which one does not part."[69] As social actors who participate in the economy but are rejected by the state, undocumented workers, for example, are abject subjects. Indeed, their incorporation in the economy is often predicated on their rejection by the state. Their simultaneous inclusion and exclusion underscore that assimilation is not only the process whereby outsiders are turned into insiders; it is also the process whereby certain social actors and groups are rendered outsiders on the inside.

The process whereby a person or a social group assimilated or is assimilated as a distinct, constitutive, and subordinate other is known as differential inclusion.[70] Examples of differential inclusion may be found in the US Supreme Court cases *Cherokee Nation v. Georgia* (1831), *Dred Scott v. Sandford* (1857), and *Downes v. Bidwell* (1901). *Cherokee Nation v. Georgia* likened the Cherokee nation's relationship to the United States to "that of a ward to its guardian."[71] *Dred Scott v. Sandford* ruled that enslaved and free African Americans were not US citizens, thereby rendering them denizens.[72] And in a nonsensical twist, *Downes v. Bidwell* determined "that whilst in an international sense Porto Rico was not a foreign country, since it was subject to the sovereignty of and was owned by the United States, it was foreign to the United States in a domestic sense, because the island had not been incorporated into the United States, but was merely appurtenant thereto, as a possession."[73]

An outsider on the inside, the figure of the model minority also exemplifies differential inclusion. As I note in chapter 4, the label was first applied to Japanese Americans and Chinese Americans in the 1960s.[74] It has also been foisted on, and in some instances embraced by, diverse groups such as Jews, West Indians, South Asians, and Dreamers. Model minorities are celebrated for being hardworking, compliant, and "able to make it on their own" (in other words, without the state's support).[75] Sociologist Lisa Sun-Hee Park points out that they do not enjoy "full citizenship rights . . . but rather, a secondary set of rights reserved for particular minorities who 'behave' appropriately and stay in their designated subsidiary space without complaint."[76]

Richard Rodriguez's 1983 memoir, *Hunger of Memory*, is a prototypical model minority tale. After earning a PhD in British literature, its narrator-protagonist, the US-born son of working-class, Spanish-speaking Mexican immigrants, rails against bilingual education, affirmative action, and identity politics. Despite his pleas for assimilation and colorblindness, Rodriguez, as literary and cultural critic Alicia Schmidt Camacho points out, enters the mainstream not as an "American" writer but as a "representative 'Hispanic.'"[77] He is assimilated, but as a racialized subject.

My definition of assimilation explores the vexed relationship between assimilation and racialization. It is by no means orthodox, but it builds on conventional understandings of the term, lay and academic alike. While my definition engages scholarship in the social sciences, it is animated by the humanities' concern with genealogy, with the recognition that things, including and especially words and concepts, have a history and that meanings change.[78] My definition is also shaped by the poststructuralist concern with the significance—by which I mean the importance and meaning—of absence and alterity. By drawing attention to what (or who) is missing in conversations about assimilation and how that absence produces meaning, I sharpen understandings of assimilation.

SITUATING ASSIMILATION IN AND BEYOND US IMMIGRATION HISTORY

The twentieth-century European experience in the United States, in which mass immigration was followed by a hiatus from 1924 until 1965, has served as the basis for dominant theories of assimilation. Indeed, the consolidation of whiteness in the United States is an effect of laws, policies, and practices that virtually shut off immigration from most of the world. The Page Act of 1875, the Chinese Exclusion Act of 1882, and the Asiatic Barred Zone Act of 1917 sought to stop immigration from Asia, the Pacific, and the Middle East. The Johnson-Reed Act slashed the influx of southern, central, and eastern Europeans by establishing a strict system of quotas based on national origins. Like its restrictionist predecessors, the Johnson-Reed Act was a racial project. It aimed for and helped usher in a demographic shift in the United States.

The ethnicity paradigm and the classical model of assimilation are responses to and articulations of the demographic shifts wrought by the restrictionist immigration legislation of the late nineteenth and twentieth centuries, the period Ngai calls the "regime of quotas and papers" (1875–1965). Situating the ethnicity paradigm and the classical model of assimilation in the context of the Second Industrial Revolution, Omi and Winant assert, "The integration of the European immigrants *may have been a one-off.*"[79] In other words, the immigration and assimilation of the "new" immigrants were effects of the political, economic, and social conditions of their time. Applying a model or theory specific to that time—namely, the ethnicity paradigm and the classical model of assimilation—to social actors of a different era is not just ahistorical; in Omi and Winant's words, it is "bad social science" and "ideological wishful thinking."[80]

This book places the emergence of assimilation as a social and cultural concept, an object of study, an academic theory, and a policy goal in the context of the regime of quotas and papers. Yet in addition to situating it in US immigration history, I locate assimilation in the context of Jim Crow, the period of de jure and de facto racial segregation from 1870 until 1965; in the allotment and assimilation era, the period from 1887 until 1943, when the US government sought to assimilate Native Americans by breaking up tribal lands and removing indigenous people from their communities; in the "new imperialism" of the late nineteenth and early twentieth centuries, an era that saw the United States acquire Puerto Rico (as well as Cuba, Guam, and the Philippines); in the Cold War (1946–91), the period that gave birth to the model minority; and in the "new nativism" of the late twentieth and early twenty-first centuries.[81] All of these overlapping epochs constitute what historian Patrick Wolfe terms "regimes of difference," systems that produce and ascribe varying values to social groups, thereby encoding and reproducing unequal relationships.[82]

The regime of quotas and papers opened with the Page and Chinese Exclusion Acts, legislation that targeted Chinese immigrants. In addition to prohibiting Chinese immigration, the Chinese Exclusion Act denied Chinese nationals US citizenship. In 1898 the US Supreme Court ruled in *United States v. Wong Kim Ark* that the Fourteenth Amendment applied to the US-born children of Chinese immigrants. This meant that the children of Chinese immigrants were US citizens by virtue of having been born on US soil. Their immigrant parents, however, remained ineligible for naturalization. In 1943 the Magnuson Act (also known as the Chinese Exclusion Repeal Act) lifted the ban on Chinese immigration and allowed some Chinese immigrants who were already present in the United States to naturalize as US citizens.

Like the Page and Chinese Exclusion Acts, the Asiatic Barred Zone Act is a defining feature of the regime of quotas and papers. Also known as the Literacy Act and the Immigration Act of 1917, the Asiatic Barred Zone Act expanded the Chinese Exclusion Act by barring immigrants not only from China but also from much of Asia, the Pacific, and the Middle East. Furthermore, it excluded immigrants over the age of sixteen who were illiterate and anyone found to be mentally, physically, or morally "defective," such as "imbeciles," "epileptics," "insane persons," alcoholics, "paupers," "vagrants," criminals, "polygamists," anarchists, and sex workers.[83]

Following efforts in San Francisco to send Japanese students to the segregated Chinese school, and amid calls throughout California to stop Japanese immigration, the Empire of Japan and the United States entered the Gentlemen's Agreement of 1907. According to the terms of that informal agreement, Japan would limit emigration to the United States. In exchange, the United States would not enact a ban on Japanese immigrants similar to that of the Chinese Exclusion Act. The Gentlemen's Agreement excluded Japanese nationals from the Asiatic Barred Zone Act. However, the Johnson-Reed Act nullified the Gentlemen's Agreement. What is more, the Johnson-Reed Act prohibited Japanese and other Asians from naturalizing as US citizens. Japanese nationals would not be eligible for naturalization until the McCarran-Walter Act went into effect in 1952.

The impact of the regime of quotas and papers on Puerto Ricans and Mexicans stands in stark contrast to that on Asians. In 1898, after the US military invaded Puerto Rico, Spain ceded the island to the United States as a spoil of the Spanish-American War. Suddenly, Puerto Ricans found themselves part of the United States. In March 1917, the same year in which it passed the Asiatic Barred Zone Act and just one month before the United States entered World War 1, Congress passed the Jones-Shafroth Act, legislation that granted US citizenship to anyone born in Puerto Rico on or after April 11, 1899. In addition to gaining 17,855 Puerto Rican conscripts, the United States affirmed its hold on the island and, by extension, the Caribbean Sea, the eastern gateway to the newly acquired Panama Canal.[84] And despite opposition from congressmen who insisted that the Puerto Rican people were a "dark race" and therefore unfit for US citizenship, Presidents Howard

Taft and Woodrow Wilson were keen to quell political unrest—in particular, socialism and a burgeoning independence movement—on the island by making Puerto Ricans US citizens.[85]

Like Native Americans and Puerto Ricans, Mexicans comprise a colonized group within the United States. The United States absorbed some 80,000–100,000 Mexicans when it invaded and defeated Mexico during the Mexican-American War (1846–48).[86] In 1848, the Treaty of Guadalupe Hidalgo extended US citizenship to Mexican nationals who found themselves living north of the new international border. As numerous scholars have shown, many of these Mexicans were citizens in name only, as they were "despoiled of their land, and their civil rights were regularly violated, often through outright racist terror."[87]

While the Chinese Exclusion Act blocked "the coming of Chinese laborers," Mexicans in Mexico continued to be recruited to the United States as workers, especially in agriculture.[88] Notwithstanding ever-expanding restrictions on immigration, the United States did not assign quotas to nationals from its neighbor to the south. Instead, it subjected them to strict visa requirements and increased border policing. Consequently, Ngai tells us, Mexicans were rendered "the single largest group of illegal aliens by the late 1920s."[89] As "illegal aliens," they were branded criminals and outsiders at once. Yet even if they remained within the purview of the law as guest workers (e.g., as braceros from 1942 until 1964), they were still regarded as transitory and disposable. Where Asian immigrants were prohibited from entering the United States and naturalizing, Mexican ones were not supposed to remain in their host country. As peoples deemed foreign, illicit, temporary, and therefore deportable, both groups were not and could never be bona fide "immigrants."

THE TAXONOMY OF MOBILE SUBJECTS

In addition to centering indigenous peoples, African Americans, Puerto Ricans, and Japanese Americans in the discourse on assimilation, this book focuses on nonnormative mobile subjects—namely, undocumented immigrants (like Dreamers), economic migrants (people who move out of economic necessity), and indigenous migrants. The social actors to whom labels such as "immigrant," "illegal alien," "economic migrant," "refugee," "N/native," and "indigenous" are ascribed comprise a hierarchy of mobile (and putatively immobile) subjects. Despite the Universal Declaration of Human Rights's (1948) proclamation that everyone "has the right to freedom of movement and residence within the borders of each state" and "the right to leave any country, including his own, and to return to his country," states frequently question and deny nonnormative mobile subjects' right to move and assimilability.[90] And unless they are model minorities and/or what political scientist Bonnie Honig terms "supercitizen immigrants," "object[s] of identification," and "the screen onto which we [Americans] project our idealized selves," undocumented immigrants are rarely protagonists in dominant narratives about immigration and assimilation in the United States.[91]

As a discursive and normative subject, the immigrant is a person from another country who has settled in the United States and has been or will be absorbed by the state and civil society. In other words, "immigrants" assimilate and are assimilable. The discourse of the "nation of immigrants," for example, assimilates them as constitutive of the nation. To paraphrase historian Oscar Handlin, immigrants *are* American history.[92] Meanwhile, nonimmigrants—for example, guest workers—are mobile subjects from other countries who are not expected to assimilate because they are not supposed to remain in the host country indefinitely.[93] In contrast, "indigenous migrant" is an oxymoron according to definitions of "indigenous" that tether the Native to a particular place. In short, nonimmigrants may be present in the nation of immigrants, but they are not considered part of it, while indigenous migrants are not supposed to exist at all.

Similarly, the "illegal alien," the mobile subject who does not have the state's permission to enter and/or to be in the receiving country, is unassimilable in the "nation of laws." Even though many immigrants and naturalized citizens were once unauthorized, stories about undocumentedness as a pre-American experience are not widely celebrated, much less acknowledged, in the United States.[94] I reckon with this absence in chapter 4.

The discursive and normative immigrant is praised for scaling the socioeconomic ladder and thereby fortifying the image of the United States as an egalitarian meritocracy, a society in which advancement is based on hard work and ability. In contrast, the economic—in other words, the poor, "unskilled"—migrant tends to be viewed with suspicion and dismissed as an opportunist. Yet according to the US master narrative of immigration, immigrants move to this country precisely because it is the land of opportunity. According to that narrative, people do not immigrate to the United States because it needs cheap, disposable labor. Nor do they immigrate because the United States is an imperial power that has destabilized their homelands by, say, interfering in an election, assassinating a political leader, arming progovernment militias or antigovernment rebels, devaluing a currency or commodity, imposing debilitating economic sanctions, or conducting a covert or full-scale military invasion. In the lore of the nation of immigrants and the nation of laws, immigrants migrate of their own volition and never without the state's consent. In contrast, "illegal aliens" move clandestinely, economic migrants move for dubious reasons, and refugees move because they must. Taken together, the ideologies and discourses of the American dream, the nation of immigrants, the nation of laws, and meritocracy gloss over, rest on, and even celebrate the foundational facts of settler colonialism, indigenous dispossession, slavery, and empire. This book examines how nonnormative mobile subjects call attention to those foundational facts, how they reinforce or trouble the relationship between immigration and settler colonialism, and how they expose the limits and contradictions—in short, the paradox—of assimilation.

CHAPTER SUMMARIES

Paying attention to the founding and growth of the United States as a settler colonial society and an empire dependent on and profiting from indigenous dispossession and slavery, the first half of this book narrates a history of assimilation beginning in the nineteenth century. The second half reflects on that history and its repercussions by analyzing enunciations of belonging and difference in literature and visual art by alien citizens, probationary citizens, and denizens since World War II.

I begin by excavating assimilation's prehistory—that is, the ways in which assimilation was conceived and defined before it came to be associated with immigrants and immigration. Drawing from archival and literary sources, including government documents, academic treatises, newspaper articles, letters, testimonies, and speeches, the first half of my book decouples immigration and assimilation and shows how the latter was implicit in pre–Johnson-Reed Act practices, policies, institutions, and narratives, such as efforts to "civilize" Native Americans, African Americans, and Puerto Ricans. This prehistory, I argue, underpins the taxonomy of mobile subjects in the twentieth and twenty-first centuries, the focus of the second half of this book. To bring that taxonomy into relief, I turn to literary and visual works, paying close attention to representations of the figures of the model minority, the Dreamer, the economic migrant, and the indigenous migrant. The title of my book notwithstanding, the history I narrate is far from exhaustive. I have opted to showcase certain moments, cases, texts, subjects, and relationships not only because they underscore the paradox of assimilation, but also because they have not received widespread attention from scholars of assimilation.

Chapter 2 explores efforts to "civilize" Native Americans, African Americans, and Puerto Ricans in the wake of the Indian, Civil, and Spanish-American Wars, moments when regimes of difference in the United States and its colonies were being challenged and consolidated.

Focusing on the Puerto Rican students who attended the Carlisle Indian Industrial School from 1898 until the school's closure in 1918, I approach assimilation as a process of entering and being situated in a racial hierarchy. In addition to underscoring the connections between African American and Native American education and the ways in which African American students were upheld as models for their Native American classmates, I show how Carlisle's Puerto Rican students were incorporated into a stratified society as racialized and colonized subjects. I also analyze how they resisted that incorporation.

Chapter 3 examines the omission of African Americans in understandings of assimilation. By putting Booker T. Washington and Robert Ezra Park's travelogue *The Man Farthest Down: A Record of Observation and Study in Europe* (1912) and George Samuel Schuyler's novel *Black No More: Being an Account of the Strange and Wonderful Workings of Science in the Land of the Free, A.D. 1933–1940* (1931) in dialogue with contemporary theories of assimilation, this chapter explores the vital and widely overlooked role African Americans have played in theories of assimilation in the United States. It also shows that African Americans have not been included in conversations about assimilation because of the long-standing discrepancy between blackness and Americanness—in other words, because of the legacy of black denizenship in the United States. I conclude by linking African American denizens to twenty-first-century Dreamers, young people who demonstrate and often claim assimilation but lack US citizenship and are therefore excluded from the polity and vulnerable to deportation.

Chapter 4 bridges the first and second halves of this book by linking the Cold War–era Japanese American model minority and the twenty-first-century Dreamer. Tracing a genealogy of deservingness, it locates the Japanese American model minority in the context of the Cold War and the discourse on the culture of poverty. Like its Cold War predecessor, the twenty-first century's iconic Dreamer bolsters the image of the United States as an egalitarian meritocracy and a benevolent nation of immigrants. Both figures serve a disciplinary function and participate in what Sébastien Chauvin and Blanca Garcés-Mascareñas call a "moral economy of deservingness," a site in which social actors demonstrate a particular kind of behavior and/or adhere to a particular set of values and ideals in exchange for rights, resources, and/or recognition.[95] Via close readings of John Okada's novel *No-No Boy* (1957) and Alberto Ledesma's graphic memoir *Diary of a Reluctant Dreamer: Vignettes from a Pre-American Life* (2017), I argue that the moral economy of deservingness offers the model minority and the Dreamer only contingent, partial, and attenuated inclusion.

The unassimilable subject is the focus of chapter 5. This chapter examines how three nonnormative mobile subjects—the dissident Dreamer, the undocuqueer, and the Oaxacalifornix—complicate and expand the lexicon of mobility and offer new possibilities for belonging and being by articulating the politics of presence, visibility, and potentiality. "Dreamer" (dissident and otherwise), "undocuqueer," and "Oaxacalifornix" are relatively new terms. To explore their meanings, I draw from queer theory, indigenous studies, and critical Latinx indigeneities as I read videos of the disruption of Barack Obama's speech by members of Asian Students Promoting Immigrant Rights through Education at the Betty Ong Recreation Center in San Francisco on November 25, 2013; digital illustrations produced from 2012 through 2018 by the self-professed undocuqueer artist Julio Salgado; and a series of murals by the indigenous Oaxacan artist collective Tlacolulokos, on display at the Central Library in downtown Los Angeles over 2017 and 2018. Because the dissident Dreamer, the undocuqueer, and the Oaxacalifornix exceed extant discursive formations and regimes of circulation, such as the "nation of immigrants" and the "nation of laws," they expose the limits not only of the United States but of arguments for inclusion that hinge on deservingness, traditional, state-bound citizenship, and the logic of multiculturalism. In doing so, they envision alternative ways of participating in society. They also offer alternative visions of society itself.

Finally, in the epilogue I summarize my book's key arguments. I point to what is at stake in debates about assimilation and stress the importance of expanding and complicating understandings of assimilation. I also contemplate the paradox of assimilation and the connection between assimilation and human worth in the context of the pandemic of 2020 and the murder of George Floyd, an African American man, by Derek Chauvin, a white police officer, in Minneapolis on May 25, 2020.

WHY ASSIMILATION MATTERS

In the twenty-first century, assimilation appears to be everywhere and nowhere at once. While writing this book I noticed that assimilation could be applied to just about any social group not deemed part of the mainstream or the majority, such as religious, linguistic, and sexual minorities and people with certain disabilities. Assimilation may also refer to the production, circulation, and consumption of cultural practices and products—for example, tacos. In this latter sense, *to assimilate* is synonymous with *to mainstream* or *to crossover.*

Despite assimilation's ubiquity, I was asked on more than one occasion about the relevance of assimilation in the twenty-first century. *Does assimilation happen in the era of multiculturalism and globalization? Is assimilation possible in a moment of xenophobia, as evinced by the Trump administration's efforts to curtail both unauthorized and authorized immigration? Does assimilation still matter?*, my interlocutors inquired. In fact, assimilation warrants attention because it is connected to ideas about belonging and merit. Whether they are native-born or newcomers, people who are not considered legitimate or deserving members of society have not enjoyed and continue to be denied the rights, resources, and recognition that the state affords to others, even when those people are present in and an integral part of a country.

My goal with this book is not to offer a narrow and precise definition of assimilation. On the contrary, I want to expand understandings of assimilation by recognizing the paradox of assimilation. The epigraphs and advertisement with which I have opened this chapter illustrate that paradox. All point to assimilation's contradictory, variegated, and shifting meanings from the late nineteenth century onward.

The ad articulates assimilation's early meaning as a physiological and biological process. The epigraphs invoke that meaning. Published in 1880, at the start of the Great Wave, the *New York Times* editorial frets about the "vast exodus" of poor immigrants from Europe and the viability of turning them "into good American citizens."[96] Echoing Pratt's call to "[t]ransfer the savage-born infant to the surroundings of civilization" so that the infant could "grow to possess a civilized language and habit," the editorial advises that "the swarms of new-comers" move out of "their East Side tenement-houses" and put themselves in "intimate contact with American people.... Foreigners.... become really good citizens only when expatriation is supplemented ... by disassociation from their race."[97]

Where assimilation is tantamount to racial uplift in the *New York Times* editorial, the ad for Dr. Pierce's Golden Medical Discovery and Pleasant Pellets equates assimilation qua civilization with discord, debasement, and loss. "Civilized man leads an unnatural and an unhealthy life," the ad reads. In contrast, the American Indian was the picture of health "when he reigned supreme over this continent."[98] By 1898, the year this ad was published, the American frontier had been declared closed and the Indian's reign over.[99] At the same time, officials in the Bureau of Indian Affairs expressed doubt about Native Americans' assimilability and concluded that they "were destined to live on the fringes of civilization."[100] Once settler colonials no longer considered aboriginal peoples a threat, they could celebrate them more easily as "noble savages" or mourn them as "vanishing Indians," as "residents of a departed past who could not live on in modern times."[101]

More than a century later, Marco Gutierrez, an immigrant from Hidalgo, Mexico, and founder of Latinos for Trump, warned about the future of the United States. Using food as a metaphor for what he saw as the dominance of Mexican culture in his adopted country, he predicted, "[W]e're going to have the White House full of taco trucks and we are going to be selling paletas on every corner around the White House" if immigration from Mexico were not curbed or stopped altogether.[102]

Tacos and paletas (popsicles) are distinctly Mexican foods. Likewise, selling tacos out of a truck and paletas on the corner is a practice associated with undocumented immigrants and the informal economy. Gutierrez's exhortation to Americans to "defend your country, our country" signals that assimilation is a power struggle, one in which the line between "your" and "our" slips and in which the proverbial tables can turn when the unchecked newcomer overwhelms the host.[103]

Widely mocked, Gutierrez's warning inspired countless memes, late-night comedy jokes, and even a wall of taco trucks outside the Trump International Hotel in Las Vegas.[104] Hillary Clinton, Donald Trump's Democratic opponent in the 2016 US presidential race, got in on the joke when she quipped, "A taco truck on every corner sounds absolutely delicious."[105] Two years into Trump's presidency, there would be no taco trucks in or *paleteros* around the White House. However, the *New York Times* would reveal that the president of the United States employed undocumented workers from Latin America at his golf course in Bedminster, New Jersey.[106]

As absurd as Gutierrez's warning and the ripostes to it were, they nod to a flexible and capacious understanding of assimilation. According to their logic, assimilation is not necessarily an imposition by the state or the dominant culture on "alien peoples." Instead, it is the negotiation of the boundary between host and newcomer, between majority and minority, between mainstream and margin, and between insider and outsider. Put another way, assimilation is the negotiation of the line that purports to separate the powerful from the less powerful. That negotiation transforms individuals and social groups and, in some cases, society itself. And as outrageous as it is for a racist and xenophobic political leader to depend on and to profit from the labor of racialized undocumented immigrants, Trump's relationship with his Latinx undocumented employees—the very fact of their copresence and dependence on one another—speaks to the paradox of assimilation. This book reckons with assimilation's messiness by confronting that paradox.

Indians and Negroes
in Spite of Themselves

Puerto Rican Students at the
Carlisle Indian Industrial School

On September 5, 1899, fifteen-year-old Vicente Figueroa of Guayama, Puerto Rico, enrolled at the Carlisle Indian Industrial School in Carlisle, Pennsylvania. During the five years that he spent at the boarding school for Native Americans, he learned English and a trade. After leaving the school in 1904, Figueroa remained in Pennsylvania. He worked for several years in Philadelphia, Bethlehem, and Pittsburgh. In 1911 he applied for a position with the Indian Service in Denver, Colorado. In a letter to Charles Dagenette, supervisor of Indian employment in Denver and a Carlisle alumnus, Carlisle superintendent Moses Friedman identified Figueroa as a machinist and concrete finisher. "He is good at the latter occupation and finds steady work in a good season," Friedman observed. He also noted that Figueroa was "a Porto Rican, mostly Negro." Figueroa did not get the job with the Indian Service. Still, he expressed gratitude to what he and many other former students called "Dear Old Carlisle." "I always speak highly of the school," he wrote in a letter to Friedman on July 31, 1912, "and I thank . . . the school for what I am."[1]

Figueroa was one of approximately sixty Puerto Rican youths who attended the Carlisle Indian Industrial School between 1898, the year

29

Figure 2. Puerto Rican students at the Carlisle Indian Industrial School. Published in *The Red Man and Helper* 19, no. 49 (July 31, 1903). Used with permission from the Cumberland County Historical Society, Carlisle, Pennsylvania.

Spain ceded Puerto Rico, along with Cuba and the Philippines, to the United States, and 1918, the year the school closed.[2] (See figure 2.) The pupils ranged in age from eleven to nineteen years.[3] Roughly thirty-eight were male and twenty-one were female.[4] The former learned farming or a trade, while the latter were trained to cook, sew, do laundry, and care for children. Carlisle aimed to produce particular kinds of workers—manual laborers and domestic servants—and normative men and women. Above all, it sought to transform Indians into Americans. So what happened to its Puerto Rican students? In addition to learning English and a trade, what did these other colonials learn about their place in an expanding empire, a nation of burgeoning immigration, and a hardening racial hierarchy defined increasingly by the so-called vanishing Indian and one-drop rule for African Americans? How did "our Porto Ricans," as they were known, fit into or frustrate that hierarchy?[5]

To address these questions, this chapter looks at the history of assimilation in the United States. Assimilation is widely seen as an outcome of immigration and as the price or reward of the American dream. Often it is defined in opposition to racialization, the process whereby racial categories are produced and understood as part of a racial hier-archy. Yet what happens when immigration and assimilation are decou-pled and assimilation is approached as racialization? Instead of framing assimilation in relation to immigration and against racialization, I look at efforts to "civilize" Native Americans, African Africans, and Puerto Ricans in the wake of the Indian, Civil, and Spanish-American Wars, moments when the polyethnic hierarchy and regime of difference, to use William McNeill's and Patrick Wolfe's terms, were being chal-lenged and consolidated in the United States.[6] I then examine the case of the Puerto Ricans at Carlisle. Using school records, letters, testimo-nies, and newspaper stories, I show how these students were incorpo-rated into a stratified society as racialized and colonized subjects. I also look at how they resisted that incorporation.

By juxtaposing efforts to civilize Native Americans, blacks, and Puerto Ricans, I draw attention to assimilation as a mutually constitutive pro-cess of categorization. In other words, assimilation is a relational process.[7] Since the 1990s, sociologists have highlighted its relational nature by the-orizing what they term "segmented assimilation." Min Zhou, for one, describes segmented assimilation as "a theoretical framework for under-standing the process by which the new second generation—the children of contemporary immigrants—becomes incorporated into the system of stratification in the host society and the different outcomes of this pro-cess."[8] However, as the experiences of so-called backward races at Carl-isle and its predecessor, the Hampton Normal and Agricultural Institute, show, segmented assimilation predates its emergence as a framework for study. In other words, segmented assimilation existed long before scholars came up with a term for it.[9] Nor have the children of immigrants been the only group to undergo segmented assimilation. Indeed, as long as there have been tiered societies, including and especially societies founded on the expropriation of land and labor, social groups have been incorpo-rated unequally into one segment or another. Approaching assimilation as a process organized around ranking, entering, and being situated in a racial hierarchy shows that it is often one and the same as subordination

or marginalization—in other words, differential inclusion.[10] By compar-
ing the experiences of African Americans, Native Americans, and Puerto
Ricans at Carlisle and Hampton, I offer a glimpse of assimilation's prehistory and show that assimilation is more than the process whereby the
boundary between mainstream and margin blurs or disappears; it is also
the process whereby that boundary is, paradoxically, reinforced.

ORIGINS AND HALLMARKS OF THE
CARLISLE INDIAN INDUSTRIAL SCHOOL

The school has long functioned as a mechanism of assimilation, particularly in settler colonial societies and migrant-receiving countries.
The establishment in 1879 of the Carlisle Indian Industrial School, the
first federally funded, coeducational, off-reservation boarding school
for Native Americans in the United States, coincided with the common school movement and Progressive-Era Americanization campaigns, both of which sought to turn immigrants and their US-born
offspring into Americans. Furthermore, Carlisle's founding coincided
with the expansion of the United States as a nation and empire. Along
with its predecessors, the Hilo School and the Hampton Normal and
Agricultural Institute, and its offshoot, the Tuskegee Normal School
for Colored Teachers, Carlisle was part of a colonial project that sought
to deracinate indigenous peoples and African Americans and to place
them in a racial hierarchy made up of "native" Americans (US-born
whites), "Negroes" (Afro-diasporic peoples), immigrants, "Indians"
(indigenous peoples), and other colonial subjects.

Louis Dalrymple's 1899 cartoon *School Begins* allegorizes the nexus of
education and colonial violence (see figure 3). Its caption reads, "School
Begins. Uncle Sam (to his new class in Civilization): Now, children,
you've got to learn these lessons whether you want to or not! But just
take a look at the class ahead of you, and remember that, in a little
while, you will feel as glad to be here as they are!" Here, Uncle Sam is
a strict teacher. The Philippines, Hawaii, Puerto Rico, and Cuba, the

Figure 3. Louis Dalrymple, *School Begins*. Published in *Puck*, January 25, 1899, www.loc .gov/pictures/item/2012647459/.

most recent US acquisitions, are small, scared, and/or surly brown students. Shoeless, disheveled, and wearing hoop earrings, they sit in the front row directly beneath Uncle Sam's massive desk and sharp pointer. Behind them, members of the class ahead sit at their desks, reading quietly. The more advanced students have lighter skin and wear long dresses or shirts with collars. Their books identify their provenance: Texas, California, Alaska, and New Mexico. Meanwhile, an African American boy perched on a ladder cleans a window and a Chinese boy wearing a cone-shaped hat and queue stands in the doorway. Both boys observe the classroom intently. In the background, a Native American boy wearing a blanket and two feathers in his hair sits by himself. He stares at a book with the letters "A-B-C" written across its cover. The book is upside down.

Just as all racial groups have their place in the US racial hierarchy, everyone has a place in Uncle Sam's classroom. Naturally, Uncle Sam is at the head of the class. Texas, California, Alaska, and New Mexico are subservient and in the background. The Philippines, Hawaii, Puerto

Rico, and Cuba are expected to follow suit. The African American's place is subsidiary. The Chinese boy's is outside. And the Native American occupies the dunce stool on the classroom's periphery.[11]

Carlisle was founded during what is known in Native American history as the allotment and assimilation era (1887–1943), a period bracketed by the Indian Wars of the second half of the nineteenth century and the Indian New Deal.[12] During this period, the US government sought to remove aboriginal peoples from the geographic and symbolic periphery—namely, from the reservations to which it had sentenced them—by breaking up communal landholding and kinship networks, prohibiting cultural expression (e.g., traditional dances and healing practices), and establishing schools for Native American youth.[13] As historian Philip J. Deloria points out, whether settlers confronted indigenous people on the battlefield or in the classroom, the settlers' goal was the same: "either to destroy Indians or to assimilate them into a white American world . . . both aimed at making Indians vanish from the landscape."[14]

The year 1879, when Carlisle was founded at a former garrison, was a turning point for Indian education. Over the next fifteen years, Congress increased spending on Native American education. Twenty off-reservation government boarding schools were established, along with dozens of new agency schools. "Perhaps most significant," historian Frederick Hoxie has observed, "instruction evolved from a haphazard affair directed by evangelical missionaries and incompetent placemen to an orderly system run by trained professionals. By the end of the 1880s federal schools operated on every reservation in the country . . . and Indian schools . . . became an integral part of the government's assimilation program."[15]

Along with the Indian school, the General Land Allotment Act of 1887 (also known as the Dawes Severalty Act and the Dawes Act) was a hallmark of the allotment and assimilation era. Named after Henry L. Dawes, a US senator from Massachusetts from 1875 to 1893 and chairman of the Senate Committee on Indian Affairs, the Dawes Act tore

tribes apart by breaking up tribal lands, then distributing the proper-
ties to individual Native Americans or selling them to white Americans. Under the Dawes Act and its 1906 amendment, the Burke Act, the
Bureau of Indian Affairs would assess allottees (Native Americans to
whom it had allotted property) after a probationary period of twenty-
five years to determine if said allottees were worthy of owning the land
and becoming US citizens. During this twenty-five-year probation, the
allottees were required to live "separate and apart from any tribe of
Indians."[16] They also had to demonstrate that they had "adopted the
habits of civilized life" and were "competent and capable of managing
[their] affairs."[17]

For Dawes, one of the most important things whites could teach
Native Americans was ownership. "The last and the best agency of
civilization is to teach a grown up Indian to *keep*," he declared in 1883.
"When he begins to understand that he has something that is his exclusively to enjoy, he begins to understand that it is necessary for him to
preserve and keep it."[18] In one fell swoop, the Dawes and Burke Acts
attempted to transform Native Americans into both capitalists (owners
of private property) and probationary citizens, individuals who must
demonstrate that they merit inclusion in the polity by fulfilling a series
of conditions. "[S]eparated from the mass, set up upon the soil, [and]
made a citizen," the Native American, Dawes predicted, would no longer be a "charge." Instead, the Native American would become "a positive good, a contribution to the wealth and strength and power of the
nation."[19] In fact, from the 1880s to 1934, lands owned by Native Americans decreased by two-thirds, from around 155 million acres to around
52 million acres, in great part as a consequence of the Dawes Act.[20]

By treating Native Americans as individuals, rather than as tribes,
and by making private ownership of land an "indispensable condition"
for assimilation and enfranchisement, the Dawes Act equated indi-
vidualism and private property with civilization and US citizenship.[21]
The sovereign individual subject and alienation from land have been
but two markers of civilization in Europe and its colonies. Among the

other markers are conversion to Christianity; farming (as opposed to hunting); and in the United States, mastery of the English language. Throughout the eighteenth and nineteenth centuries, politicians, military leaders, missionaries, and teachers maintained that the achievement of one would lead to the achievement of another, and that once Native Americans gave up their "savage" ways, they would be absorbed into the dominant society. A report from the House Committee on Indian Affairs in 1818 predicted that indigenous children who had been introduced to "the primer and the hoe" would "naturally, in time, take hold of the plough; and as their minds become enlightened and expand, the Bible will be their Book, and they will grow up in habits of morality and industry, leave the chase to those whose minds are less cultivated, and become useful members of society."[22]

For European settlers and their creole progeny, the school was a catalyst for transforming Native Americans into "useful members of society." Indeed, the various arms of the civilizing effort often converged in the Indian school, with the missionary doubling as teacher and a curriculum that included not only catechism but reading, writing, arithmetic, farming, animal husbandry, blacksmithing, carpentry, sewing, weaving, and housework. With the Civilization Fund Act of 1819, Congress boosted the efforts of "capable persons of good moral character," such as missionaries and other "humanitarians," to impart "the habits and arts of civilization" to Native Americans.[23] The Civilization Fund Act did not grant the state direct control of Indian education, but it allowed the federal government to control the purse strings for Indian education and, by extension, to influence individuals and organizations vying for federal money to civilize Indians.

Carlisle's founder, Richard Henry Pratt, was one such individual. As he put it, the school's goal was to civilize, assimilate, and "citizenize" Native American youth by removing them from their homes and families.[24] In its thirty-nine years, approximately eight thousand students passed through Carlisle.[25] In addition to learning English, if they did not already know it, and basic academic skills, students received vocational training and participated in the school's "outing program," a hallmark of its curriculum. Dubbed the "supreme Americanizer," the outing program aspired to put indigenous youth in closer proximity to whites and to augment their vocational training by placing them in white homes and workplaces throughout the northeastern United States.[26] Girls and young women performed domestic work. Boys and young men apprenticed under their hosts. Some toiled in shops and on farms. Others worked in the factories of Ford, General Electric, and Bethlehem Iron and Steel.

Unlike contemporaries who subscribed to the adage that the only good Indian was a dead one, Pratt believed that the so-called Indian problem could be solved by "killing the Indian and saving the man."[27] Put another way, Native Americans needed to be saved from themselves. They had to be cut off from their homes, families, and traditions; pulled from the nation's literal and figurative periphery; and immersed in the white mainstream. "It is a great mistake to think that the Indian is born an inevitable savage," Pratt contended. "He is born a blank, like all the rest of us. Left in the surroundings of savagery, he grows to possess a savage language, superstition, and life. . . . Transfer the savage-born infant to the surroundings of civilization, and he will grow to possess a civilized language and habit."[28]

For Pratt, civilization was both a place and an achieved state. To demonstrate Carlisle's ability to convert what one teacher called "blanket Indians" into "civilized" men and women, school administrators used the before-and-after portrait.[29] Newly arrived students were photographed in a studio or on campus wearing either traditional regalia, such as feather headdresses and breastplates, or the disheveled clothes that they had worn on the journey from their homes to Carlisle. Then they were photographed after they had bathed, had their hair shorn, and been issued the school's stiff, military-like uniform. Both the before and the after photos were staged, and many were sold as cabinet, boudoir, or stereoview cards and postcards. Pratt was keenly aware of their value and used them to convince lawmakers, government bureaucrats, potential donors, and "friends of the Indian" of Carlisle's "civilizing effects."[30] And while he claimed to detest Wild West shows for encouraging Indians "to remain Indians," the more barbaric the indigenous pupil appeared in the before photo, the better.[31] The juxtaposition of the before-and-after images purported to testify to Carlisle's success.[32]

As the number of schools on reservations jumped in the last decades of the nineteenth century, enrollment at Carlisle fell, and the flagship off-reservation boarding school became less cost-efficient and less relevant. In 1904 Pratt resigned as school superintendent, a consequence of having locked horns repeatedly and very publicly with the Bureau of Indian Affairs. Ten years later the school was under investigation by Congress for mismanagement of funds. There were also complaints about excessively harsh disciplinary measures to which students were subjected, as well as lax supervision of students both on and off campus. In 1918 the army repossessed the campus for use as a hospital for soldiers returning from World War I. The school closed, but it remains a salient feature of the allotment and assimilation era.

RICHARD HENRY PRATT: FROM BATTLEFIELD TO PRISON TO CLASSROOM

Carlisle's founder was a laborer, tradesman, and military man who likened his mission as an educator to his work as a soldier. Indeed, as school superintendent, Pratt claimed to confront "a greater number of the 'enemies of civilization'" in the classroom than he had encountered on the battlefields of Indian Territory.[33] Tellingly, his memoir, published posthumously in 1964, is titled *Battlefield and Classroom: Four Decades with the American Indian, 1867–1904.*

Pratt was born in 1840 in Rushford, New York, and raised in Logansport, Indiana. When he was thirteen years old, his father was murdered. Pratt left school and went to work as a printer, tinsmith, and rail splitter to support his widowed mother and two younger brothers. When the Civil War erupted in 1861, he enlisted in a volunteer regiment of the

Union Army and was promoted to first lieutenant of the cavalry.[34] In 1867 he returned to military service and was dispatched to the western frontier. He spent the following eight years commanding Indian scouts and the newly formed 10th Cavalry, the first African American cavalry and original Buffalo Soldier regiment.

In *Battlefield and Classroom*, Pratt recalled pondering the contradiction of having to support and defend the US Constitution as an army officer and at the same time being charged with leading a racially segregated regiment in a war that sought to contain and control Native Americans. "It seemed plain that under [the new Fourteenth] amendment the Negro could not be relegated in army service to the Negro units of enlisted men solely," he observed, "and the Indian could not [continue to] be ... imprisoned on separate tribal reservations."[35] In short, he was unable to reconcile the role of racial segregation in what would be called, in twenty-first-century parlance, a multicultural democracy. Yet that multicultural democracy was not egalitarian. For Pratt and many of his white contemporaries, whites were naturally superior to Negroes and Indians. A self-professed friend of the Indian, he made it his mission to uplift so-called savages by imposing civilization on them.

In 1875 Pratt was presented with the opportunity to transfer a group of Native Americans from "the surroundings of savagery" to "the surroundings of civilization." Following the Red River War in Oklahoma and Texas, he was charged with transporting seventy-two captive Kiowa, Comanche, Cheyenne, Arapaho, and Caddo to Fort Marion in St. Augustine, Florida. Once they arrived at the fortress, Pratt proceeded to turn "his prison into a school for teaching civilization to the Indians."[36] First, he had his prisoners' hair cut and replaced their clothing with secondhand army uniforms. He removed their shackles and replaced the prison's white guards with a Native American patrol. Then he recruited white volunteers to teach the prisoners English and Christian fundamentals. By the summer of 1876, Fort Marion boasted "a two-hour school daily with an average of fifty pupils, divided into four classes," plus a weekly prayer meeting.[37] To instill a work ethic in his prisoners, Pratt had them collect seeds, from which they made neck-laces. Then they sold the necklaces to local curio dealers. The necklaces were so popular that the prisoners were soon making and selling other handicrafts, like canes, bows, arrows, and painted fans. Eventually they were hired out as laborers. They earned money for carrying bags at the train station, picking oranges, clearing land, caring for horses, and milking cows for local farmers. Some taught archery lessons and led tourists on fishing expeditions. To cultivate a spirit of entrepreneurial-ism and thrift among his prisoners-cum-workers, Pratt kept individual savings accounts for each of them and permitted them to spend their earnings on purchases in St. Augustine.[38] His ability to "tame" Native Americans, some of whom were reputed to be among the most incor-rigible of their time, garnered positive attention from philanthropists, clergymen, lawmakers, scholars, and educators, including Spencer Baird, the Smithsonian Institution's first curator, and Samuel Chapman Armstrong, founder of the Hampton Normal and Agricultural Institute in Hampton, Virginia.[39]

In 1877 Pratt arranged to send a group of his prisoners to Hamp-ton so they could continue their education. Armstrong had established Hampton in 1868 "to train selected Negro youths who should go out and teach and lead their people."[40] From 1877 to 1923, the school also admitted over thirteen hundred Native American students from sixty-five tribes.[41] During this period, it claimed to be "devoted to the Negro and Indian Races."[42] In fact, Hampton was compensated by the federal government for the Native American pupils it received. Black students, meanwhile, were expected to "earn ... their own way through school."[43] Hampton's Indian program came to an end after Congress withdrew funding for it.[44] Today, Hampton University is a federally designated historically black college and university (HBCU).

Armstrong was born in 1839 to missionary parents on the island of Maui in the Kingdom of Hawaii. He graduated from the elite Puna-hou School in Honolulu and Williams College in Massachusetts, but modeled Hampton after the Hilo Boarding and Manual Labor School in Maui. A boarding school for boys of the general population, the Hilo School stressed vocational training, including farming, baking, fishing, and sewing, over the study of Greek and Latin. Its alumni went on to work as teachers, government bureaucrats, and ordained ministers.[45]

Similarly, Hampton aimed "to fit selected youth of the Negro and Indian races to be examples to, and teachers of, their people" by "training the hand, the head and the heart."[46] In turn, Hampton served as a model for Carlisle and the Tuskegee Normal School for Colored Teachers, another HBCU. Tuskegee University, as it is known today, was founded by Booker T. Washington, Armstrong's protégé and a celebrated Hampton alumnus. After 1898, Puerto Rican students would find themselves not only at Carlisle, but at Hampton and Tuskegee as well.[47]

Despite their different class and educational backgrounds, Armstrong and Pratt had more than a little in common. Both were Civil War veterans who reinvented themselves as educators in the wake of the Civil and Indian Wars. Pratt commanded an African American regiment on the frontier during the latter war, while Armstrong led African American troops in the Union Army during the former. After the Civil War, Armstrong joined the Freedmen's Bureau, the federal agency charged with aiding newly freed slaves in the South during Reconstruction. Just as Pratt held that the Indian savage could "grow to possess a civilized language and habit" under the right circumstances, Armstrong maintained that "blacks had emerged from slavery culturally and morally inferior to whites and only under the benevolent tutelage of whites could they hope to make genuine racial progress."[48]

Similarities notwithstanding, there were considerable differences between the two men and the institutions they led, in great part because they saw distinct and disparate destinies for their respective students. Where Armstrong understood that African Americans had a clear and fixed place in an increasingly segregated society, Pratt endeavored to uproot Native Americans and to scatter them among whites. Detribalization, acculturation, proselytization, and miscegenation would make indigenous people disappear; assimilation was tantamount to vanishing.

Meanwhile, African Americans would remain a conspicuously separate but putatively equal faction under Jim Crow, a regime that actively prohibited their "detribalization" and mingling with whites.[49] Armstrong rationalized racial segregation on the grounds that "[b]eing kept out of white men's societies of all kinds create[d] independent, healthy organizations" for the southern Negro. And although he longed to see more of his black pupils travel to Africa as missionaries, he dismissed the colonization movement—proposals to remove African Americans from the United States—as a "stupid" and "outrageous" pipe dream.[50]

ASSIMILATION AS RACIAL AND CULTURAL RANKING

On April 13, 1878, Pratt arrived at Hampton with sixty-two Native Americans in tow.[51] He had misgivings about educating them in isolation from whites and openly fretted about the school's "remoteness from the observations of our best people."[52] Anticipating late-twentieth-century theories of the culture of poverty and the belief that "the Black underclass serves as a cauldron of contagious social ills," he also expressed concern about the proximity and potential influence of what he deemed "degraded negroes" in the nearby woods.[53] After only one year at Hampton, and with the financial backing of the federal government, he moved what he considered "his" Indians to Carlisle. As he put it, he did not want "to further the segregating and reservating process."[54] That Native Americans would be further segregated and "reservated" at an *all*-Indian school was no hindrance to him.

For decades, the "co-education of Negroes and Indians at the Hampton Institute [was] watched with interest," despite measures to keep the two groups of students apart, such as separate curricula, classrooms, dormitories, dining halls, and social activities.[55] "[S]ocial intercourse between the races of opposite sexes [was also] limited and guarded. Trouble might come of it," Hampton teacher Helen Ludlow acknowledged in 1888. She quickly added, "None ever has."[56] Meanwhile, heterosexual relations between Native Americans and whites ensued, with two of Ludlow's star female Native American students marrying white men and two white female teachers marrying Native American men.[57] In the final years of Hampton's Indian program, after congressional funding for Native American students and their number—in particular, the number of Native American males—had dwindled, rumors that "Indian girls flirted so with the colored boys" continued to besiege the school.[58] While "friends of the Indian" worried about and attempted to prevent the union of Native Americans and African Americans, they expected and even welcomed "amalgamation" between Native Americans and whites.

According to Wolfe, "territorial expropriation was foundational to the colonial formations into which Europeans incorporated" Native Americans. Meanwhile, "blacks' relationship with their colonizers—from the colonizers' point of view at least—centered on labor. In this light, the varying miscegenation policies make immediate sense, since assimilation reduces an Indigenous population with rival claims to the land, while an exclusive strategy enlarges an enslaved labor force."[59] In short, from the point of view of the colonizer, miscegenation between white and Indian would hasten the latter's inevitable extinction and bolster the settler's "rights to the soil."[60] In contrast, the one-drop rule of *Plessy v. Ferguson*, the US Supreme Court decision in 1896 upholding racial segregation, dictated that black-indigenous unions would only produce more blacks or "mongrels." Whether the union was white and indigenous or black and indigenous, the offspring was no longer indigenous.

Even though, African American and Native American students at Hampton were assigned separate curricula, classrooms, dormitories, dining halls, and social activities Pratt and some of his contemporaries saw value in Native Americans' relationship with and to African Americans. Black students at Hampton were not only charged with orienting newly arrived Native Americans; they were upheld as exemplars of assimilation. Not unlike Carlisle's outing program, slavery was deemed a "supreme Americanizer," for it had brought blacks into

"close contact . . . with the white's civilization, language, labor, and religion."[61] Pratt saw blacks' interaction with whites not only as a "tremendous advantage" for the former group, but as "the greatest blessing that
ever came to the Negro race."[62] "[B]rought from the Torrid Zone across
a great ocean in vast numbers" and "[t]ransferred into . . . new surroundings and experiences," African slaves, he pontificated, "became
English-speaking and civilized, because forced into association with
English-speaking and civilized people; became healthy and multiplied,
because they were property; and industrious, because industry, which
brings contentment and health, was a necessary quality to increase
their value."[63]

By being uprooted and forced into contact with their white masters,
African slaves and their New World descendants had lost their "aboriginal habits" and "old languages."[64] They underwent what Pratt termed,
quite baldly, "assimilation under duress."[65] They were better off for it,
he insisted, and Native Americans would be, too, if he had his way.
His contradictory views of the African American as both pariah and
model point to assimilation's contradictions. What is more, they underscore its violence as a process that can involve not only displacement
and the eradication of culture and language, but an enforced jockeying
among groups as they scramble to gain proximity to the powerful and
to put distance between themselves and the less powerful or powerless.
In other words, assimilation is a process of what anthropologist Aihwa
Ong terms "racial and cultural ranking."[66] To bring that ranking into
relief, let us turn to the Puerto Rican students at the Carlisle Indian
Industrial School.

INDIOS PUERTORRIQUEÑOS

Carlisle's first Puerto Rican student, Juan Santano, enrolled on November 23, 1898, six months after the US Navy invaded San Juan. He
remained a student at the school until April 24, 1904.[67] According to
Pratt, "soldiers returning from serving in that island" brought the boy,

who was around sixteen years old and spoke no English, to the main-land.[68] Nearly sixty Puerto Ricans followed, with the majority arriving between 1900 and 1910.[69]

The United States wasted little time in attempting to Americanize the island's inhabitants, strategically setting its sights on children. As early as 1898, a US-style public school system was already in place in Puerto Rico. A normal school, modeled after normal schools for Native Americans and African Americans, followed in 1900. The University of Puerto Rico was founded in 1903. At all levels of education, English was the primary language of instruction, a policy that would last until the 1940s. In addition, from 1898 to 1903, Congress set aside money for scholarships that would transport Puerto Rican youths to the mainland for study. Carlisle was one of several educational institutions to tap that scholarship fund.[70] Puerto Ricans, particularly Afro-Puerto Ricans, also enrolled at Hampton and Tuskegee.[71]

Like Pratt and Armstrong, John Eaton, Puerto Rico's first education minister, had served in the Union Army during the Civil War. And like Armstrong, Eaton oversaw the establishment of schools for newly freed slaves. As US commissioner of education between 1870 and 1886, Eaton made numerous visits to the Carlisle Indian Industrial School.[72] His successor in Puerto Rico (and governor of Pennsylvania from 1915 to 1919), Martin Grove Brumbaugh, targeted the children of elite families—"lo mejorcito que tiene Puerto Rico," in the words of one alumna—for enrollment at Carlisle, much in the same way that Pratt actively worked to enroll the children of tribal leaders at his school.[73] Their privileged status notwithstanding, the Puerto Ricans who landed at Carlisle would find themselves in a bedeviling racial hierarchy, one in which they were rendered "Indians" and "Negroes."

Evidence of enunciations of this racial hierarchy is found in Carlisle's long, albeit incomplete, paper trail. To obtain federal funds, school documents required students to avow their "Indianness" and to state their tribal affiliation. Many of the Puerto Ricans' forms are marked with cross-outs and added text. For example, in the application for enrollment of Emilio de Arce Pagán, an eighteen-year-old who arrived at Carlisle on February 7, 1911, "Indian" is crossed out and replaced with "Porto Rican."[74] Likewise, "Tribe" is crossed out on José Gonzalo's July 23, 1912, application for enrollment and replaced with "Spain," while "Spaniard" and "Porto Rican" substitute for "Indian."[75] Vicente Figueroa and Delores Nieves were identified in school records as "Negroes." However, like many of their compatriots, Nieves wrote "Porto-Rican" after "Tribe" on a postcard the school sent to check up on former students, and Figueroa self-identified on forms as "Porto Rican" and "Spanish."[76] José Prado plainly stated, "I am not an Indian," on a form dated May 5, 1915.[77] And in a letter to the school's superintendent on January 20, 1914, former student Adela Barrelli noted, "I always like to hear from [the] school although I am not an Indian."[78] These cross-outs, added text, and explanations point to the expanding empire's effort to incorporate its newly conquered subjects in an intelligible way. Moreover, they illuminate Puerto Ricans' refusal to be classified as Indian, an inferior racial category throughout Latin America.

Indeed, a number of the Puerto Ricans who attended Carlisle were dismayed, if not horrified, to find themselves grouped with and as Indians. Some reiterated racist stereotypes about Native Americans in their recollections about the school. In a letter to Superintendent Friedman on June 16, 1911, Providencia Martinez of Ponce, Puerto Rico, reported that she was shocked to encounter Native Americans when she arrived at Carlisle on November 8, 1901. "Really, we did not know that the school was a regular school for Indians when we went there," she recalled. "We thought that there were [A]mericans[,] as well as [P]orto [R]icans [there]." In the three years she spent at Carlisle, she "lernt [*sic*] to like the Indians very much. That is some of the refine one [*sic*]. They were very nice to the [P]orto [R]ican[s,] although at first they hated us." Martinez's father was less sanguine about his daughter's stint at the school. "[H]e used to cry thinking that that place was not a place where we could be happy," she informed Friedman. "You can imagine why he thought so. Down here we do not know anything about good [I]ndians but of those you read in books that are regular animals."[79]

Angela Rivera Tudó, Martinez's classmate, arrived at Carlisle in November 1901 harboring many of the same racist suspicions about Native Americans. In an article that appeared in *La Correspondencia de Puerto Rico* on January 3, 1931, she remembered her first night at the boarding school as "una pesadilla" (a nightmare). She was so scared that her Native American roommates would scalp her that she clutched her head all night to ensure that it remained intact ("me agarraba la cabeza para ver si todavía estaba en su puesto"). Although some former students, like Figueroa, expressed fondness for "Dear Old Carlisle," Tudó charged that the school had abused Puerto Ricans by equating them with "savages" ("poniéndonos al nivel de unos salvajes"). She was glad she learned English while living on the mainland and even went on to pen *Idioms and Other Expressions in English and Spanish* (1940).[80] However, thirty years later she was still smarting at having been reduced to an "indio puertorriqueño" by the island's new, patently ignorant masters. "Nos tomó por Indios puesto que Puerto Rico es parte del grupo de islas los americanos llaman West Indies" (They mistook us for Indians simply because Puerto Rico is part of the West Indies), she complained.[81] "To . . . remember those 'good' times" at Carlisle, she noted with more than a hint of sarcasm, she invited her former classmates, fellow "'Indios' Puertorriqueños," to a reunion to be held at her house in San Juan on January 5, 1931.[82]

The following year, Juan José Osuna published "An Indian in Spite of Myself," an autobiographical essay about his experience at Carlisle. In 1901, at the age of fifteen, he left his widowed mother and eight siblings in Caguas and set out with a group of Puerto Rican youths for "that half-mythical land of promise, the United States of America . . . to study, master a profession, and return to serve our native land." The apprentice bookkeeper and future dean of the College of Education at the University of Puerto Rico aspired to be a lawyer. He believed that he was heading to a school that would set him on the appropriate path and was stunned by what and whom he encountered upon his arrival at Carlisle:

> We looked at the windows of the buildings, and very peculiar-looking faces peered out at us. We had never seen such people before. The buildings seemed full of them. Behold, we had arrived at the Carlisle Indian School! The United States of America, our new rulers, thought that the people of Puerto Rico were Indians; hence they should be sent to an Indian school, and Carlisle happened to be the nearest. Our lives as Indians began May 2nd, 1901, at six o'clock in the morning.[83]

Reminiscent of Frantz Fanon's celebrated 1967 essay, "The Fact of Blackness," "An Indian in Spite of Myself" points to a process of racialization, or, more precisely, to what critical race theorist Devon Carbado has termed "racial naturalization": the "social practice wherein all of us are Americanized and made socially intelligible via racial categorization."[84] Where the Martinican Fanon became a "Negro," a fabrication of a white supremacist empire, when he arrived in France, Osuna became an "Indian," a fabrication of yet another white supremacist empire, when he arrived at Carlisle. Meanwhile, his compatriots, Figueroa and Nieves, became (or perhaps remained) "Negroes," a subordinate category traversing multiple imperial racial hierarchies—French, Spanish, and US alike—despite their self-identification as Puerto Rican and/or Spanish. Whether classified as "Negro" or "Indian," the Puerto Rican youths who landed at Carlisle found themselves "objects in the midst of other objects," as Fanon writes.[85]

As future laborers, Carlisle's Puerto Rican students were inducted into a regime of difference that was not only raced but also classed, as evinced by the work they were required and trained to do. "All the large boys had to choose a trade, while we smaller ones were assigned all sorts of duties from house-cleaning to serving as orderly to General Pratts [*sic*]," Osuna recounted.[86] One of his first tasks after arriving at Carlisle was to weed a large onion field. "We were strung out in a long line with taskmaster Bennett, the farmer, keeping the line of progress as straight as he could by the aid of a whip," he recalled. "[T]his type of education was not exactly in keeping with my preconceived ideas of the 'land of promise.'"[87] Instead, this type of education relied on and reproduced violence and subjugation, as taskmaster Bennet's whip made clear. Indeed, in Osuna's colonial education, violence and subjugation *were* "progress."

Some Puerto Rican students at Carlisle took umbrage at having to do manual and domestic labor, perhaps because they hailed from well-to-do families and were unaccustomed to such work. For instance, José Prado grumbled that he should not have to do kitchen work since his father was paying his tuition. His parents also sent the school extra money for his violin lessons.[88] The students' complaints reached Luis Muñoz Rivera, editor of the *Puerto Rico Herald*, who took it upon himself to visit Carlisle in August 1901. His report, titled "Una visita a Indian School," concluded that Carlisle was a first-rate school for vocational training but no place for "la abstracción mental de estudios" (academics, in other words).[89]

Coincidentally, Puerto Ricans arrived at Carlisle at a moment when questions were being raised about the Dawes Act and the "Indian question" was undergoing revision. Policy makers and "friends of the Indian," like Pratt, had maintained throughout the nineteenth century that Native Americans could and would be absorbed by the mainstream. However, by the turn of the twentieth century, a growing number of government bureaucrats had reached the conclusion that the Native American was "destined to live on the fringes of civilization," just as Dalrymple had portrayed him in *School Begins*.[90] For example, Francis Leupp, commissioner of Indian affairs from 1904 to 1909, recommended in his first annual report that the assimilation program lower its sights from transforming Native Americans to merely improving them. As far as he was concerned, the Indian would "always remain an Indian."[91] Meanwhile, Estelle Reel, superintendent of Indian schools from 1898 to 1910, revamped the Indian Office's curriculum so that it emphasized basic manual and domestic labor, like fixing tools and doing light chores.[92] Likewise, the Hampton publication *Southern Workman* dismissed efforts to educate Native Americans among whites at institutions like Harvard, Dartmouth, and William and Mary as "a dismal failure" and lamented the return of one "Indian girl" to her "rude Indian home with a knowledge of French and music but without any instruction in cooking, sewing, or the care of the home."[93] Expectations that Native Americans would be simple manual and domestic workers may have been deemed practical by some. Yet those expectations not only reflected ideas about the limited and subordinate role Native Americans should play in society; they also produced that very role. By the start of the twentieth century, "[a]ssimilation was no longer an optimistic enterprise born of idealism or faith in universal human progress," Hoxie has noted; "the term now referred to the process by which 'primitive' people were brought into regular contact with an 'advanced' society."[94]

In keeping with contemporary policies regarding Native American education, Osuna was issued his "working outfit" on his second day at Carlisle. The "overalls," "checkered shirt," and "heavy shoes" the school provided him marked his absorption into the host society not as a scholar or future lawyer but as a menial laborer.[95] In 1902 he was sent to work on the farm of Dr. J. P. Welsh in Orangeville, Pennsylvania, as part of the school's outing program. Welsh was the principal of the Bloomsburg State Normal School in nearby Bloomsburg, Pennsylvania. Instead of returning to Carlisle, Osuna remained with his employer and attended school in Orangeville. Then he enrolled at the Bloomsburg State Normal School. "I did not want to return to Carlisle," he admitted. "Frankly, I did not like the place. I never thought it was the school for me. I was not an Indian; I was a Puerto Rican of Spanish descent."[96] Despite being away from Carlisle for three years, he was invited to participate in the school's commencement ceremony and was issued a diploma in 1905. Of the roughly sixty Puerto Ricans who attended Carlisle, he and Tudó were two of only seven to graduate.[97] "I am an alumnus of the Carlisle Indian Industrial School," Osuna reminded his reader, and perhaps himself, at the end of his essay. "I am an Indian in spite of myself."[98]

The Puerto Rican students who attended Carlisle disavowed Puerto Rico's indigenous past and present when they claimed that they had never seen an indigenous person before arriving at the school, when they dismissed their identification as and association with Native Americans as Yankee ignorance and/or geographical error, and when they insisted that they simply were not Indians. As the students and their guardians reiterated, they were Puerto Ricans "of Spanish descent," as opposed to Puerto Ricans of Taíno, African, or mixed origin. Ultimately, Carlisle's Puerto Ricans made a familiar assimilationist move, one taken by more than a handful of other groups in the United States, from the Irish in the nineteenth century to Mexican Americans in the twentieth: they asserted their claim to whiteness.[99]

THE PARADOX OF ASSIMILATION

The Jones-Shafroth Act of 1917 conferred US citizenship on anyone born in Puerto Rico after April 11, 1899. In 1924 the Snyder Act gave US citizenship to "Indians born within the territorial limits of the United States."[100] Both pieces of legislation enshrined jus soli citizenship. Latin for "right of soil," jus soli citizenship maintains that citizenship is more than a legal status; it is also a place.

Similarly, for Pratt, civilization was both an achieved state and a place. To learn how to be civilized, Native Americans needed to be brought to civilization, whether they wanted to or not. To remain civilized, they needed to stay in civilization. Similarly, Armstrong reminded his contemporaries who concocted plans to rid the United States of black people by shipping them overseas that the "Afro-American is here to stay."[101] Yet the place, physical and otherwise, of African Americans and Native Americans following the Civil and Indian Wars would not be the same as that of white Americans. Jim Crow mandated that blacks be excluded from the mainstream (white society, in other words). In contrast, Native Americans were to be absorbed and disappeared by that mainstream. Meanwhile, Puerto Ricans' puzzling status as outsiders on the inside would be articulated via the infamous and inherently contradictory statement that the island was "foreign to the United States in a domestic sense."[102] These seemingly different responses to the so-called Negro and Indian problems and the debate over the status of Puerto Rico in the expanding empire underscored the perceived inferiority of racialized and colonized peoples. Above all, they shed light on assimilation as a process that is often violent and unequal and always relational.

In its thirty-nine years, Carlisle produced more than claims to whiteness. It also came to be a wellspring of modern pan-Indianism, an identity and approach to political organizing based on a sense of commonality and solidarity among indigenous peoples. Historian Hazel W. Hertzberg has described modern pan-Indianism as "the crucible in which elements in the larger society combine with elements in Indian life to produce new definitions of identity within the American," and, one might add, hemispheric and global "social order."[103] Writing about her own Ojibwe family members who attended Indian boarding schools, historian Brenda J. Child notes that her relatives encountered not only "government teachers, matrons, and bureaucrats," but "Lakotas, Oneidas, and Poncas and other students from Indian country." This "rich cross-cultural exchange"—an encounter with both sameness and difference—helped spark modern pan-Indianism.[104] Contrary to Pratt's goal to annihilate the Indian by removing Native Americans from their homes and communities and thrusting them together, Carlisle, paradoxically, helped foster a sense of shared Indianness among some of its pupils precisely by removing them from their homes and communities and forcing them to see themselves in relation not only to the dominant society but to one another. The students hailed from different tribes and places. They spoke different languages and had different religious beliefs and practices. What they shared was the experience of being Indian at Carlisle and all that entailed.

While Puerto Ricans like Tudó and Osuna tried to distance themselves from Carlisle and its Native American students, the very fact of their presence at the Indian school exposes what literary and cultural critic Juan Flores has identified as the cultural convergence and divergence of shared "histories of conquest, enslavement and forced incorporation at the hands of the prevalent surrounding society."[105] These shared histories sometimes produce disavowal, as Tudó's and Osuna's words make clear. Yet they can also produce affirmation and sometimes even alliance, as pan-Indian movements like the Red Power movement and the Indigenous Environmental movement show. The chapters that follow deepen the exploration of convergent and divergent histories of assimilation and the disavowals and affirmations those histories engender.

CHAPTER THREE

Demography Is Destiny

Negroes, New Immigrants,
and the Threat of Permanence

Demography is destiny, so we are told. First used by Ben Wattenberg and Richard Scammon in 1970 in *The Real Majority: An Extraordinary Examination of the American Electorate*, this well-worn maxim has been applied not only to electoral politics but also to myriad subjects, such as financial markets, aging populations, fertility and birth rates, and immigration.[1] Irrespective of context or application, "demography is destiny" holds that population trends and distributions portend or even determine the future.

Whether they are celebratory or full of trepidation, attitudes toward immigration bring the putative relationship between demography and destiny into stark relief. Take, as one example, Theodore Roosevelt's 1905 warning that an influx of "new" immigrants—namely southern, central, and eastern European Jews and Catholics—and low birth rates among "old stock" Americans (Protestant, of northwestern European descent) would result in "race suicide."[2] Two years later, the twenty-sixth president tasked a committee of congressmen and presidential appointees with studying immigration and assimilation and recommending legislation.

Chaired by Vermont senator William Paul Dillingham, the Dillingham Commission, as that committee came to be known, launched its investigation in May 1907 with a tour of Europe, where its members met heads of state and members of the landed elite, who lamented the exodus of peasants from their homelands. They also interviewed migrants who had gone to the United States then returned to their countries of origin.[3] In 1911 the commission presented its findings in a forty-one-volume report. Among its conclusions was that immigrants from southern, central, and eastern Europe were so different from "old stock" Americans, they could not assimilate. "While the American people, as in the past, welcome the oppressed of other lands," Dillingham and his colleagues wrote, "care should be taken that immigration be such both in quality and quantity as not to make too difficult the process of assimilation."[4] Ultimately, the Dillingham Commission's findings helped lead to more restrictive legislation, such as the Immigration Act of 1917 (also known as the Literacy Act and Asiatic Barred Zone Act) and the Immigration Act of 1924 (also known as the Johnson-Reed Act).

More than a century later, US president Donald Trump echoed Roosevelt and the Dillingham Commission when he complained about too much immigration from what he called "shithole countries," like Haiti and countries in Africa, and not enough from Norway.[5] His attorney general, Jeff Sessions, questioned why the United States should welcome "someone who's illiterate[,] has no skills, and is going to struggle in our country and not be successful."[6] White supremacists fulminated about "white genocide" and chanted "You will not replace us!" at rallies in cities like Charlottesville, Virginia.[7] Right-wing television and radio talk show host Laura Ingraham mourned the destruction of "the America we know and love" by "both illegal and legal immigrants."[8] And the ostensibly less tendentious, former NBC news anchor Tom Brokaw claimed that Americans "'don't . . . want brown grandbabies.'"[9] The immigrants' origins have changed, but the fear of a nonwhite country endures.

Since its founding, the United States has been envisioned as a white nation. The people of color who have inhabited this land, indigenous and imported alike, have been imagined as disappearing, temporary, or demographically insignificant, as the label "minority" signals. Writing in the early 1780s in *Notes on Virginia*, Thomas Jefferson, for example, predicted that slavery would be abolished, but like many of his white contemporaries, he maintained that there would be no place for free blacks in the new republic. In addition to "[d]eep rooted prejudices entertained by the whites" and "ten thousand recollections, by the blacks, of the injuries they have sustained[,] the real distinctions which nature has made" would forever prevent the two groups from living together in harmony.[10] So the statesman and future president proposed that following emancipation, African American children "continue with their parents to a certain age, then be brought up, at the public expense, to tillage, arts or sciences... till the females should be eighteen, and the males twenty-one years of age, when they should be colonized to such place as the circumstances of the time should render most proper."[11] Put another way, free blacks should be made wards of the state. Then, after acquiring the skills to live independently, they should be deported. To replace them, Jefferson recommended recruiting "an equal number of white inhabitants."[12]

His was but one of many pitches in the eighteenth and nineteenth centuries to make the United States an all-white nation. Schemes to deport African Americans were called colonization, and the American Colonization Society helped found Liberia as a colony for free blacks in 1822. At the same time, the federal government deported indigenous peoples via policies and practices known quite baldly as Indian removal.[13] Native Americans could also be disappeared via miscegenation, an option that Jefferson and many of his countrymen ruled out for African Americans. "Are not the fine mixtures of red and white... preferable to ... that immovable veil of black?" the founding father (and father of six mixed-race, African American children) asked.[14] White could and would absorb and, ultimately, erase red, while black was deemed fixed and unassimilable.

Exploring the vital and widely overlooked role African Americans have played in understandings of assimilation in the United States, this chapter contemplates the real and imagined connections between demography and destiny—that is, between assimilation and futurity. To do so, I approach Booker T. Washington and Robert Ezra Park's 1912 coauthored travelogue, *The Man Farthest Down: A Record of Observation and Study in Europe* (1912), and George Samuel Schuyler's novel, *Black No More: Being an Account of the Strange and Wonderful Workings of Science in the Land of the Free, A.D. 1933–1940* (1931), as parallels to the Dillingham Report and *Notes on Virginia*. Like the members of the Dillingham Commission, Washington and Park traveled to Europe and wrote their book in order to better understand the immigrants who were arriving to the United States during the Great Wave (1880–1924). Of particular concern was the newcomers' impact on the US racial hierarchy during Jim Crow (1870–1965), a period of de jure and de facto racial segregation when both blackness and whiteness were contested and consolidating. *Black No More*, not unlike *Notes on Virginia*, proposes a far-fetched solution to what by the end of the nineteenth century had come to be known as "the Negro problem."[15] Where Jefferson's fantasy of a post-black future recalls the story of Noah's ark—African Americans are sent away with tools, utensils, and "pairs of . . . domestic animals"—Schuyler's novel imagines a near future in which millions of African Americans undergo a medical procedure that turns them white.[16]

Black No More is an early example of Afrofuturism, speculative fiction by and about Afro-diasporic peoples that grapples with questions regarding the relationship of black people to science, technology, humanity, and the future.[17] It is also a political satire and a racial passing narrative. Yet even though its African American protagonist moves from the margin to the center of American society by becoming white, Schuyler's novel is generally not read as a tale of assimilation. Similarly, *The Man Farthest Down* has not been regarded as a commentary on mobility, by which I refer to movement not only through space (e.g., travel and migration) but within the US racial hierarchy. Indeed, of Washington's and Park's many writings, *The Man Farthest Down* has received scant attention from scholars. And Washington, while widely recognized as an African American leader, is generally not seen as an authority on immigration and assimilation. In contrast, Park, a white man and a founder of the Chicago school of sociology, has been upheld as one of the twentieth century's most prominent scholars of immigration, assimilation, and race.[18]

Since the late nineteenth century, assimilation has been associated with immigration, especially European immigration, to the United States. To be sure, there are and have long been black immigrants to this country. However, as Ethiopian American poet Samuel Getachew has astutely observed, "an ingrained American inability to think about both blackness and immigration simultaneously" persists.[19] And although early scholars of assimilation studied US-born African Americans, that group has not figured prominently in conversations about assimilation since the last decades of the twentieth century, the moment when the discipline of sociology splintered into the sociology of race and the sociology of immigration.[20]

Indeed, scholars have bracketed off African Americans or excluded them altogether in theorizing assimilation, against which they have defined racialization. For example, sociologist Milton M. Gordon maintained in his 1964 study, *Assimilation in American Life: The Role of Race, Religion, and National Origins*, that "the Negro, one of America's oldest minorities," had achieved "cultural assimilation, or acculturation" (e.g., by adopting the English language and Christianity) but had yet to assimilate fully.[21] As long as they faced prejudice and discrimination and were "barred from the cliques, social clubs, and churches of white America," Gordon averred, African Americans would "construct . . . their own network of organizations and institutions, their own 'social world,'" and remain outside the mainstream.[22] More than a generation later, sociologist Nathan Glazer attributed "the failure of assimilation to work its effects on blacks as on immigrants . . . to the strength of American discriminatory and prejudiced attitudes and behavior toward blacks."[23]

This chapter probes the omission of African Americans in theories and understandings of assimilation. By putting *The Man Farthest*

Down and *Black No More* in dialogue with Park's contemporary writings, I argue that African Americans have not been included in conversations about assimilation because of the ways assimilation has been defined against racialization. Specifically, African Americans have not been included in conversations about assimilation because of the longstanding discrepancy between blackness and Americanness—in other words, because of the legacy of black denizenship in the United States. Simultaneously an insider and an outsider, the figure of the denizen brings the paradox of assimilation into relief: assimilation via differential inclusion, with differential inclusion referring to the incorporation of members of a social group as distinct and subordinate subjects, rather than as identical peers.[24] This chapter illuminates a widely overlooked history of black assimilation narratives that ironically highlight differential inclusion. I conclude by connecting *The Man Farthest Down* and *Black No More* to twenty-first-century debates about immigration and assimilation and by highlighting the parallels between African American denizenship and the denizenship of the undocumented.

BOOKER T. WASHINGTON, ROBERT EZRA PARK, AND THE US RACIAL HIERARCHY

African American activists and intellectuals paid attention to how immigrants were reshaping the US racial hierarchy during Jim Crow and the Great Wave.[25] Perhaps none did so as closely as Washington, founder and principal of the Tuskegee Normal and Industrial Institute, a school for African Americans in rural Tuskegee, Alabama. In 1910 Washington embarked on an eight-week tour of Europe, "visiting those parts of the country from which the majority of our immigrants are now coming to America."[26] He recalled, "I wanted to see these people in their home in order to compare them with the condition of the Negro people in the Southern states."[27] Following in the footsteps of the Dillingham Commission, he visited modern-day England, Scotland, Germany, the Czech Republic, Austria, Hungary, Serbia, Bulgaria, Turkey,

Italy, France, Denmark, Poland, and Russia.[28] In addition to meeting landless peasants, miners, ghetto merchants, slum-dwelling artisans, and prospective and returned emigrants, he hobnobbed with the European elite. For example, he was honored at a luncheon of the Anti-Slavery and Aborigines Protection Society in London, dined with the king and queen of Denmark, and played golf with Andrew Carnegie at his castle in Scotland.[29] Washington traveled with Park, his publicist and ghostwriter. Park, having completed his doctoral degree in philosophy at Heidelberg University in 1903, planned their itinerary and translated between English and German, "the language which was of greatest use in most of the countries," on their tour.[30]

Washington and Park met each other around 1904 via the Congo Reform Association, an international organization dedicated to ending King Leopold II's rule in the Congo Free State. Washington was the organization's vice president; Park, a former reporter and newly minted PhD, its secretary. According to Washington, the two men shared an interest in the power of education to uplift the "backward races," a label applied to nonwhite and non-Western peoples during the Progressive Era.[31] Just as Richard Henry Pratt, the founder of the Carlisle Indian Industrial School, the first off-reservation boarding school in the United States, maintained that Native Americans could be civilized if they were brought to civilization, Park saw "the backwardness of peoples" as "on the whole, a historical and not a biological phenomenon."[32] In other words, Park believed that nonwhite and non-Western peoples, along with poor, rural whites, were not intrinsically inferior to "metropolitan peoples."[33] With the right sort of education, they could be reformed.

A graduate of the Hampton Normal and Agricultural Institute, Washington presented himself and was upheld as a product of the right sort of education. As I note in the previous chapter, Hampton, the model for Carlisle and Tuskegee, was founded in the wake of the Civil War as a vocational school for African Americans. Washington's celebrated 1901 autobiography, *Up from Slavery*, attests to his transformation from slave, to student, to educator. "[W]ith an optimism characteristic of other self-made Americans," Park observed, "Washington was disposed to believe that all men were predestined to rise and those who found themselves behind were, in all probability, merely those who, like the Negro, had started late and were now, or would soon be, on their way."[34]

When Park and Washington first met one another, Park was interested in Christian missions in Africa. "He had a notion," Washington recollected, "that the conditions of the natives in the Congo, as well as in other parts of Africa, could not be permanently improved only through a system of education, somewhat similar to that at Hampton and Tuskegee."[35] Yet instead of studying Christian missions in Africa, Park embarked on a "study of the Negro and the race problem" when he moved from Boston to Tuskegee in 1905.[36] He worked closely with Washington for nine years. After leaving Tuskegee in 1914 for the University of Chicago, Park quickly rose as an expert on the American Negro (the title of the first class he taught) and, more generally, "cultural and racial contacts."[37] At Chicago, he developed his famous race relations cycle, the theory that when social groups encounter one another—for example, via conquest, colonialism, enslavement, or migration—four phases ensue, always and everywhere: competition, conflict, accommodation, and assimilation. The race relations cycle posited that assimilation was a result of contact and that "savage" peoples could be elevated, quite ironically, when subjugated by more advanced ones.[38] For example, slavery, according to Park (1914), was

> the usual method by which peoples have been incorporated into alien groups. When a member of an alien race is adopted into the family as a servant, or as a slave, and particularly when that status is made hereditary, as it was in the case of the Negro after his importation to America, assimilation followed rapidly and as a matter of course.... [T]he Negro in the southern states, particularly where he was adopted into the household as a family servant, learned in a comparatively short time the manners and customs of his master's family.[39]

Park attributed his insights to his stint at Tuskegee, musing, "I proba- bly learned more about human nature and society, in the South under Booker Washington, than I had learned elsewhere in all my previous studies."[40]

Unlike Park, Washington is generally not regarded as an authority on immigration and assimilation. However, their coauthored travelogue, *The Man Farthest Down*, is a commentary on both subjects. Although their book "contains the observations of two different individuals," it is unclear where one man's observations end and the other's begin.[41] As Washington acknowledged, "[A] large part of what I saw and learned about Europe is due directly to the assistance of Doctor Park.... I do not believe I am able to say now how much of what I have written is based upon my own personal observations and what is based upon those of Doctor Park."[42] Likewise, Park explained that as he and Washington "travelled about," they had "the same ideas; and it was because ... we understood each other, were interested in the same things, that the book came to be written."[43]

The Man Farthest Down not only prefigures Park's race relations cycle; it also echoes Washington's famous Atlanta Compromise speech. Wash- ington delivered that speech to a predominantly white audience at the Cotton States and International Exposition in Atlanta on September 18, 1895. His speech is generally read as a narrative of accommodation. It is also a condemnation of migration, *em*igration and *imm*igration alike. Washington assured white southerners that in exchange for basic edu- cation and due process, black southerners would work and submit to white political rule rather than agitate for equality or integration. He called on African Americans to remain in the South and not to consider "bettering their condition in a foreign land"—be it Africa, the industrial North, or the industrializing West.[44] Likewise, he urged white south- erners not to "look to the incoming of those of foreign birth and strange tongue and habits for the prosperity of the South."[45] To both blacks and whites, he reiterated the imperative, "Cast down your bucket where you are."[46] If they did so, he avowed, blacks would befriend "the peoples of all races, by whom [they were] surrounded." In turn, whites would find among "the eight millions of Negroes[,] habits you know, fidelity and love." He implored whites, "Cast down your bucket among these people who have without strikes and labor wars tilled your fields, cleared your forests, builded [*sic*] your railroads and cities, [and] brought forth treasures from the bowels of the earth."[47] Put another way, African Americans were not the same as whites, but they were not unfamiliar and unruly foreigners, either. They were lesser Americans, but Americans nonetheless.

When read in this light, we see that the Atlanta Compromise is not only accommodationist but also nativist. It reflects both Jim Crow and the mounting nativism of the late nineteenth century.[48] Undeniably, African Americans had reason to fear immigrants. After all, "one of the first things aliens learned upon arriving was the norms of the American caste system."[49] As they jockeyed for a position within that system, immigrants whose own whiteness was tenuous refused to live and to work with African Americans, barred them from labor unions, and supported the white supremacist Democratic Party. Writer and cultural critic Toni Morrison has described "pressing African Americans to the lowest level of the racial hierarchy" as the "most enduring and efficient rite of passage into American culture."[50]

THE MAN FARTHEST DOWN

As its title alone signals, *The Man Farthest Down*, like the Atlanta Compromise, is an intervention in the American caste system and racial hierarchy. And like Washington's well-known speech, *The Man Farthest Down* is an argument against an anti-black present and a post-black future. At the outset, Washington explained that he traveled to Europe "to find the man farthest down," a synecdoche for the social group with "the narrowest outlook," "the hardest work," and the "greatest need of education" that is most "removed from influences which are everywhere raising the level of life among the masses of the European people."[51] To find that most downtrodden and isolated of peoples, he determined to acquaint himself "with the condition of the poor and working classes in Europe, particularly in those regions from which an ever-increasing number of immigrants are coming to our country each year"; "to learn why it was that so many of these European people were leaving the countries in which they were born and reared"; and "to study the methods which European nationals were using to uplift the masses of the people who were at the bottom of the scale of civilization."[52] Above all, he set out to refute the contention that the European immigrant could "substitute for the Negro labourer and that in this direction a solution for the race problem would be found."[53]

Washington acknowledged similarities between African Americans in the rural South and European peasants. However, by "compar[ing] the masses of the Negro people of the Southern States with the masses in Europe," he sought to show that African Americans were closer, and therefore more similar, to white Americans—especially white southerners—than Europeans were.[54] "Whatever else one may say of the Negro, he is, in everything except his color, more like the Southern white man, more willing and able to absorb the ideas and the culture of the white man and adapt himself to existing conditions, than is true of any race which is now coming into this country," he insisted.[55] As evidence of African Americans' assimilability and adaptability, he upheld their adoption of Christianity and English, "a language that the civilized world respects and that the civilized world is learning more and more every year."[56]

Furthermore, Washington warned that the threat of revolution and war loomed large in Europe and that European immigrants brought with them anarchism, socialism, and "labour insurrection."[57] Meanwhile, "the Negro in America" only wished "to seek his salvation by developing himself . . . through education."[58] In an echo of his Atlanta Compromise speech, he assured his readers, "The Negro is not, at the present time, either an anarchist, nor a socialist, nor is he anywhere seeking to organize or overthrow or undermine the government."[59] Indeed, the

Negro "is just as proud to be an American citizen as he is to be a Negro. He cherishes no ambitions that are opposed to the interest of the white people, but is anxious to prove himself a help rather than a hindrance to the success and prosperity of the other race."[60]

According to Washington, compared to the European masses, African Americans, rural and urban alike, were flourishing. He noted that despite Jim Crow; *Plessy v. Ferguson* (the 1896 US Supreme Court ruling upholding racial segregation); voter disenfranchisement; and white supremacist terrorism, as evinced, for example, by the resurgence of the Ku Klux Klan (KKK) in the early twentieth century, African American birth and literacy rates were rising, and an increasing number of African Americans owned property. Not only was there more land to buy in the United States; there was more food and plenty of work to be had. The rural "Negro is better off," he asserted, because "even when his home is little more than a primitive one-room cabin, he is at least living in the open country in contact with the pure air and freedom of the woods, and not in the crowded village where the air and the soil have for centuries been polluted with the accumulated refuse and offscourings of a crowded and slatternly population."[61] Similarly, "the coloured people" in "the slums and poorer quarters of... New Orleans, Atlanta, Philadelphia, and New York" were "in every way many per cent. [*sic*] better off."[62]

Reiterating contemporary ideas about a hierarchy of peoples and presaging Park's race relations cycle theory, Washington insisted that African Americans' greatest advantage was their "contact with... the best and ripest civilization that the world knows anything about": white America.[63] In contrast, what he called Europe's "under-races" lacked "contact with the educated classes, the rich classes, the cultured classes.... They do not have the close contact with the progressive, the intelligent classes that the Negro has here in the South."[64] He concluded that the African American was not "the man farthest down." To the poor, slum-dwelling European woman he bequeathed that ignominious distinction.

Washington's rosy appraisal of black life in the United States was met with skepticism, if not outrage, by contemporary civil rights activists. For example, in their "Open Letter to the People of Great Britain and Europe" on October 26, 1910, W. E. B. Du Bois and twenty other African American leaders lambasted Washington for "giving the impression abroad that the Negro problem in America is in process of satisfactory solution."[65] They surmised that the Tuskegee Institute's dependence on wealthy white donors had "compelled [Washington] to tell, not the whole truth, but that part of it which certain powerful interests in America wish to appear as the whole truth."[66] Even Park, by no means a radical, took note of his traveling companion's insistence that "everything in America surpassed anything in Europe. He just wanted to get the dirt on them that was all, to discover for himself that the man farthest down in Europe had nothing on the man farthest down in the U.S."[67]

The Man Farthest Down does not just paint a cheerful picture of relations between white and black Americans in the early twentieth century; it predicts an even brighter future. Washington tapped Progressive-Era ideas of evolution, modernity, and futurity, declaring that "the Negro is not, as a rule, a degenerate. If he is at the bottom in America, it is not because he has gone backward and sunk down, but because he has never risen."[68] Where the peoples of the Old World continued to toil with primitive tools, African Americans were not "stuck so fast in their old traditional ways of doing things that they refuse to change."[69] On the contrary, he declared, they belonged "to a new race that was not burdened with traditions and past—to a race, in other words, that is looking forward instead of backward, and is more interested in the future than in the past."[70]

In fact, the United States would not rid itself of African Americans, and the European immigrants of Washington's time would not replace them. However, African Americans would not be folded into the American polity in quite the same way as the "new" immigrants and their white descendants. As Park pointed out in 1930, despite having been in the United States for three-hundred years, "[t]he Negro ... ha[d] not been assimilated. This is not because he has preserved in America a foreign culture and an alien tradition.... To say that the Negro has not assimilated means no more than to say that he is still regarded as in some sense a stranger, a representative of an alien race."[71]

According to Park, the unassimilated remain conspicuously alien, while the assimilated vanish into the majority. Assimilation, or, more precisely, inassimilability, was "a function of visibility."[72] "In America it is proverbial that a Pole, a Lithuanian or a Norwegian cannot be distinguished in the second generation from the older American stock," he observed.[73] In contrast, people of color—namely Asians and blacks—bore what he described as a "distinctive racial mark," one that amounted to a "racial uniform."[74] "It is not because the Negro and the Japanese are so differently constituted that they do not assimilate," Park contended. "The trouble is not with the Japanese mind but with the Japanese skin. The 'Jap' is not the right color."[75]

As I note in the following chapter, Japanese Americans would be christened the first US model minority in the 1960s. They were absorbed as "good" (meaning docile) citizens, but they still retained their racial uniform, as the "minority" in "model minority" signals. In contrast, European immigrants and their white progeny moved closer to and eventually merged with white Americans via a process known as assimilation. Policy makers, politicians, activists, and artists came to understand and to articulate African Americans' differential inclusion via concepts like segregation, isolation, alienation, subpopulation, and underclass, as well as double consciousness, race pride, black pride, and black nationalism.[76] For example, in his commencement speech at Howard University on June 4, 1965, President Lyndon B. Johnson warned that the "great majority of Negro Americans—the poor, the unemployed, and the dispossessed are another nation. Despite the court orders and the laws, despite the legislative victories and the speeches, for them the walls are rising and the gulf is widening.... The isolation of Negro from white communities is increasing rather than decreasing, as Negroes crowd into the central cities and become a city within a city."[77] Put another way, while European immigrants and their white offspring moved closer to and became the American mainstream, African Americans moved further away. White Americans and black Americans appeared to be separate peoples.

Published a year after Park declared inassimilability a function of visibility, George Schuyler's *Black No More* imagines a world in which one's "racial uniform" can be changed to "the right color." Set primarily in New York City and Atlanta in the 1930s, the novel chronicles the adventures of Max Disher, a fast-talking hustler and the first person to undergo the "powerful and dangerous treatment" at Black-No-More, Incorporated, a clinic owned and operated by Dr. Junius Crookman, an enterprising African American scientist who has developed a process that turns black people white.[78] After Max becomes white, he changes his name to Matthew Fisher and relocates from Harlem to his native Atlanta to pursue Helen Givens, an attractive, dim-witted white woman who rejected him because he was black when they first encountered one another at a Harlem speakeasy. In addition to winning Helen's heart and hand in marriage, Matthew rises to the top of the Knights of Nordica, a parody of the KKK, by posing as an anthropologist—in other words, as a student of man. He also amasses a fortune by advising white capitalists on how to subdue their increasingly restive employees, poor whites who fear that "white Negroes" (blacks who have become white) have infiltrated the workplace and are stealing their jobs.[79]

Black-No-More proves to be so successful that Dr. Crookman and his associates open clinics across the country. Sales of Madame Sisseretta Blandish's hair straighteners and skin lighteners, stand-ins for the real Madame C. J. Walker's cosmetics, dwindle as the lines outside Dr. Crookman's clinics grow.[80] Black-owned banks shutter after customers withdraw all their money. Donations to the National Social Equality League, a spoof of the National Association for the Advancement of Colored People (NAACP), dry up. Race leaders, like Shakespeare Agamemnon Beard, a caricature of Du Bois, find themselves out of work. Harlem and other African American enclaves are reduced to ghost towns. The white population suddenly swells, and black people disappear from the American landscape.

To distinguish "imitation whites" from "pure whites," Arthur Snobb-craft and Samuel Buggerie, leaders of the elitist Anglo-Saxon Associ-ation, launch an investigation into all Americans' family trees.[81] They are horrified to discover that their own lineage is not as white as they had believed. After newspapers expose the self-proclaimed bluebloods as Negroes, they are set upon and burned at the stake by a bloodthirsty mob of Christian white supremacists in rural Mississippi.

When the novel closes, Dr. Crookman, the new US surgeon general, publishes a report on skin pigmentation, noting that "the new Cau-casians" (blacks who have undergone his Black-No-More treatment) tend to be "two to three shades lighter than the old Caucasians."[82] In other words, "the blacks [a]re whiter than the whites."[83] His discovery prompts a backlash against very pale people, with employers paying them less and public institutions segregating them. To defend the newly maligned very white whites, Karl von Beerde, the former Shakespeare Agamemnon Beard, founds the Down-With-White-Prejudice-League. Mrs. Sari Blandine, a.k.a. Madame Sisseretta Blandish, strikes it rich with a cosmetic that imparts "a long-wearing light-brown tinge to the pigment."[84] "Everybody that was anybody had a stained skin," Schuy-ler's narrator observes. "A white face became startlingly rare. Amer-ica was definitely, enthusiastically mulatto-minded."[85] Emblematic of the new face of America, "dusky," little Matthew Crookman Fisher is born to Helen and Max.[86] Upon learning that his beloved son-in-law, baby grandson, and he himself are all Afro-descendants, Henry Giv-ens, Helen's father and the Imperial Grand Wizard of the Knights of Nordica, concludes, "I guess we're all niggers now."[87]

In summary, Max/Mathew's transformation—his name change, movement out of the ghetto, marriage to a white woman, and ascent in the work world—are all hallmarks of the assimilation process as it is generally understood and frequently narrated in the United States. And while African Americans were stereotyped as a "scab race" as early as the 1890s, a consequence of labor unions' refusal to admit them, the immigrant has long been seen as a cheaper and more productive substitute for the American worker.[88] As a tale of metamorphosis, physical and social mobility, and the struggle between putative insiders and interlopers, *Black No More* is, without a doubt, a story of assimilation and Americanization.

PASSING AND ASSIMILATION

Published during the heyday of eugenics and on the cusp of the Nazis' rise to power, *Black No More*, like previous and contemporary works by James Weldon Johnson, Nella Larsen, and Fannie Hurst, points to the mutability and fiction of race. In Schuyler's novel, race is not just a social construct; it is a simulacrum, a copy for which there is no original. Yet unlike Johnson's *The Autobiography of an Ex-colored Man* (1912), Larsen's *Passing* (1929), and Hurst's *Imitation of Life* (1933), Schuyler's novel has a comedic tone. Much of its humor revolves around transgressions, impurities, and role reversals: blacks become white; so-called pure whites find that they are black; putatively white women give birth to black babies; erstwhile black people "out-white" white people; and the very light-skinned are discriminated against in the same ways that the very dark-skinned were discriminated against.

Like assimilation, passing involves mimesis and mobility—sameness and movement, in other words. As literary critic Elaine K. Ginsberg points out, passing is "about the boundaries established between identity categories," particularly racial, gender, sexual, and class identities, and "about the individual and cultural anxieties induced by boundary crossing."[89] As a story about racial passing, *Black No More* is part of a narrative tradition dating back to the nineteenth century. While stories of reverse passing tend to garner considerable attention, as the case of civil rights activist Rachel Dolezal has demonstrated, many narratives about racial passing in the United States are about "the assumption of a fraudulent 'white' identity by an individual culturally and legally defined as 'Negro' or black by virtue of percentage of African ancestry."[90]

The nexus of mimesis and mobility is evident in *Black No More*. Once Max crosses over from black to white—that is, once he moves from one social category to another—he finds that his literal, physical movement is practically unimpaired. His new power and privilege become apparent to him immediately after he undergoes Dr. Crookman's treatment, when he is interviewed by an attractive, white, female reporter. Together, "[t]hey walked down Broadway in the blaze of white lights to a dinner-dance place. To Max it was like being in heaven. He had strolled through the Times Square district before but never with such a feeling of absolute freedom and sureness. No one now looked at him curiously because he was with a white girl. . . . Gee it was great!"[91] As a white man, Max is free to pass through spaces that were dangerous or off-limits to him previously. What is more, the reporter has paid Max a handsome sum to get the scoop on his transition from black to white, so he is suddenly rich. In short, he is able to move through physical and social spaces that were once out of his reach. "[H]e could go anywhere, associate with anybody, be anything he wanted to be," now that he was "free, white and . . . [in] possess[ion of] a bankroll!"[92] "At last," Schuyler's narrator adds, Max "felt like an American citizen."[93]

Despite the parallels between racial passing and assimilation, narratives in which an African American attempts to pass or successfully passes as white are usually not read as stories about Americanization and the pursuit of the American dream. Instead, they are seen as tales of imitation, appropriation, and guile. As literary critic and poet Harryette Mullen points out:

> Passing is not so much a willful deception or duplicity as it is an attempt to move from the margin to the center of American identity. That such movement has been systematically blocked to the mass of black people is perhaps the primary reason that the ability to do so is almost invariably

interpreted as inauthenticity when managed by an African-American, but as an exemplary instance of cultural assimilation when accomplished by European immigrants who shed language, culture, and tradition in order to become, or allow their offspring to become true (white) Americans.[94]

In other words, some people—namely, European immigrants and their white descendants—become Americans, while those barred from that category can only try to approximate or appropriate Americanness. If whiteness is a privilege, a possession, and a form of property, as scholars like Cheryl I. Harris and George Lipsitz have argued, and Americanness is whiteness, then Americanness is also a privilege, a possession, and a form of property.[95]

DENIZENSHIP AND THE PARADOX OF ASSIMILATION

Efforts to bar certain groups from the category "American" extend back to this nation's founding. As noted previously, African Americans and Native Americans were not envisioned as legitimate parts of the polity or even as permanent members of society during Jefferson's lifetime. Their exclusion was formalized with the first US naturalization law, the Naturalization Act of 1790, which limited citizenship to "free white" persons and laid the groundwork for the Chinese Exclusion and Johnson-Reed Acts and other restrictive legislation.[96] Until the ratification of the Fourteenth Amendment in 1868, African Americans, including those who were free, were ineligible for US citizenship.

African Americans were in and of the United States but were not considered real Americans. Instead, they were denizens: people who are present in the space of the nation-state but are not and are never supposed to be full members of the polity. As Park observed, "The first Negroes were imported into the United States in 1619.... By 1860... it is safe to say, the great mass of Negroes were no longer, in any true sense, an alien people. They were, of course, not citizens. It might, perhaps, be more correct to say that they were less assimilated than domesticated."[97] Despite claims that assimilation results in homogeneity and racialization conserves difference, Park's observation indicates that certain social groups are incorporated ("domesticated," to use his word) into a stratified society precisely as racialized subjects. Incorporation via marginalization or subordination—differential inclusion, in other words: this is the paradox of assimilation.

Contrast Park's remarks regarding African American assimilation (or lack thereof) with those of writer and literary critic Samuel Delany, an heir to the Afrofuturist literary tradition Schuyler helped establish:

> The historical reason that we [African Americans have] been so impoverished in terms of future images is because, until fairly recently, as a people, we were systematically forbidden any images of our past. I have no idea where, in Africa, my black ancestors came from because, when they reached the slave markets in New Orleans, records of such things were systematically destroyed. If they spoke their own languages, they were beaten or killed. The slave pens in which they were stored by lots were set up so that no two slaves from the same area were allowed to be together. Children were regularly sold away from their parents. And every conceivable effort was made to destroy all vestiges of what might endure as African social consciousness.... That some musical rhythms endured, that certain religious attitudes and structures seem to have persisted, is quite astonishing, when you study the efforts of the white, slave-importing machinery to wipe them out.[98]

In addition to underscoring the need for future images of, for, and by Afro-diasporic peoples, Delany offers a pointed commentary about assimilation and the violence it often entails. Indeed, the "powerful and dangerous treatment" to which aspiring whites subject themselves at the Black-No-More clinics serves as a metaphor for the violence of assimilation. Schuyler likens the chair into which Dr. Crookman's patients are strapped to "a cross between a dentist's chair and an electric chair" and describes the Black-No-More treatment as "the beginning or the end," as a process that involves both gains and losses.[99]

Without a doubt, *Black No More* is a misanthropic and dystopian satire. The novel presents a dim view of the future, one in which the present's problems endure, but in new form. Moreover, all of its characters are self-serving. They are either slow and stupid or bold and crafty. That said, the novel offers not only villains but also heroes. The elitist WASPs, Snobbcraft and Buggerie, occupy the former camp. Their names alone articulate arrogance, deceit, and nonnormative sex. They get their comeuppance when they are assailed by the white supremacist gang in an isolated corner of the deep South. Reminiscent of lynching reports, with which Schuyler, as a reporter for the black press, was all too familiar, the grisly description of their torture and murder stands out in a narrative that is, up until that harrowing scene, quite tongue-in-cheek.

The novel's heroes, Max and Dr. Crookman, are rewarded for their chutzpah and wiliness with wealth and power. The story ends on a high note, with Max and his family and friends sunbathing at Cannes, all just as brown and carefree as Max and Helen's mixed-race son. In the end, *Black No More* envisions not only a post-black but a post-white world. With Dr. Crookman's skin- and face-altering technology, blacks and whites alike disappear and are replaced by people with a "light-brown tinge to the pigment." No longer a threat or tragedy, the "mulatto," to use Schuyler's word, is embraced, celebrated, and upheld as the embodiment of a better future.

NEW DENIZENS, NEW SLOGANS

Despite assertions that multiculturalism had killed or would kill assimilation in the second half of the twentieth century, the term continues to circulate in academia, policy circles, and the mainstream media, especially in debates about the so-called Hispanic and Islamic challenges (the contention that Latinxs in the United States and Muslims in North America and Europe are unable or unwilling to integrate fully). The subject of Latinx, Asian, and, more recently, Muslim assimilability (or inassimilability, depending on one's point of view) has figured prominently in debates about immigration and citizenship in the twenty-first century. In contrast, African Americans are rarely included in these conversations, especially outside cities with relatively high concentrations of black immigrants, like New York, Miami, and Minneapolis-St. Paul.

By reading *The Man Farthest Down* and *Black No More* as narratives about immigration and assimilation, I have endeavored to detangle these terms and to draw attention to the ways people who are not generally associated with them—in this case, African Americans—are, in fact, assimilated as racialized others and internal outsiders. Furthermore, I show that, although the concept of denizenship has come to be associated with late capitalism, its history in the United States goes back much further, to the very founding of this country.[100] The discrepancy between African Americanness and Americanness persists in the twenty-first century. Take, for example, the conspiracy theory that Barack Obama was not born in the United States and therefore was ineligible to be president. As long as African Americans are disassociated from Americanness, stories about racial passing will not be considered stories about assimilation and Americanization. Instead, they will be read as tales about people who claim something that is not supposed to be theirs: the power and privilege of full citizenship.

In the twenty-first century, stories about passing—about duplicity and trespassing—continue to circulate. Literary critic Kirsten Silva Gruesz observes that "the slave and the undocumented migrant share similar conditions of legal vulnerability as non-citizens. One parallel emerges when the body in question moves into a space where it is not supposed to be: a refugee whose request for asylum has not been approved; a fugitive from the slave regime or from federal immigration authorities."[101] Just as Frederick Douglass used forged papers to escape slavery in 1838, immigrants have used forged documents to enter, remain, and work in the United States since those documents were required of them.[102] And where the Progressive-Era protagonist was African American, the hero of the twenty-first-century passing narrative tends to be a young, undocumented immigrant.

Like Park's "domesticated" Negroes, these new protagonists are in and of the United States, but because they are not US citizens, they are not real Americans from the state's point of view. For example, participants in Deferred Action for Childhood Arrivals (DACA), a program established by executive order in 2012 that allows certain undocumented youth to remain and to work in the United States, may be "less illegal" than undocumented immigrants who do not have DACA.[103] Still, as noncitizens, the DACA-mented are not authorized or documented enough, or in quite the right way, as far as the state is concerned. In fact, because DACA does not lead to any form of permanent regularization, it formalizes its participants' marginalization, thereby rendering them denizens.

Nonetheless, these twenty-first-century denizens have a deep connection to their adopted homeland. If, as several sociologists have asserted, assimilation is a process of identification and attachment, one "in which persons and groups acquire the memories, sentiments, and attitudes of other persons or groups" and the "newcomer ... comes to assume the outlook shared by his new associates," then these denizens are highly assimilated.[104] Many grew up and attended (or still attend) school in the United States. Many are fluent in English. Many are familiar not only with US popular culture but with this country's institutions, history, narratives, and proclaimed values and ideals, especially as related to hard work, opportunity, and merit.[105] Some—for example, Dreamers, would-be beneficiaries of the abortive DREAM Act—follow in the footsteps of not only the Japanese American model minority but the talented tenth, the label applied to promising and accomplished young black men in the early twentieth century.

So fluent and familiar are these twenty-first-century denizens that they pass as bona fide Americans. Indeed, some do not realize that they are not US citizens until they reach a milestone of adolescence, such as applying for a driver's license, graduating from high school, or applying to college. By unhinging Americanness from formal belonging, these self-proclaimed undocumented Americans challenge the state's monopoly on citizenship.[106] They offer a broader and more inclusive vision of the United States.

Despite their insistence that they truly are Americans, albeit without papers, undocumented Americans live in a state of "permanent temporariness."[107] They remain vulnerable to deportation, a mechanism that renders certain individuals and groups temporary and, to paraphrase indigenous futurist writer and scholar Lou Cornum, unworthy of the future.[108] That many of the undocumented, the deportable, and the deported are indigenous Mexicans and Central Americans and other people of color warrants scrutiny, especially in the context of cries of white genocide; laments about too many poor black and brown immigrants; the detention and caging of migrant children; the diversion of asylum-seekers to Mexico and Guatemala, "safe third countries" in twenty-first-century doublespeak; the overhauling of the US immigration system so that it is merit (read: money) based rather than family based; and efforts to add a citizenship question to the US Census. Against this backdrop, the imperative to "Make American Great Again" (MAGA) comes into relief as a sinister campaign to maintain the white majority, numerically and otherwise, by driving people of color to the margins or out. In short, MAGA is a method of asepsis and a milder form of ethnic cleansing.[109]

The Man Farthest Down is a plea to white Americans to accept African Americans as Americans, albeit as unthreatening, second-class citizens, while *Black No More* offers a vision in which the US Negro problem is solved by getting rid of Negroes. By twenty-first-century standards, neither of these works is affirming, liberating, or politically correct. At the same time, neither is an illogical response to the exigencies of its time, an era of de jure and de facto racial segregation in public schools, public spaces, and public transportation; of poll taxes and literacy tests; and of lynching, a form of ethnic cleansing if ever there was one.

MAGA conjures up a violent past that terrifies many Americans, or it mourns a past that never was. Either way, the slogan nods to an earlier maxim, "demography is destiny," as it attempts to reshape the future. Yet despite deracination, disease, slavery, family separations, exclusion acts, quotas, Jim Crow, lynching, tribal disenrollment, voter suppression, internment, border walls, workplace raids, incarceration, poisonous water, travel bans, cages, and deadly encounters with law enforcement, the people of color who were never envisioned as a real, legitimate, or permanent part of this settler colony-cum-nation of immigrants have persevered. In the wake of Trump's 2016 presidential election, old slogans, like the post-Holocaust cry, "Never Again," have taken on new meaning as migrant detention facilities have been likened to the Nazi and US concentration camps of the Second World War.[110] All the while, new calls, like #heretostay, defiantly envision a black and brown present and future.[111]

CHAPTER FOUR

The Moral Economy of Deservingness, from the Model Minority to the Dreamer

ASSIMILATION UNDER DURESS, REDUX

In April 1947, *Mademoiselle* published a story about the reintegration of Japanese Americans into US society following their incarceration during the Second World War. Titled "The Nisei Discover a Larger America" and penned by Nisei (second-generation Japanese American) Sono Okamura, the story spotlighted five Japanese American women who were successfully pursuing careers in the arts in New York City. Okamura acknowledged that "[f]or the great bulk of the Nisei, relocation meant disillusionment and frustration."[1] Nonetheless, she contended, the women in her story were successful because of their experiences of "evacuation" and "segregation," euphemisms for removal to and incarceration in the concentration camps that the War Relocation Authority (WRA) had established specifically for Japanese nationals and Japanese Americans. "[I]n spite of the hardships of evacuation and segregation," she averred, "the war served to widen the horizon of this group."[2]

One of the former internees Okamura profiled, Miné Okubo, worked as an illustrator for *Fortune* magazine. In 1946, Columbia University Press published *Citizen 13660*, Okubo's celebrated graphic memoir of internment. According to Okamura, "Miné ... was too much the artist to remain idle" while incarcerated at the Tanforan Assembly Center in San Bruno, California, and the Topaz War Relocation Center in northwest Utah from 1942 until 1944.[3] "Instead, she made capital of her camp experiences and produced some two thousand drawings objectively recording every detail of camp life."[4] In addition to removing Japanese Americans "from those sections of the country where traditional discrimination against them had been the strongest," such as small towns and "little Tokyos" along the West Coast, the experience of displacement provided them with "new opportunities for social and economic life."[5] Okubo, for one, had traveled a long way from her sleepy hometown of Riverside, California, to New York City, "the ideal market place for [her] talent."[6] Okamura's story ended on a high note. "Scattered all over the country, the Nisei are discovering America for the first time," she proclaimed, "and America is discovering them."[7]

Some seventy years after the publication of Okamura's article and Okubo's book, eighteen-year-old Larissa Martinez revealed that she was "one of the eleven million undocumented immigrants" living in the United States, in her June 3, 2016, valedictory speech at McKinney-Boyd High School in McKinney, Texas, an exurb of Dallas-Fort Worth.[8] The aspiring neurosurgeon was graduating with a 4.95 grade point average and a full scholarship to Yale University. "When people see me standing up here, they see a girl who is Yale-bound and who seems to have her life figured out," she observed. In fact, she lived with fear, uncertainty, and deprivation. "We are here without official documentation because the U.S. immigration system is broken," she declared. "I myself have been waiting seven years for my application to even be processed." She shared some of the obstacles she had overcome since she had left her abusive and alcoholic father in her native Mexico and arrived in the United States with her mother and sister on a tourist visa seven years earlier. Along with "having to embrace and fit into a new culture," Martinez recalled giving "up a part of [her] childhood to help raise [her] little sister" while their mother "worked from morning until late at night."[9]

The three of them crammed themselves into a one-bedroom apartment without internet or a washing machine. Martinez did not even have her own bed. School became her "safe haven."[10] Upending then-presidential candidate Donald Trump's slogan, "Make America Great Again," and his promise to build a wall along the US-Mexico border, she insisted that "people like me, people who have become a part of the American society and way of life ... yearn to make America great again, without the construction of a wall built on hatred and prejudice." She concluded, "[B]y sharing my story, I hope to be able to convince all of you that if I was able to break every stereotype based on what I'm classified as— Mexican, female, undocumented, first-generation, low-income—then so can you. . . . I am living proof that beating the system is possible."[11]

Even though Trump would win the county in which McKinney is located, as well as the rest of Texas, in the race for the US presidency in November 2016, Martinez received a standing ovation for her speech.[12] She drew the attention of both local and national media and received praise and scorn alike on social media.[13] Scott Martin, a teacher at McKinney-Boyd who professed to come from a "Republican background," acknowledged that not all Americans would be pleased with his student or her words. Still, he gushed, "[W]hen kids from these backgrounds outperform kids who come from so much, it blows my mind. . . . It's like a book or a movie."[14]

Indeed, Okamura's article and Martinez's speech tap and reproduce a well-known and widely beloved narrative in the United States: that of the model minority and the Dreamer, as the would-be beneficiary of the abortive DREAM Act is known. The heroines in these stories—the productive, resilient, and uncomplaining Nisei and the young, scrappy, and bright undocumented immigrant—achieve success despite formidable hurdles, including racism, wartime hysteria, xenophobia, poverty, and a "broken" immigration system. In line with Martinez's claim that she is "living proof that beating the system is possible," tales about successful racial minorities and immigrants hold out the promise of upward mobility for all.

The Japanese American internee was what historian Mae M. Ngai has termed an alien citizen, "an American citizen by virtue of . . . birth in the United States but whose citizenship is suspect, if not denied, on account of the racialized identity of . . . immigrant ancestry."[15] Dreamers, in contrast, are not US citizens, but they are what I call probationary citizens, people who must show that they merit inclusion in society. The federal DREAM Act and its successor, DACA, bring their probation into relief.

First introduced in Congress in 2001, the DREAM Act seeks to grant certain young undocumented immigrants conditional residency and, upon their meeting further qualifications, such as attending an institution of higher learning and/or serving in the military for at least two years, legal permanent residency. In response to Congress's refusal to pass the DREAM Act, President Barack Obama implemented DACA, an executive order, in 2012. DACA grants certain young undocumented immigrants temporary permission to work in the United States and a temporary stay of deportation. Like the DREAM Act, DACA does not lead to citizenship. It does not lead to legal permanent residency, either. DACA is a temporary, revocable, and precarious status. Although the DREAM Act and DACA are distinct, DACA participants are often referred to as Dreamers. They are also sometimes called DACA-mented.

Differences in status notwithstanding, both alien citizens and probationary citizens are participants in what sociologists Sébastien Chauvin and Blanca Garcés-Mascareñas call a moral economy of deservingness, a site in which social actors demonstrate a particular kind of behavior and/or adhere to a particular set of values and ideals in exchange for rights, resources, and/or recognition.[16] Just as Richard Henry Pratt, the founder of the Carlisle Indian Industrial School, claimed that Native Americans had to undergo "assimilation under duress" to earn US citizenship, WRA officials saw internment as a form of "benevolent" and "coercive assimilation."[17] Ngai has shown that they envisioned the camps as "'Americanizing projects' that would speed the assimilation of Japanese Americans through democratic self-government, schooling, work, and other rehabilitative activities."[18] Similarly, the Dreamer's exclusion and marginalization function as a proving ground of Americanness. The DREAM Act's champions argue that because Dreamers contribute to society, they have earned a place in the polity, if not as formal citizens, then as legal permanent residents, and if not as legal permanent residents, then as DACA-mented immigrants, a status they must renew every two years.

Linking the Cold War–era Japanese American model minority to the twenty-first-century Dreamer, this chapter traces a genealogy of deservingness. I locate the Japanese American model minority in the context of the Cold War and the discourse on the culture of poverty. While Japanese Americans were labeled the first model minority in 1966, Latinxs (in particular, Mexicans and Puerto Ricans) and African Americans were branded "problem minorities." The figure of the model minority was upheld as evidence that the United States was a racial democracy and an egalitarian meritocracy, a society in which advancement is based on talent, effort, or achievement. What is more, the figure of the model minority served a disciplinary function during the Cold War: it helped justify the social, economic, and political status quo and linked success with virtue. In so doing, it reinforced a hierarchy of deserving and undeserving subjects, of good citizens and model minorities on the one hand, and failed citizens and problem minorities on the other.

Like the Cold War–era model minority, the twenty-first-century Dreamer bolsters the image of the United States as an egalitarian meritocracy and a benevolent nation of immigrants, as opposed to a fickle and calculating capitalist nation in need of labor—in other words, economic migrants. In addition, the archetypal Dreamer disciplines citizens and noncitizens who fail to live up to neoliberal ideals of autonomy, self-entrepreneurialism, personal responsibility, and deservingness.[19] Because DACA is temporary and revocable, it disciplines its own participants. Proponents of the DREAM Act and DACA stress the Dreamer's superhuman work ethic, self-reliance, and contributions to society. This is a well-meaning, albeit misguided, dangerous, and as of this writing, unsuccessful strategy for reforming US immigration policy. Ultimately, I argue, the moral economy of deservingness has not offered the model minority full citizenship or the Dreamer formal citizenship. Rather, it has offered them only contingent, partial, and attenuated inclusion.

To connect the first and most recent US iterations of the model minority, I begin by scrutinizing the relationship between Americanness and prosperity and between non/un-Americanness and poverty. After discussing the racialization of poverty as Latinx and African American and the invention of the model minority, I turn my attention to John Okada's 1957 novel *No-No Boy* and Alberto Ledesma's 2017 graphic memoir *Diary of a Reluctant Dreamer: Vignettes from a Pre-American Life*, two texts that grapple with the themes of deservingness and belonging. Both works also express an ambivalent Americanness, thereby troubling the figures of the model minority and Dreamer and calling attention to the exigencies of their social and political contexts.

AMERICANNESS AND WEALTH

In narrating the history of the DREAM Act, Walter J. Nicholls notes that the "authors of the original piece of legislation developed the DREAM acronym ... to create a direct connection between the [DREAM Act] cause and core national values associated with the American dream."[20] Although it has been linked to the founding of the United States—specifically, to the Declaration of Independence's proclamation about life, liberty, and the pursuit of happiness—and has been identified as a "central ideology of Americans," the concept of the American dream is a relatively recent invention.[21] The American historian James Truslow Adams is credited with coining the term in his 1931 book *The Epic of America*.[22] Writing in the midst of the Great Depression, he defined the American dream not as a "a dream of merely material plenty" but as "a social order in which each man and each woman shall be able to attain to the fullest stature of which they are innately capable, and be recognized by others for what they are, regardless of the fortuitous circumstances of birth or position."[23] The United States was exceptional, Adams insisted, because it was a meritocracy that allowed men and women "to grow to fullest development . . . unhampered by the barriers which had slowly been erected in older civilizations."[24] Similarly, political scientist Jennifer L. Hochschild has defined the American dream as "not merely the right to get rich, but rather the promise that all Americans have a reasonable chance to achieve success as they define it— material or otherwise—through their own efforts, and to attain virtue and fulfillment through success."[25]

Hochschild's definition indicates that the American dream does not necessarily refer to material success. Still, ideas about property and ownership have long been entangled with conceptions of Americanness and whiteness. As a status conferring the right or privilege to own property, be it in the form of a slave or a house in the "right" neighborhood, whiteness is a form of property.[26] So, too, is US citizenship. Not unlike money or a parcel of land, US citizenship is a status that can be passed from one generation to the next. In other words, US citizenship is an inheritance. Yet until the adoption of the Fourteenth Amendment in 1868, whiteness was a requirement for US citizenship. As media scholar Hector Amaya observes, US citizenship "is inherently a process of uneven political capital accumulation and that unevenness follows ethno-racial lines."[27]

To highlight the imbrication of race, citizenship, and property ownership, I look to instances in which the state has permitted, imposed, or denied property ownership. In addition to converting black bodies into property, the regime of slavery, for example, denied African Americans the right or privilege to own property. Similarly, as "aliens" ineligible for citizenship, Asians were prohibited from owning property in several states. Internment also forced many Japanese Americans to sell their property at a loss or to give it up altogether during the Second

World War.[28] In contrast, the Dawes Act of 1887 broke up tribal lands and required individual Native Americans to own private property, rather than hold it in common, as a condition for US citizenship. Senator Henry L. Dawes, author of the Dawes Act, maintained that by owning private property, Native Americans would go from being burdens to contributors to society.[29]

Arguments linking property ownership and contributions to society continue to reverberate in discourse on DACA and the DREAM Act. Take, for example, a photo essay that appeared in the *New York Times* in November 2019, one week before the US Supreme Court ruled on the validity of the Trump administration's decision to terminate DACA. Titled "They Achieved the American Dream: Will the Supreme Court Let Them Keep It?," the photo essay featured Jorge Garcia Alvarez and Evelyn Duron Guerra, a young undocumented couple. As small children, Alvarez and Guerra "were illegally brought across the border with Mexico."[30] With the support of DACA, they attended college. Jorge studied finance; Evelyn, business. They went on to earn a combined $90,000 annually in the white-collar sector. Alongside pictures of their tidy, beige, clapboard house, the story reported, "After growing up in trailer parks in Indiana, the couple bought their first home in a Nashville suburb. It has three bedrooms, plenty for a family."[31] From slavery to DACA, property ownership in the United States has signaled full personhood; acceptance of, absorption into, and/or contribution to a capitalist socioeconomic order; assimilation; the threat or promise of permanence; and the achievement of the American dream.

The *New York Times* photo essay identified Alvarez and Guerra as Dreamers, young, undocumented immigrants who had risen from humble origins. Despite poverty and their "alien" status, they had "built an American life."[32] However the script is written—as a story about the achievement of virtue or "striking it rich"—the American dream, like its stage, meritocracy, articulates reward and deservingness.[33] In his history of poverty policy in the United States, Michael B. Katz locates the transmutation of poverty into a condition of morality and, by extension, deservingness in the transition to capitalism and democracy in the early nineteenth century. In addition to prodding people to work, thereby helping ensure a "supply of cheap labor in a market economy increasingly based on unbound wage labor," the moralization of poverty identified "market success with divine favor and personal worth. Especially in America, where opportunity awaited anyone with energy and talent," Katz observes, "poverty signaled personal failure."[34] As I show in the following discussion, being poor is tantamount not only to failure but also to a racialized form of un-Americanness.

THE RACIALIZATION OF POVERTY

In 1962 socialist activist and writer Michael Harrington introduced the US mainstream to poor Americans with the publication of *The Other America: Poverty in the United States.* To be sure, there have always been poor people in the United States. Harrington's goal was to draw attention to them and to transform US politics in order to abolish poverty. "That the poor are invisible is one of the most important things about them," he announced.[35]

The Other America followed the publication of David M. Potter's *People of Plenty: Economic Abundance and the American Character* in 1954 and, four years later, John Kenneth Galbraith's celebrated *The Affluent Society.* Galbraith asserted that over the course of the twentieth century, the United States had come to enjoy "great and quite unprecedented affluence" and the "ordinary" American, "access to amenities—foods, entertainment, personal transportation, and plumbing—in which not even the rich rejoiced a century ago."[36] Such "economic abundance," Potter concluded, had shaped "the whole, broad general range of American experience, American ideals, [...] American institutions," and "the American character."[37] In the midst of the Cold War, social scientists defined that character as acquisitive, individualistic, and oriented toward achievement and the future. "In this context," Katz observes, "the 'lower class' emerged" not only as an aberration, but "as un-American."[38]

While prosperity has been linked to Americanness, poverty has been associated with the not-yet-, non-, or un-American. Think, for example, of Emma Lazarus's tired, poor, huddled masses and the category Third World. Yet poverty has also been attached to the "failed" citizen. Unlike the "law-abiding and hard-working" "good" citizen, the failed citizen, sociologist Bridget Anderson tells us, is "incapable of achieving, or failing to live up to, national ideals."[39] Similarly, Harrington characterized poor Americans as "the rejects of society and of the economy."[40] Decades before scholars would theorize the concept of precarity, an existence defined by vulnerability, unpredictability and insecurity, Harrington pointed out that the poor "never had the right skills in the first place, or they lost them when the rest of the economy advanced."[41] "[C]ondemned to the economic underworld— to low-paying service industries, to backward factories, to sweeping and janitorial duties," they comprised a separate and "underdeveloped nation" within the United States.[42] They were, in Harrington's words, "internal aliens" and "alien citizens."[43] "To be impoverished is... to grow up in a culture that is radically different from the one that dominates the society," he declared.[44]

By the late 1950s, American social scientists, educators, and policy makers had labeled the putatively radically different culture of the American poor the "culture of poverty." Distinguishing the culture of poverty from poverty plain and simple, anthropologist Oscar Lewis defined the former as "a culture in the traditional anthropological sense in that it provides human beings with a design for living, with a ready-made set of solutions for human problems, and so serves a significant adaptive function."[45] Among the adaptations were "feelings of dependency and helplessness, a present-time orientation, unemployment, a lack of class consciousness, out-of-wedlock child-rearing, female-headed households, and a general mistrust of institutions."[46] According to Lewis, these adaptations calcified into "a way of life handed on from generation to generation along family lines," thereby creating a cycle of poverty "that is difficult to escape even when structural conditions change."[47]

The idea of the culture of poverty arose in the aftermath of the Second World War, a moment that saw a split between welfare qua "entitlements" and welfare qua "charity." Programs benefiting white men primarily, such as workmen's compensation, Federal Housing Authority loans, and the G.I. Bill, fell into the former category, while programs used by women and children, such as Aid to Families with Dependent Children, fell into the latter.[48] Entitlements were disassociated from and thus not recognized as welfare. Welfare, meanwhile, became a dirty word, a signifier of women's and people of color's dependence, laziness, opportunism, and pathology.

In the years following the Second World War, social scientists looked to culture and behavior to explain differences among social groups as theories of biological inferiority fell out of favor.[49] At the same time, racial minorities were growing more vocal in demanding civil, political, and labor rights, and race riots erupted in cities across the United States. Although they by no means had a monopoly on being poor, African Americans and Latinxs—in particular, Mexicans and Puerto Ricans— came to be associated with the culture of poverty and were branded "problem minorities," a category preceding that of the failed citizen.[50]

Latinxs loomed especially large in Lewis's theorization of the culture of poverty. He introduced the idea of the culture of poverty in his 1959 ethnography, *Five Families: Mexican Case Studies in the Culture of Poverty*, then developed it further in *La Vida: A Puerto Rican Family in the Culture of Poverty—San Juan and New York*.[51] Meanwhile, Daniel Patrick Moynihan, assistant secretary of labor under President Lyndon B. Johnson, issued "The Negro Family: The Case for National Action," "one of the most controversial documents in the history of American social science."[52] The Moynihan Report, as it came to be known, maintained that African Americans expected equal opportunities but would never achieve "roughly equal results, as compared with other groups ... unless a new and special effort is made."[53] While acknowledging "the racist virus in the American bloodstream," Moynihan attributed what he saw as an enduring and distinctly African American cycle of poverty to "the breakdown of the Negro family." He presented out-of-wedlock births and female-headed households as consequences of slavery and evidence of the black family's dysfunction. Characterized by a matriarchal family structure, poor school performance, low test scores, crime, delinquency, and widespread alienation among African American youth, the African American "subculture," he concluded, amounted to a "tangle of pathology."[54]

THE MODEL MINORITY

Against the backdrop of the black and brown culture of poverty and the Moynihan Report, William Petersen, a sociologist at the University of California, Berkeley, invented the figure of the model minority. He first used the label in "Success Story, Japanese-American Style," a story in the January 9, 1966, issue of the *New York Times Magazine.* Over eight pages, he extolled Japanese Americans for overcoming "the worst injustices," including "color prejudice," "fear and hatred," and the denial of "their elementary rights—most notoriously in their World War II evacuation to internment camps."[55] Because they had achieved upward mobility by assimilating into particular institutions, social spaces, and occupations, such as the university and "white-collar" professions, Japanese Americans, he concluded, were "better than any other group in our society, including native-born whites."[56]

Just as important to Petersen's model minority construct is its antithesis: the problem minority and failed citizen. While the model minority stereotype would be extended to Chinese Americans and, over the ensuing decades, other Asian Pacific Americans, the Asian Pacific American qua model minority would always be distinguished from the white majority. Above all, historian Ellen D. Wu points out, the Asian Pacific American model minority would be upheld as *"definitively not-black."*[57]

The not-blackness of Japanese Americans is both explicit and implicit in "Success Story, Japanese-American Style." Echoing theories of the culture of poverty and the Moynihan Report, Petersen posited that African Americans were hopelessly locked in a cycle of poverty. "For all the well-meaning programs and countless scholarly studies now focused on the Negro," he maintained, "we barely know how to repair the damage that the slave traders started." "Barely more than 20 years after the end of the wartime camps," Japanese Americans, in contrast, had "risen above even prejudiced criticism." That they had "established this remarkable record . . . by their own almost totally unaided effort" further distinguished them from the problem minorities and failed citizens who demanded or had come to depend on assistance, such as welfare. Where the matriarchal African American family passed dysfunction from one generation to the next, Japanese immigrants, according to Petersen, had "developed a family life both strong and flexible enough to help their children cross a wide cultural gap."[58] In addition, Japanese Americans were "distinguished by their greater attachment to family, their greater respect for parental and other authority."[59] And where African Americans were associated with crime and delinquency, "the Japanese were exceptionally law-abiding," an effect, Petersen claimed, of their vulnerability as "aliens ineligible" for naturalization until the passage of the McCarren-Walter Act in 1952.[60] So different were Japanese American youth and African American youth that "only occasionally" did members of the former group show an interest in "anything even as slightly off the beaten track"— and black—"as jazz music."[61] Nisei, he quipped, "were squares."[62]

Petersen attributed Japanese Americans' success not to their Americanness but to what he saw as "their meaningful links with an alien culture"—in other words, with Japanese culture and values.[63] Put another way, their enduring difference from the dominant American culture facilitated their partial—what a later generation of sociologists would call segmented—assimilation.[64] "Buddhist moral values," he avowed, lent themselves to "adaptation to American institutional forms," and Japanese "diligence in work" and "simple frugality" were akin to the Protestant ethic.[65] In contrast to Harrington's impoverished internal alien and alien citizen, the American Negro, according to Petersen, was "[t]he minority most thoroughly imbedded in American culture." Consequently, African Americans lacked "meaningful ties to an overseas fatherland," and "a Negro who knows no other homeland ... has no refuge when the United States rejects him."[66] Paradoxically, African Americans were unmoored precisely because they had been tethered to an anti-black America, while Japanese Americans had assimilated successfully, albeit incompletely, because they maintained ties to an "alien culture."

As scholars in Asian Pacific American studies have shown, the model minority is not a full citizen. Rather, the model minority occupies a secondary space. "This secondary space," sociologist Lisa Sun-Hee Park observes, "is a socially marginal one in which Asian Americans, despite their legal citizenship, continue to hold a foreigner status."[67] In addition to being an alien citizen (in Ngai's sense), the model minority is a myth that ignores or dismisses Asian Pacific American activism and masks disparities among and within Asian Pacific American groups.[68] This myth also serves a disciplinary function by helping justify the social, economic, and political status quo. According to its logic, if the docile, patient, hardworking, and self-reliant model minority can achieve material success, then the failed citizen and problem minority should be able to do so as well without protest or an advantage. The model minority's success is upheld as proof that the United States is a colorblind meritocracy, while the failed citizen's and problem minority's failure to rise out of poverty and into the mainstream is chalked up to an inferior culture or to personal or moral failure.

In addition to manifesting the perception of Japanese Americans as perpetual foreigners, "Success Story, Japanese-American Style" reproduced stereotypes that pathologized those deemed failed citizens and problem minorities—in particular, African Americans. The African American, according to Petersen, was everything that the Japanese American was *not*: lazy, dependent, demanding, antiauthoritarian, criminal, hip, tragically assimilated, bereft, angry, and undeserving.

Contrasting John Okada's *No-No Boy*, the first novel by a Japanese American ever published, with the works of the African American writer James Baldwin, Petersen described the former as "a novel of revolt against revolt."[69] In other words, *No-No Boy*, he tells us, is a defense of the status quo.

In contrast, writer Karen Tei Yamashita (2019) would write of *No-No Boy's* "anger" and "aggressively violent" and "ironically masked" treatment of race and citizenship when Okada's novel was re-released in 2019.[70] In a sort of rejoinder to Petersen, she would liken *No-No Boy* to Richard Wright's 1939 classic *Native Son*. First published in 1957 by a Japanese publisher (after being rejected by several American publishers) and then republished in its entirety by the University of Washington Press in 1976 during "a literary moment of political protest and cultural recuperation" among Asian Pacific Americans, Okada's groundbreaking novel is both a defense of the status quo and an aggressive and ironic treatment of race and citizenship.[71] It is to *No-No Boy* that I now turn.

NO-NO BOY: THE PRODIGAL SON

Okada's novel is about the struggle of Ichiro Yamada to reintegrate into US society after the Second World War. Like Okada, who was incarcerated at a WRA camp in Minidoka, Idaho, Ichiro is a former internee.[72] Yet unlike Okada, a Second World War veteran, Ichiro is a no-no boy, a young Japanese American man who replied "no" to questions 27 and 28 on a questionnaire that the War Department and WRA gave to all adults of Japanese ancestry who were incarcerated in concentration camps in the late winter and spring of 1943. Known informally as the Loyalty Questionnaire, the survey was supposed to assist in the recruitment of Nisei into the US military and to assess the loyalty of Japanese and Japanese Americans. To those ends, the two questions asked:

27. Are you willing to serve in the armed forces of the United States, or combat duty wherever ordered?

28. Will you swear unqualified allegiance to the United States of America and faithfully defend the United States from any or all attack by foreign or domestic forces, and forswear any form of allegiance or obedience to the Japanese emperor, to any foreign government, power or organization?[73]

When the novel opens, Ichiro is twenty-five years old. Having spent the past two years in prison for refusing to profess loyalty to the United States, he has just returned to Seattle, his (and Okada's) hometown. Upon his arrival, he encounters Eto Minato, an acquaintance and a Nisei veteran. When he realizes that Ichiro is a no-no boy, Eto spits on Ichiro. Unable to look Eto in his "hate-churned eyes," Ichiro wishes he could "gouge out his own eyes." He averts his gaze and notices "his accuser's" pants: "God in a pair of green fatigues, U.S. Army style. . . . Beseech me, they seemed to say, throw your arms about me and bury your head between my knees and seek pardon for your great sin."[74]

A tale of guilt, penitence, and redemption, *No-No Boy* is rich with Christian imagery. Ichiro's sin is his betrayal of the United States, and his homecoming is a sort of violent baptism. After Ichiro wishes he could gouge out his own eyes, an act of self-flagellation reminiscent of the martyrdom of Saint Lucy, a group of African Americans calls him "Jap" and tells him to "[g]o back to Tokyo."[75] He has returned home not as a hero but as "an intruder in a world to which he ha[s] no claim."[76] His "cross" is the "unrelenting condemnation" he feels from others and, most of all, himself: "[H]e had driven the nails with his own hands."[77]

Not unlike the prodigal son of Jesus's parable, Ichiro is tormented by feelings of guilt, shame, infidelity, and undeservingness. After the prodigal son leaves home and squanders his inheritance, he begs his father to take him back as a servant. Similarly, Ichiro has denied and been denied both his Japanese heritage and "the gift of his birthright": his rights as a US citizen.[78] It was out of loyalty to his Japanese mother, an immigrant ineligible for naturalization under US immigration law and an unwavering supporter of her homeland, that he answered no to questions 27 and 28 on the Loyalty Questionnaire. "It was she who opened my mouth and made my lips move to sound the words which got me two years in prison," he tells himself.[79] At the same, time, he blames himself for his decision. "[O]f his own free will," the narrator recounts, "he had stood before the judge and said that he would not go in the army. At the time there was no other choice for him."[80] At the time Ichiro, along with some 110,000 other Japanese Americans, was held captive by his own government in a concentration camp.[81] The experience of internment showed him that it was "all right to be German and American or Italian and American or Russian and American," but "it wasn't all right to be Japanese and American."[82] Nor was it "enough to be American only in the eyes of the law"—in other words, an alien citizen.[83] He blames his mother, himself, and "the world which is made up of many countries which fight with each other and kill and hate" for his loss.[84] Neither Japanese nor American, all that is left of him, he concludes, is an "empty shell."[85]

No-No Boy narrates Ichiro's effort "to find his way back to that point of wholeness and belonging."[86] In his quest, he encounters new people, like Emi and Carrick, and loses others, including his friend Kenji Kanno and his own mother. Emi, a pretty Nisei woman, is a "striking sensual contrast" to Ma.[87] Ma has "the awkward, skinny body of a thirteen-year-old which had dried and toughened," while Emi is "slender, with heavy breasts . . . rich, black hair . . . and long legs" that are "strong and shapely like a white woman's."[88] Unlike Ma, Emi is patient and forgiving, two qualities associated with normative femininity and the model minority. Emi is also a patriotic American. She has lost her Japanese immigrant father to repatriation, and her Nisei husband has abandoned her for a career in the US military, so desperate is he to prove his patriotism. Still, she urges Ichiro to stop being angry at himself or the United States. "They made a mistake when they made you do what you did," she concedes, "and they admit it by letting you run around loose. Try, if you can, to be equally big and forgive them and be grateful to them and prove to them that you can be an American worthy of the frailties of the country as well as its strengths."[89]

Shortly after Emi delivers this rousing speech, Ichiro travels to Portland with the thought of starting a new life there. When he applies for a job as a draftsman, he meets Carrick, a white American man who affirms Emi's claim that the United States is a fallible and forgiving country deserving of forgiveness. After describing Japanese American internment as a "big black mark in the annals of American history," Carrick offers Ichiro the job at an unusually high salary.[90] Carrick's admission is, in effect, "a sincere apology from a man who had money and position and respectability."[91] His generous job offer is a kind of penance. However, Ichiro is convinced that the "job did not belong to him, but to another Japanese who was equally as American as this man who was attempting in a small way to rectify the wrong he felt to be his own."[92]

Notwithstanding his feeling of undeservingness, Ichiro's encounter with Carrick is a turning point. It allows Ichiro to glimpse "the real nature of the country against which he had almost fully turned his back" and to see that "its mistake was no less forgivable than his own."[93] In other words, it prompts him to begin to forgive himself for betraying the United States and the United States for betraying him. Moreover, he realizes that he cannot run from his Japanese identity, as represented by his parents. If he rejects them, he "render[s] himself only part of a man."[94]

While Ichiro's "intrapsychic division" leaves him feeling that he is only part of a man, Kenji, a Nisei veteran whose right leg has been partially amputated due to a combat injury, is physically part of a man.[95] The US military has given Kenji a Silver Star Medal and a new Oldsmobile customized to accommodate his disability. As a veteran, he is able to give his father, a widower "who had known only poverty and struggle after his wife died leaving six children," a two-story, seven-room house with "new rugs and furniture and lamps and [a] big television set."[96] Yet Kenji has never fully recovered, and his health is declining. A strong, physically intact no-no boy, Ichiro is the wounded veteran's antithesis.

Ichiro is also poor. Like Kenji's father, his parents migrated to the United States with the intention of making money, then returning to Japan. Yet unlike Kenji's father, the Yamadas do not live in middle-class comfort. Their cramped, one-bedroom apartment in the back of a grocery store stands in stark contrast to the Kannos' house. Riding as a passenger in the Oldsmobile, Ichiro gazes at "the big, roomy houses of brick and glass which belonged in magazines and were of that world which was no longer his to dream about." He envies Kenji and insists he "would have given both legs to change places with" him.[97] As literary critic and writer Viet Thanh Nguyen has pointed out, "commodities such as cars, televisions, houses, and furnishings are signs not only of prosperity but also of loyalty" in *No-No Boy*. "The reward for loyalty, both during World War II and then implicitly during the Cold War, is the participation in America's bounty of plenty."[98] Kenji's new car and middle-class house indicate that he has achieved the American dream, but his eventual death from his combat wound highlights the cost of loyalty and America's bounty of plenty.

Similarly, Ichiro's mother's suicide underscores the psychic toll of migration. She is not only fiercely loyal to Japan in an inhospitable—indeed, overtly anti-Japanese—host country; she is also mentally ill. Ma believes that Japan has defeated the Allies; that the Japanese government will send a ship to "return to Japan those residents . . . who have steadfastly maintained their faith and loyalty to our Emperor"; and that the letters she receives from distressed relatives in Japan are fraudulent.[99] Both her vehement patriotism for her homeland and her madness may be read as symptomatic of her formal exclusion from the American polity and the persecution by the state to which she, Japanese immigrants, and Japanese Americans were subjected during the Second World War. As Ichiro's alcoholic father puts it, "Mama sick. Papa sick. . . . Everybody sick."[100]

When he returns home from Portland, Ichiro finds his drunk father passed out, their apartment flooded, and Ma's body floating "half out of the tub."[101] After receiving a letter from her sister in Japan in which her sister begged for food, Ma had withdrawn, then drowned herself. Her suicide is a second baptism in *No-No Boy*. With it, Ichiro is reborn an American. He does not mourn her death. Instead, he feels "a little bit freer, a bit more hopeful."[102] After leaving Ma's memorial service early, he goes dancing with Emi at a roadhouse on Seattle's outskirts. Anonymous and on the dance floor, he thinks:

> This is the way it ought to be . . . to be able to dance with a girl you like and really get a kick out of it because everything is on an even keel and one's worries are only the usual ones of unpaid bills and sickness in the family and being late to work often. Why can't it be that way for me? Nobody's looking twice at us. Nobody's asking where I was during the war or what the hell I am doing back on the Coast. There's no trouble to be had without looking for it. Everything's the same, just as it used to be. No bad feelings except for those that have always existed and probably always will. It's a matter of attitude. Mine needs changing.[103]

For writer Stan Yogi, the dance floor in this scene is "a metaphor for America."[104] Likewise, it is a site of assimilation, a place where the erstwhile racialized minority disappears and becomes an unmarked subject with "the usual" (majoritarian) worries, not extraordinary (minoritarian) ones, like prohibitions against naturalizing or owning property, orders to evacuate, or loyalty tests. The dance floor is also a site of individualized consent. Instead of trying to change the social structures that produce and maintain exclusion, marginalization, and persecution, Ichiro opts to change his attitude. He becomes the model minority.

After Ichiro and Emi dance, an older, white, male stranger approaches them and buys each of them a drink. The couple are puzzled by his generosity. Contrary to his feeling of anonymity while on the dance floor, Ichiro first speculates that the stranger has treated them to drinks out of guilt or nostalgia because they are Japanese. Then he stops second-guessing the stranger's motives—looking for trouble, in other words—and changes his attitude. "I want to think," he tells Emi, that the stranger "saw a young couple and liked their looks and felt he wanted to buy them a drink and did."[105]

Just as the prodigal son was lost and is found, Ichiro at first rejects and then ratifies the dominant narrative of assimilation in the United States. Because *No-No Boy* is a bildungsroman that narrates its protagonist's development from tormented and fragmented to calm and more whole, it has been read as a reaffirmation of the Nisei's Americanness.[106] Yet several literary critics have pointed out "the cultural tensions" surrounding it.[107] Jinqi Ling, for example, notes that Okada "wrote and published the novel in an era when Cold War ideological drives toward U.S. nationalism and legitimation of material abundance promoted tendencies to embrace a common national character and a 'seamless' America.... In this political climate a few American publishers began to develop a market for Japanese American and Chinese American writers" who would "refute Communist bloc charges of racial discrimination and class oppression" by functioning "as cultural mediators" and telling "stories of successful assimilation."[108]

Cold War imperatives notwithstanding, *No-No Boy* is by no means a wholesale celebration of the Japanese American model minority, the United States as an egalitarian meritocracy, or the American dream.[109] The Yamadas' poverty, Ma's madness and suicide, and Kenji's premature death undermine all of these myths. Ichiro, meanwhile, remains "an ambiguous protagonist," however reformed.[110] When the novel ends, he is far from the homogenizing utopia of the roadhouse dance floor. Instead, he is in an alley in Seattle's Asian and black ghetto, comforting Bull, a Nisei who, like Eto, detests no-no boys. Bull has just been in an altercation with Freddie, another no-no boy. Freddie is dead after crashing his car and being "cut ... in two," a physical manifestation of "his shattered life."[111] Even though Ichiro sympathizes with Bull, the novel closes on an uncertain note. "In the darkness of the alley of the community that was a tiny bit of America," the narrator reports, Ichiro "chased that faint and elusive insinuation of promise as it continued to take shape in mind and in heart."[112] Okada's tentative language belies resolution and nods to his protagonist's enduring ambivalence, while the final setting, a dark alley in a tiny bit of America, makes clear the Nisei's ongoing marginalization.

DIARY OF A RELUCTANT DREAMER:
THE AMBIVALENT AMERICAN

Like *No-No Boy*, *Diary of a Reluctant Dreamer* is a *bildung* narrative. Alberto Ledesma's memoir chronicles its protagonist's transition from poor, "nervous undocumented immigrant kid" to middle-class US citizen and "university professor and administrator."[113] Yet despite his achievement of normative success—of, some might say, the American dream—*Diary of a Reluctant Dreamer* does not celebrate the United States as a nation of immigrants or an egalitarian meritocracy. Like Ichiro, Ledesma is "afflicted . . . by a profound ambivalence about [his] Americanness."[114] While Ichiro is an alien citizen, Ledesma's protagonist is a probationary one. Undocumented, he is besieged by feelings of fear, guilt, and undeservingness. Yet even after he naturalizes as a US citizen, he continues to suffer from a kind of post-traumatic stress disorder. "The twelve years that I spent living . . . as an undocumented immigrant conditioned me in a profound way," Ledesma has acknowledged.[115]

The illustration *Who's the Leader of the Club Who Wants to Deport You and Me . . . ?*, provides a glimpse of that conditioning (see figure 4). In this 2013 self-portrait, Ledesma sits on a green bench, a diminutive pair of Mouseketeer ears by his side. A grown man, he wears dark-rimmed glasses, a watch, a black shirt, mustard trousers, and sneakers. With one arm resting on the back of the bench, he appears relaxed. He is on vacation with his wife and daughter at Disneyland, home to It's a Small World, a ride that celebrates the diversity of peoples and international unity. Parodying the ride's theme song, "It's a Small World (After All)," the text at the top of the drawing reads, "It's a scary world after all . . . We are at Disneyland for our summer vacation. A policeman passes by and I feel him stare me down. That's when I realize that nothing has changed." Around Ledesma's neck hangs a sign reading, "NO LONGER UNDOCUMENTED BUT STILL SCARED SHITLESS."[116] His seemingly calm composure belies the sign's panicked message.

Figure 4. Alberto Ledesma, *Who's the Leader of the Club Who Wants to Deport You and Me . . .?* (2013). Used with permission from Alberto Ledesma/Mad Creek Books.

A "hybrid book," in its creator's words, *Diary of a Reluctant Dreamer* combines text and illustrations, political and social commentary and autobiography.[117] Using words and images that tap visual traditions as varied as twentieth-century Mexican social realism, New Deal social documentary photography, and DC Comics, Ledesma informs his reader that he was born in the Mexican state of Jalisco in 1965. Although he regularized years before the DREAM Act was first introduced in Congress and therefore was never a Dreamer per se, he resembled the archetypal Dreamer when he was young and undocumented. In the summer of 1974, at the age of eight years, he arrived in the United States with his mother, Josefina, and his two sisters. They crossed the border in Tijuana, "in the back seat of some strange lady's red Camaro."[118] The children pretended to sleep as they passed through the checkpoint to avoid having to speak to the guard who looked over their fraudulent birth certificates.[119] When they arrived in Oakland, where Ledesma's father, Adalberto, was already living, Ledesma was under the impression that he, Josefina, and his sisters were simply visiting. He had no idea that the small, blue house on 82nd Avenue that his father was renting was their new home and that for the next twelve years, it would be their prison.

In his pioneering study of nineteenth- and twentieth-century autobiographies by European immigrants to the United States, literary critic William Boelhower contends, "In immigrant autobiography, there is always a new birth."[120] In *Diary of a Reluctant Dreamer*, in Oakland Ledesma is reborn, not as an American but as an undocumented immigrant. He describes his pre-American life as one of both confinement and transgression. Worried that they could be picked up by law enforcement and deported at any time, Josefina and Adalberto limit the family's excursions and are loath to permit their children to leave home alone. "The only times we seem to go out are when we go to Los Mexicanos Market for the week's groceries," Ledesma relates. "We travel as a group, always within sight of each other."[121] As a teenager, he clashes with his father when his father prohibits him from going out with friends or attending his first high school dance. In 1984 Ledesma is offered admission to Berkeley, but his parents are reluctant to let him go, even though the campus is merely "a BART-ride away" from their home.[122] "I want to go places by myself, to explore this new world and the people in it," he recounts, "to be the kind of teenager . . . in a John Hughes movie."[123] The discrepancy between his identification with Hughes's white, mostly affluent, suburban, and US citizen adolescent heroes and the reality of his situation is stark.

During an extraordinary outing on a Saturday afternoon in April 1977, Ledesma and his family travel in their green, 1969 Ford Country Squire station wagon from their home "in the heart of East Oakland's African American ghetto" to the suburban Hayward Hills.[124] They stop at a vacant lot overrun with what appear to be weeds. While Adalberto makes his way across the lot picking cactus leaves, Ledesma notices that the buildings in the Hayward Hills are tidier than those in East Oakland. The cars are also newer, and many of the passing motorists seem to be "blondes wearing sunglasses."[125] Ledesma is only eleven, but he quickly realizes, "We are an oddity in this place—a Mexican family making its home among the weeds. We should just go back."[126] His suspicion that they are out of place is confirmed when his sister, Silvia, spies a faded "No Trespassing" sign. "¿Qué quiere decir TRES-PASSIN?" ("What does TRES-PASSIN mean?"), Josefina asks, amplifying their extraneousness with her limited English.[127] When Silvia informs her that the sign says that they can be jailed for being there, the family promptly leaves, but not before Adalberto has gathered "a mountain of cactus leaves."[128] On the drive home, Josefina talks excitedly about the chile con nopalitos that she will cook and eat. "It's been years since I had good cactus, she says and laughs, as if nothing has happened."[129] Meanwhile, Ledesma sits silently in the backseat, stunned by what he sees as his parents' unusual carelessness.

The fear of trespassing and getting caught shapes Ledesma's pre-American experience. That fear is compounded with a sense of undeservingness when he wins a scholarship that sends him to Washington, D.C. He is in high school and his teacher, Mrs. Wolfe, has nominated him for the award. "I felt honored and did not want to disappoint Mrs. Wolfe," he recalls, but he recognizes the danger travel poses. He accepts her nomination, then tries to "tank . . . the interview" by responding to the questions "with nonsensical gibberish."[130] Instead, he comes off as diplomatic and polite. To his shock, he wins the scholarship.

The trip is "an extremely stressful experience." In addition to touring famous landmarks, like the White House and the Capitol, Ledesma and the other awardees visit the headquarters of the Federal Bureau of Investigation. "I thought that if I were going to be caught anywhere," he recollects, "it would be there, in the home of the best detectives on Earth." As he nervously waits to pass through security in the building's lobby, he notices that everyone is staring at him. He assumes that they know that he is undocumented. He is on the verge of confessing his status when another boy informs him that his trousers' zipper is open. Ironically, the trousers that have brought Ledesma so much unwanted attention and that have nearly exposed him as undocumented are part of a suit that Adalberto purchased for his son so he could "'blend in'" in Washington, D.C.[131]

In 1986 Ledesma and his family were able to legalize their status after President Ronald Reagan signed the Immigration Reform and Control Act (IRCA). In addition to increasing border security and penalizing employers for hiring undocumented workers, IRCA allowed approximately 2.7 million undocumented immigrants to "wipe the slate clean" and regularize.[132] Also known as Amnesty, it was a reprieve. Still, "while we were now legal, while we now had permission to work and go to school," Ledesma has insisted, "the carefulness that resulted from those twelve years of conditioning did not disappear."[133] He believes that the feelings of fear, guilt, and undeservingness with which he lived for so many years compelled him "to become a man who was overly cautious, nauseatingly polite, always worried about offending others."[134] Like the iconic Dreamer, he racked up honors and awards in his quest for acceptance. "Hyperdocumented," he earned three degrees, including a doctorate in ethnic studies from Berkeley.[135]

The hyperdocumented undocumented immigrant—in other words, the hardworking, accomplished, and promising Dreamer—figures prominently in *Diary of a Reluctant Dreamer*. So, too, does the economic migrant. The economic migrant, the migrant who moves out of economic necessity, is the Dreamer's antithesis. In many instances, the economic migrant is also the Dreamer's parent. Distinguishing the economic migrant from the refugee, the United Nations High Commissioner for Refugees (UNHCR) defines the former as a person who leaves the "countr[y] of origin purely for economic reasons not in any way related to the refugee definition, or in order to seek material improvements in their livelihood. Economic migrants do not fall within the criteria for refugee status and are therefore not entitled to benefit from international protection as refugees."[136]

Like the UNHCR's refugee, the archetypal Dreamer is a victim, not only of a broken immigration system but of the undocumented immigrant parent's decision to transport the Dreamer to the United States in the first place. Walter J. Nicholls and Tara Fiorito explain that advocates of the DREAM Act have "sought to assert the innocence of [Dreamers] and exonerate them of their 'illegality' by stressing their status was 'no fault of their own.'"[137] In contrast, the economic migrant is an agent and therefore a threat. As writer Dina Nayeri puts it, if you are born poor "in the Third World, and you dare to make a move before you are shattered, your dreams are suspicious. You are a carpetbagger, an opportunist, a thief."[138] Driven and self-reliant, the economic migrant, ironically, resembles the "bootstraps" immigrant of lore, the model minority, and the neoliberal subject. However, because economic migrants are perceived as people who take (specifically, jobs) and who do not give back—for example, as workers or consumers—they are not deemed deserving of inclusion or protection.

The son of a poor Mexican who migrated to the United States without papers to work in a piston factory, Ledesma reckons with "the reality of economic migration."[139] In doing so, he calls into question the putative out-of-place-ness and undeservingness of the economic migrant. Rather than celebrate the United States as a nation of immigrants, he lambasts his adopted homeland as a greedy, draconian, and mercurial migrant-receiving country "that only values papers and stamps and hides the fact that only our limbs are allowed to be present in this economy, that only our arms are valued for the labor they can exert."[140] *Diary of a Reluctant Dreamer* is full of images of immigrants at work. They harvest, scrub, sew, and mop. In Ledesma's *M Is for Machine*

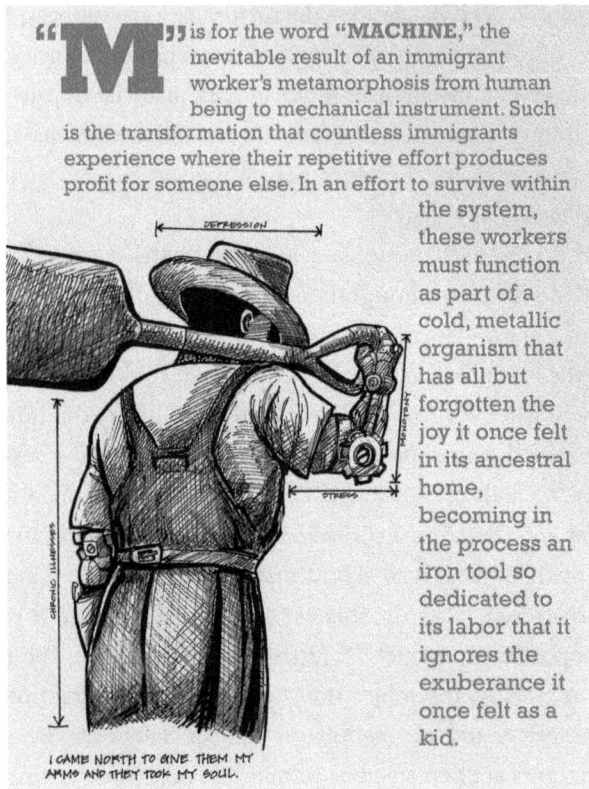

"**M**" is for the word "**MACHINE**," the inevitable result of an immigrant worker's metamorphosis from human being to mechanical instrument. Such is the transformation that countless immigrants experience where their repetitive effort produces profit for someone else. In an effort to survive within the system, these workers must function as part of a cold, metallic organism that has all but forgotten the joy it once felt in its ancestral home, becoming in the process an iron tool so dedicated to its labor that it ignores the exuberance it once felt as a kid.

I CAME NORTH TO GIVE THEM MY ARMS AND THEY TOOK MY SOUL.

Figure 5. Alberto Ledesma, *M Is for Machine* (2016). Used with permission from Alberto Ledesma/Mad Creek Books.

(2016), a man wearing overalls and a broad-brimmed hat carries a shovel (see figure 5). The man's back is turned to the viewer, and his face appears to be downcast, but we can see that his arms and right hand are those of a robot. His mechanical limbs evoke not only the bracero, the worker who has been reduced to his arms, but Karl Marx and Frederick Engel's nineteenth-century factory worker, an "appendage of the machine."[141] They illustrate the "metamorphosis from human being to mechanical instrument."[142]

Diary of a Reluctant Dreamer actively rehumanizes the undocumented immigrant—in particular, the undocumented worker and undocumented immigrant parent. Where the man with the mechanical limbs is faceless, the woman and small child in Ledesma's *Resolve* (2016) confront the viewer (see figure 6). Written from the point of view of the woman and addressed to the child, the text that accompanies this illustration debunks the image of the United States as a meritocracy:

> There, there, little girl. Everything will be alright. . . . But it is good for you to learn that all this talk of fairness and opportunities was all just an illusion. The truth is that there has never been any progress we could depend on and that you will have to work even harder than I did to get even a little ahead. God knows what senseless obstacles will be put in front of you. But I will teach you how to persevere as I always have.[143]

Reminiscent of Florence Owens Thompson, the woman at the center of Dorothea Lange's iconic 1936 black-and-white photograph *Migrant Mother, Nipomo, California* (see figure 7), the woman in Ledesma's illustration has a very serious look on her face. With a furrowed brow, Thompson looks away from the viewer distractedly. She holds an infant in her lap as two small children hide their faces in and behind her slumped shoulders. The children's clothes appear to be rough and soiled. In contrast, Ledesma's drawing contains rich, warm hues, like gold, emerald, and crimson. Ledesma's migrant mother stares directly at or past the viewer. Meanwhile, the child in her arms looks warily over her own shoulder. With fear and uncertainty, she peeks at the viewer and perhaps at the ominous future before her.

Because silence is often read as a sign of docility or complicity, it has come to be associated with the model minority. However, "[f]or the undocumented," Ledesma observes, "silence is almost always meaningful, not the absence of complaint, but the sign of how thoroughly oppression works."[144] Assuming the voice not only of the Dreamer but of the Dreamer's parent and the economic migrant, he shatters that silence in *Diary of a Reluctant Dreamer.* By acknowledging the Dreamer's parent and the economic migrant, he also calls attention to the limitations of meritocracy, the DREAM Act, and arguments for immigration

THERE, THERE, LITTLE GIRL. EVERYTHING WILL BE ALRIGHT. AFTER ALL, IN THE END, ALL WE REALLY HAVE IS EACH OTHER.

BUT IT IS GOOD FOR YOU TO LEARN THAT ALL THIS TALK OF FAIRNESS AND OPPORTUNITIES WAS ALL JUST AN ILLUSION. THE TRUTH IS THAT THERE HAS NEVER BEEN ANY PROGRESS THAT WE COULD DEPEND ON AND THAT YOU WILL HAVE TO WORK EVEN HARDER THAN I DID TO GET EVEN A LITTLE AHEAD.

GOD KNOWS WHAT SENSELESS OBSTACLES WILL BE PUT IN FRONT OF YOU. BUT I WILL TEACH YOU HOW TO PERSEVERE AS I ALWAYS HAVE.

Figure 6. Alberto Ledesma, *Resolve* (2016). Used with permission from Alberto Ledesma/Mad Creek Books.

reform that hinge on the immigrant's contributions to society and, by extension, the immigrant's deservingness. What counts as a contribution to society, and who is deemed deserving? Who makes those determinations? These are the questions with which *Diary of a Reluctant Dreamer* leaves the reader.

FROM DREAM TO TEST

In August 2019 Kenneth T. Cuccinelli, the great-grandson of an Italian immigrant and acting director of US Citizenship and Immigration Services (USCIS), a division of the Department of Homeland Security (DHS), announced that beginning the following October, USCIS would begin denying permanent legal status to legal immigrants who

Figure 7. Dorothea Lange, *Migrant Mother, Nipomo, California* (1936). Library of Congress, https://www.loc.gov/item/2017762891/.

are likely to become a public charge.[145] USCIS defines "public charge" as "an individual who is likely to become primarily dependent on the government for subsistence, as demonstrated by either the receipt of public cash assistance for income maintenance or institutionalization for long-term care at government expense."[146] Since the implementation of the Personal Responsibility and Work Opportunity Reconciliation Act (a.k.a. welfare reform) in 1996, legal immigrants have been prohibited from receiving more than half their income from cash benefits, such as Temporary Assistance for Needy Families or Supplemental Security Income from Social Security.

Under the new policy, titled Inadmissibility on Public Charge Grounds (IPCG), but known informally as the wealth test, prospective legal permanent residents must demonstrate that they "are self-sufficient, *i.e.,* do not depend on public resources to meet their needs, but rather rely on their own capabilities, as well as the resources of family members, sponsors, and private organizations." In addition, the new policy expands the definition of "public charge" to include anyone who has used public benefits, like Medicaid, public housing assistance, or food stamps, for more than twelve months over a thirty-six-month period.[147] Days before ICPG was set to go into effect, US District judge George Daniels of Manhattan blocked it from being implemented on the grounds that the need to expand the definition of public charge had not been justified. He also declared the wealth test "repugnant to the American Dream of the opportunity for prosperity and success through hard work and upward mobility."[148] On January 27, 2020, the US Supreme Court ruled against Daniels's injunction and permitted USCIS to move forward with ICPG.[149] The new rule went into effect on February 24, 2020.[150]

In addition to reinforcing the link between Americanness and material wealth, the wealth test brings into plain sight the moral economy of deservingness. Similarly, while the Civil Liberties Act of 1988 was a form of redress for Japanese American internees, it also exposed belonging as a kind of transaction: in exchange for having been incarcerated by their own government, Japanese Americans received some financial compensation.[151] Where the Japanese American internee-cum-model minority and the DACA participant trade docility, hard work, and loyalty for contingent, partial, attenuated, and revocable inclusion (and a cash payout, in the internee's case), the ICPG beneficiary converts money into a green card. I do not blame the authors and supporters of the DREAM Act for the ICPG, but the wealth test is a logical extension of the argument that those who contribute to society in a way that is recognized as valuable merit a legitimate place in that society. With their alien citizen and probationary citizen protagonists, *No-No Boy* and *Diary of a Reluctant Dreamer* are cautionary tales. Both works testify to the toll—social and psychic alike—of the moral economy of deservingness.

CHAPTER FIVE

Impossible Subjects

Dissident Dreamers, Undocuqueers,
and Oaxacalifornixs

In *Tourists vs. Refugees*, German photographer Jörg Brüggemann juxtaposes tourists and refugees. Shot on the Greek island of Kos in the summer of 2015, his series of photographs presents European holidaymakers alongside Syrian, Iraqi, and Afghan refugees, or signs of these refugees. For instance, in one photo, two pale, barefoot, bikini-clad women walk past soggy, discarded lifejackets strewn across a beach (see figure 8).[1]

In an interview in 2018, Viet Thanh Nguyen explained why he calls himself a refugee, not an immigrant. "We [the people of the United States] call ourselves a 'Nation of immigrants,'" the Vietnamese American writer and scholar remarked. "If you call yourself an immigrant here, you fit. People will want to hear your heartwarming story about getting to this country." In contrast, "refugees are different. Refugees are unwanted where they come from. They're unwanted where they go."[2]

Brüggemann's photos and Nguyen's comments share a concern with semantics as they distinguish "refugees" from other moving bodies, namely "tourists" and "immigrants." According to the United Nations High Commissioner for Refugees (UNHCR), a refugee is "a person forced to flee their country because of violence or persecution."[3] Since

Figure 8. Jörg Brüggemann, *Tourists vs. Refugees* (2015). Used with permission from Jörg Brüggemann/OSTKREUZ.

the ratification of the UN Refugee Convention in 1951, refugees have comprised "a special category of protection," one that aligns with what philosopher Thomas Nail calls a "regime of social circulation," such as a set of principles (e.g., human rights) or a particular foreign policy.[4] The UNHCR's definition frames the refugee exclusively in international, rather than domestic, terms. Similarly, exiles and émigrés are people who are coerced to move from one country to another, often for political reasons. As literary critic Kirsten Silva Gruesz points out, all three terms—"refugee," "exile," "*émigré*"—invoke "a claim to sympathy."[5] A tourist, in contrast, is "a person who is traveling or visiting a place for pleasure."[6] Whether they remain within the boundaries of a particular nation-state or cross international lines, tourists enjoy the power, privilege, and prestige of elected movement, especially when they bear the right passport, currency, and mode of transportation, be it a reliable car or a private jet.

Differences notwithstanding, refugees and tourists are mobile subjects.[7] Immigrants are, too, but because they are defined by the place they arrive at, the receiving or host country in the lexicon of migration studies, they are "understood from the perspective of stasis."[8] At the same time, *e*migrants are defined by sending countries, the places they leave. In the nation of immigrants, immigrants land and stay put. In other words, they are settlers. As such, they are agents and beneficiaries of settler colonialism, as scholars in Native American and indigenous studies have noted. Political scientist Haunani-Kay Trask, for example, points out that "'immigrant' . . . is, itself, a particularly celebrated American gloss for 'settler.'"[9] Yet immigrants not only settle; they "fit," to use Nguyen's word. In short, they assimilate and, in doing so, burnish the image of the United States as a "land belonging to no one" and as a multicultural democracy and meritocracy.[10]

To this taxonomy of mobile subjects add "arrivant," a person forced into a settler society "through the violence of European and Anglo-American colonialism and imperialism around the globe"; "nonimmigrant," a status designating a range of sojourners in the United States, including international tourists, diplomats, foreign students, and guest workers; "illegal alien," a dehumanizing invective for foreigners who enter or remain in a country without the state's authorization; and "migrant." Although "migrant" is an ostensibly broad and neutral term referring to "any person who is moving or has moved across an international border or within a State away from his/her habitual place of residence," it has become shorthand for "one of the global poor."[11] There is quite a bit of gray area between these labels, but states and nongovernmental organizations still attempt to distinguish one from the other.[12] Taken together, these terms comprise a hierarchy. The social actors to whom they are ascribed are accorded different values and different contexts of reception.[13] Put bluntly, the state and civil society's dominant institutions do not consider these people equals and, therefore do not treat them the same.

If the refugee is intelligible to a global moral and political order, and the immigrant can be absorbed by the nation of immigrants, who gets to be a refugee or an immigrant? That is, who is welcomed or tolerated as a refugee, celebrated as an immigrant, or branded an illegal alien? In short, which mobile subjects are deemed valuable, worthy, or nonthreatening, and which are seen as a burden, failure, or threat? By the same token, who is recognized as native if, as Nail asserts, society itself "is always in motion" and "there is no social stasis, only regimes of social circulation"?[14] And how are mobile subjects challenging those regimes—specifically, state-sanctioned forms of movement and belonging—by articulating new ontologies and relationships?

To address these questions, this chapter takes as its objects of study both words and images. Of particular concern are three nonnormative mobile subjects—the dissident (also known as the bad, reluctant, or unbounded) Dreamer, the undocuqueer, and the Oaxacalifornix—and their representation in visual culture.[15] Dreamer (dissident and otherwise), undocuqueer, and Oaxacalifornix emerged in the United States in the 1990s and early 2000s in conversations about immigration. To illuminate these relatively new labels' meanings, I read videos of the disruption of Barack Obama's speech by members of Asian Students Promoting Immigrant Rights through Education (ASPIRE) at the Betty Ong Recreation Center in San Francisco on November 25, 2013; digital illustrations produced from 2012 through 2018 by the self-professed undocuqueer artist Julio Salgado; and a series of murals by the Oaxacan artist collective Tlacolulokos, on display at the Central Library in downtown Los Angeles over 2017 and 2018.

I put these works in dialogue with each other because they articulate the politics of presence, the politics of visibility, and the politics of potentiality. The politics of presence emphasizes the fact of a social group's existence in the face of marginalization or erasure. Similarly, the politics of visibility counteracts invisibilization. A rallying cry of undocumented immigrants in the United States since the election of Donald Trump as president in 2016, #heretostay enunciates a politics of presence and visibility. While these politics affirm resistant identities and an antiassimilationist stance, both can reproduce the logic of multiculturalism in their demand for recognition, and/or they can reaffirm the authority of the state in their petition for rights. In the case of undocumented immigrants, the politics of presence and visibility can bring exposure that results in detention and deportation.[16]

In contrast, the politics of potentiality, as theorized by performance and visual studies scholar José Esteban Muñoz, "is essentially about the rejection of a here and now and an insistence on potentiality or concrete possibility for another world."[17] Muñoz grounds his theory of potentiality in an explicitly queer framework and applies it to "queers and other people who do not feel the privilege of majoritarian belonging, normative tastes, and 'rationale' expectations."[18] Connecting concrete, rather than abstract, utopias to "historically situated struggles," his is a politics of vision *and* action animated by hope.[19]

The primary sources I study in this chapter engage the politics of presence, visibility, and potentiality by highlighting the voices and bodies of dissident Dreamers, undocuqueers, and Oaxacalifornixs. In doing so, these texts complicate and expand the lexicon of mobility and offer new possibilities for belonging and being. Just as "[q]ueerness is not yet here . . . yet exists for us as an ideality that can be distilled from the past and used to imagine a future," the figures of the dissident Dreamer, the undocuqueer, and the Oaxacalifornix embody and envision forms of belonging and being that do not correspond with and even defy a Trumpist United States.[20] Because they exceed extant regimes of circulation, such as the nation of immigrants and the nation of laws, the dissident Dreamer, the undocuqueer, and the Oaxacalifornix are impossible subjects, to borrow from the title of historian Mae M. Ngai's book.[21] Unassimilable in the here and now, they point us to another world.

THE DISSIDENT DREAMER

The figure of the Dreamer rose to prominence in the discourse on immigration in the United States in the first years of the twenty-first century. To make the case for the DREAM Act, legislation that sought to provide a select group of young, unauthorized immigrants with citizenship or legal permanent residency, activists, political strategists, policy makers, politicians, and artists presented Dreamers as young, educated, accomplished, assimilated, and patriotic immigrants. Because Dreamers were brought to the United States at a young age by their parents, they were cast as innocent. Above all, Dreamers promised to make a valuable contribution to their adopted homeland, in particular, to its economy and military. "This framing strategy rested on an effort to cleanse the youths of the stigmas attributed to them," Walter J. Nicholls and Tara Fiorito point out, "while simultaneously stressing the attributes that made this group exceptionally deserving of the right to stay in the country."[22]

Nicholls and Fiorito describe the figure of the exceptionally deserving Dreamer as "bounded" and contrast it with that of the "unbounded" Dreamer: "Whereas the 'bounded Dreamer' emphasized the narrow boundaries that distinguished youths from others in the immigrant population, the 'unbounded Dreamer' blurred those lines and stressed broader identities, ties, and goals."[23] Put another way, bounded Dreamers are presented and understood according to "a single-axis framework"—their undocumentedness—and as solitary social actors whose only goal is to obtain citizenship for themselves.[24] In contrast, unbounded Dreamers embody and enact intersectionality, "the relationships among multiple dimensions and modalities of social relations and subject formations," and do not ignore or cover up their ties to other people, such as parents, siblings, spouses, and lovers.[25] "This fluidity allows them to cut across movements . . . develop new alliances, and play vibrant roles in a variety of social justice campaigns," including opposing deportation and advocating for undocumented immigrants who do not adhere to the model of the bounded Dreamer.[26] "As Dreamers have become more drawn into anti-deportation and enforcement campaigns," Nicholls and Fiorito observe, "their public frames shifted from stressing the attributes that made youths uniquely deserving of legality to frames stressing why all undocumented immigrants deserved a right to reside in the country."[27] Moreover, dissident Dreamers do not celebrate the United States as an egalitarian nation of immigrants and the land of opportunity. Instead, they draw attention to this country's disparities, enforced marginalizations and exclusions, and key role in displacing peoples globally.[28]

Coordinated by members of ASPIRE, a San Francisco–based organization of undocumented Asian Pacific Islander youth, the disruption of Obama's speech at the Betty Ong Recreation Center in San Francisco's Chinatown on November 25, 2013, emblematized young undocumented activists' shift in focus from deservingness to deportation.[29] The direct action was led by Ju Hong, a twenty-four-year-old participant in DACA, a program that grants certain undocumented youths permission to remain and to work in the United States on a temporary and renewable basis. Hong and other ASPIRE members were invited by the White House to attend the speech, the focus of which was immigration reform. Placed on the dais directly behind the president's podium, they presented "a diverse mix of immigrants."[30]

Hong, a graduate student in public administration at San Francisco State University, appeared to be a poster boy for DACA and the DREAM Act. He had traveled at age eleven with his mother and older sister from their native South Korea to San Francisco on a tourist visa after his parents' business and marriage fell apart. Hong, his mother, and his sister remained in the Bay Area after their visas expired. At Alameda High School he ran cross-country and played on the basketball, volleyball, and rugby teams, all the while maintaining a 3.8 grade point average. Before transferring to the University of California, Berkeley, he was the first Asian student body president at Laney College in Oakland. By the time he confronted Obama, he was a seasoned activist. In fact, in August 2013, in a sort of run-up to the direct action he would take at the Betty Ong Recreation Center, he was arrested for disrupting a meeting of the Regents of the University of California as they appointed Janet Napolitano, former secretary of DHS, president of the university.[31]

Hong interrupted Obama just as the president was wrapping up his speech. "If we get immigration reform across the finish line," Obama stated, "we're going to grow our economy. We're going to make our country more secure. We'll strengthen our families." At that moment, Hong shouted, "But Mr. Obama. . . . My family's been separated. . . . .I need your help! There are thousands of undocumented immigrants . . . torn apart every single day!"[32] In videos, Hong is not always visible, nor are his words always clear. Still, it is evident that the urgent and unwavering voice emanates from a man standing on the dais behind the president. The heckler, as he came to be known, wears a conservative gray business jacket and a blue shirt with a collar. Within seconds of his outburst, a hand, presumably belonging to a security guard, appears from behind him and grips his right shoulder. Some of the people surrounding the speaker look stunned and uncomfortable. Others smile and nod their heads in affirmation.

At first Obama ignores Hong, but the young man persists. Then Obama turns around and engages his interlocutor, stating, "That's exactly what we're talking about. That's why we're here." Unyielding and unflappable, Hong urges him to "please use your executive order to halt deportations for all 11.5 [*sic*] undocumented immigrants in this country right now!" Obama attempts to regain control of his speech, but Hong cuts him off, shouting, "We agree that we need to pass comprehensive immigration reform! At the same time, you have a power to stop deportations of all undocumented immigrants!" Some members of the audience begin chanting "Obama!" and "Stop Deportations!" and clapping rhythmically.

During the chanting and clapping, two security guards apprehend Emmanuel Valenciano, another ASPIRE member on the dais.[33] Obama instructs the guards to leave the protestors alone. The president then turns around to face the podium, and the crowd erupts in applause. He acknowledges "the passion of these young people." However, he explains, "[I]f ... I could solve all these problems without passing laws in congress, then I would do so. But we're also a nation of laws. That's part of our tradition." To those committed to "democratic processes," he vows "to make sure that we are welcoming every striving, hardworking immigrant who sees America the same way we do, as a country where no matter who you are or what you look like or where you come from, you can make it if you try." Turning to Hong and using a tone veering between challenging and chiding, he adds, "And if you're serious about making that happen, then I'm ready to work with you. But it is gonna require work. It is not simply a matter of us just saying we're going to violate the law. That's not our tradition." Obama ends his speech on a high note, assuring his audience that "ultimately justice and truth win out." Meanwhile, Valenciano, the young man who was nearly escorted away, can be seen standing prominently behind the president, where the security guards left him. Valenciano's plaid shirt has been unbuttoned. Beneath it he is wearing a white T-shirt with the words "not one more deportation" printed across it in black ink.[34]

Despite Obama's insistence that he and the protestors shared the same goal and viewpoint, the videos of his speech are a lesson in Bakhtinian polyphony and dialogism; they contain a multiplicity of unreconciled voices and perspectives.[35] The president attempted to neutralize the protest. First, he assured Hong that they were on the same page. Then the president folded the protestors' utterances into the master narrative of immigration in the United States. However, Hong's words and the inscription on Valenciano's shirt tell another story, one that has less to do with bootstraps and democratic processes and more with the power of the state to make and to break families. Indeed, in a November 25, 2013, press release, May Liang, ASPIRE campaign organizer, expressed frustration with process and protocol and reiterated ASPIRE's concern with detention and deportation. Despite having "organized countless lobby visits in Washington D.C." and "townhalls supporting just and humane reform," she wrote, "the suffering of our communities who are facing deportation and languishing in detention centers continues unabated."[36] Fed up and refusing to be silent "props," the members of ASPIRE took it upon themselves to engage Obama, "using our voices to tell you directly what our community needs and what you can do today."[37]

Yet by insisting that the United States is "a nation of laws" and that violation of the law is "not our tradition," Obama not only attempted to silence the young undocumented immigrants' dissent but also disregarded this country's rich and complicated history of civil disobedience. In doing so, he painted a narrow and inaccurate picture of the United States, one that marginalizes those who challenge the status quo via civil disobedience or excludes them altogether. In interviews, Hong noted that "the law itself" was "wrong," "inhumane," and "broken."[38] And in an open letter published in *Huffpost*, he reminded Obama, "With the stroke of a pen, you dramatically changed the lives of hundreds of thousands of young people like me" with the establishment of DACA.[39]

The ASPIRE activists' disruption of Obama's speech and the videos documenting it speak to the politics of presence and visibility. By catapulting himself into the media spotlight, Hong has "put an Asian face to a contentious debate that often is focused on Latinos."[40] In other words, he has brought visibility to the struggles of undocumented Asian immigrants, thereby debunking the myth that undocumented immigration is a Latinx issue exclusively and shattering the stereotype of the Asian model minority. However, that visibility has not always been well received. Hong's mother, for one, has expressed ambivalence about his activism. Regarding his disruption of Obama's speech, she asked him in Korean, "Why did you have to step up when there are other kids? I thought we could just let things be the way they are."[41] Without the protection of DACA, his mother was in no position to commit a very public act of civil disobedience. Yet being visible also functioned as a form of protection for Hong and the other protestors at the Betty

Ong Recreation Center. By instructing the security guards not to eject them, Obama shrewdly avoided an ugly spectacle, one in which the protestors' concern—the state's power to remove people by force—would have been manifest. Thus, like the ASPIRE activists' direct action, the video of that action is a strategy in and of itself.

One year after his speech, Obama introduced Deferred Action for Parents of Americans and Lawful Permanent Residents (DAPA), an executive order modeled after DACA that would have granted some undocumented parents of US citizen and permanent resident children permission to work and a reprieve from deportation. Hong was credited with helping "spark a national discussion" about presidential authority.[42] However, DAPA was suspended by the courts. Then the Trump administration rescinded it on June 15, 2017. Three months later, Attorney General Jeff Sessions announced DACA's termination. Echoing Obama's speech, Sessions characterized the American people as a "people of law."[43] In contrast, DACA recipients were, in his words, "mostly-adult illegal aliens."[44] Sessions claimed that the Obama administration had circumvented the law when it implemented DACA, so its recipients were always already illegal. Despite their deservingness and demands, Dreamers, bounded and unbounded alike, would not be absorbed by the nation of laws. With Trump, the state to which Hong had appealed would turn a deaf ear to—but train its sights on—undocumented immigrants.

THE UNDOCUQUEER

Like the figure of the dissident Dreamer, the figure of the undocuqueer brings into relief divisions and inequalities among the undocumented. Both the dissident Dreamer and the undocuqueer are subjects of the work of Julio Salgado, a self-taught multimedia artist who was born in Ensenada, Mexico, in 1983 and raised in Long Beach, California. A self-described "undocumented queer 'artivist,'" he has produced much of the iconography of the twenty-first-century immigrant youth movement.[45] His work has been exhibited at galleries, colleges, and universities, but much of it originates and circulates online, especially on social media. Bright colors and cartoon-like drawings are hallmarks of his illustrations. His colorful palette and simple renditions appear to be, in the words of one observer, "non-threatening," "resolutely cheerful," and "optimistic."[46] However, in the tradition of Chicanx protest art, many of his illustrations contain copy with a serious and overt political message. "The art I put out there is really trying to change the culture of migrant hate," Salgado has affirmed.[47]

The figure of the undocumented LGBTQ immigrant—the undocuqueer—figures prominently in his vast oeuvre. In 2010 the Immigrant Youth Justice League in Chicago established National Come Out of the Shadows Day.[48] One year later, the national immigrant youth advocacy organization United We Dream launched the Queer Undocumented Immigrant Project (QUIP).[49] "When a lot of undocumented folks started coming out, I just had to document the folks that were at the forefront of this movement," Salgado recalled. "A lot of them were fellow queer brothers and sisters that made me feel like I wasn't alone."[50] Working with QUIP and the California-based Undocumented Queer Youth Collective, he inaugurated his *I Am Undocuqueer!* series in 2012.[51] Via social media, he invited fellow undocuqueers to send him "a photograph from the waist up ... and a quote telling us what it means to be both undocumented and queer."[52] The objective of the series was "to give us undocumented queers more of a presence in the discussion of migrant rights."[53]

Reminiscent of Emory Douglas's drawings and graphic designs in the late 1960s and early 1970s in *The Black Panther*, the newspaper of the Black Panther Party, each *I Am Undocuqueer!* portrait presents a cartoon-like rendering of a self-proclaimed undocuqueer against a bright, colorful background.[54] Beneath "I AM UNDOCU-QUEER" in large, black, capital letters, each model wears a white shirt with the words "UNDOCUMENTED and UNAFRAID" and "QUEER & UNASHAMED" written across the chest. In addition, all are presented alongside a brief text. For example, Seleny's 2012 portrait reads, "UNDOCUQUEER. TAKING CONTROL OF MY OWN IDENTITY. I EXIST!"[55]

Just as Hong has sought to draw attention to the plight of undocumented Asian immigrants, Salgado has reiterated that one of his goals as an artist has been to bring visibility to people who are often overlooked by the mainstream, including mainstream gay and lesbian and immigrant advocacy movements. To that end, he launched his *I Exist* series in 2012.[56] In addition to "challeng[ing] people who might not know about the immigration experience," he has endeavored "to make art that other people," especially other undocuqueers, "can see themselves in."[57] However, representation is not enough for him. He has stressed that "we get to be the ones who drive our narratives" and that those narratives need not be "digestible for audiences. We are complicated human beings."[58]

Salgado's 2013 self-portrait, *Queer Butterfly*, brings that complexity to light (see figure 9). In this drawing, a young, bare-chested man with fuchsia skin and pierced nipples stands before a bright, yellow background. He faces the viewer with open arms. The words "I EXIST/YO EXISTO" are written across his chest and abdomen. Behind him, two red, orange, blue, and green butterfly wings are unfurled. They read, "JOTERIA/MIGRANTE/AMOR/FAMILIA/UNIDAD/PAZ" and "MIGRANT/QUEERNESS/LOVE/FAMILY/UNITY/PEACE." By incorporating words in Spanish and English, colors associated with LGBTQ struggles and pride, and the image of a butterfly, a symbol of migration and metamorphosis, *Queer Butterfly* visualizes intersectionality. Moreover, it moves beyond the binary of the deserving and undeserving immigrant. Where the inscription across Valenciano's chest, "not one more deportation," is a plea, demand, or argument that simultaneously defies and appeals to the state, the words across Salgado's are, quite simply, a factual statement.

Like the other illustrations in his *I Exist* series, Salgado's self-portrait enacts a politics of presence and visibility. However, his works do not appeal to the state or the heteronormative and cis-gender

Figure 9. Julio Salgado, *Queer Butterfly* (2013). Used with permission from Julio Salgado.

mainstream. "For many years, when I started doing a lot of these art-works, my message—and the message for a lot of us—was to show this country that we're good immigrants," he recalled in an interview in 2018.[59] However, as Congress dragged its feet on the Dream Act and comprehensive immigration reform and the number of deportations soared, his work grew more defiant, irreverent, and iconoclastic. "I use words like 'illegal' and 'faggot' all over my work with a very intentional purpose of throwing back the hate to those who wish I would disappear," he declared in 2018, a year after Trump's inauguration.[60]

By using these terms, Salgado breaks from the bounded Dreamer paradigm. Illustrations like *I'd Rather Be Undocumented* (2012) (see figure 10) and *No Longer Interested in Convincing You of My Humanity* (2018) reject that paradigm altogether. In the former, a young, brown man in a green graduation cap and gown stands beneath the words "I'D RATHER BE UNDOCUMENTED THAN DIE FOR YOUR ACCEPTANCE." He looks directly at the viewer with his middle finger extended. The

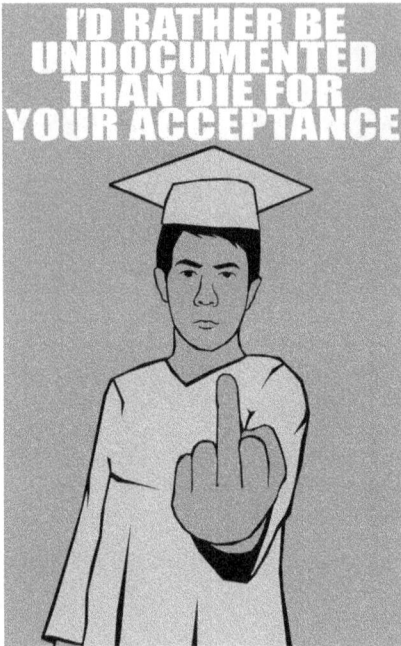

Figure 10. Julio Salgado, *I'd Rather Be Undocumented* (2012). Used with permission from Julio Salgado.

illustration's bright, *Simpsons*-esque colors belie its angry tone and sober message, a rejection of the Dream Act's requirement that undocumented youth attend college or enlist in the US military in order to be eligible for legal permanent residency. Similarly, the latter work invokes the figure of the student, the representative deserving immigrant, by presenting a blue mortarboard beneath the words "NO LONGER INTERESTED IN CONVINCING YOU OF MY HUMANITY." Rather than showcase the supplicant immigrant, this illustration shifts the gaze to "you," the viewer, and exposes the hostility of those who need to be convinced of another human's humanity.

Not only does Salgado's work spurn the iconic Dreamer and the DREAM Act; it rejects the nation-state as grantor and protector of rights and as framework for community. In an interview about *Queer Butterfly*, the artist reflected on the monarch butterfly's ability to "travel across Canada, the United States and Mexico," and asked, "'Wouldn't it

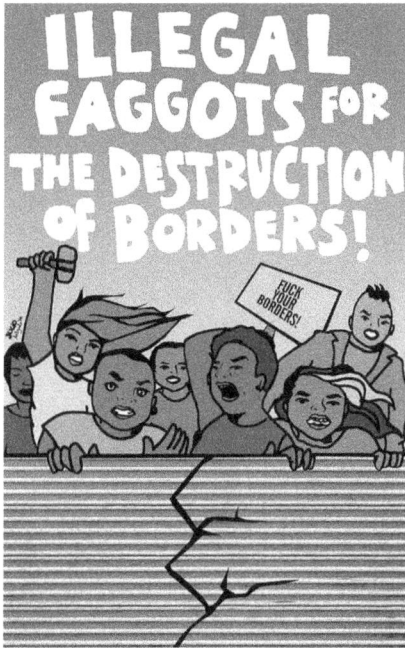

Figure 11. Julio Salgado, *Illegal Faggots for the Destruction of Borders!* (2014). Used with permission from Julio Salgado.

be great if human beings could do the same, without borders?'"⁶¹ Evoking Gabriel García Márquez's 1955 magical realist story, "A Very Old Man with Enormous Wings," his self-portrait appears to be a fantasy. In fact, illustrations like *Queer Butterfly, Illegal Faggots for the Destruction of Borders!* (2014), and *Bigger Than Any Border* (2015) offer a radical vision by enunciating a queer, gender nonbinary politics of no borders and by representing solidarity among seemingly disparate social groups (see figures 11 and 12).

Illegal Faggots presents a group of people of color storming a cracked fence. Some are gender fluid. All are angry. A person wearing a bright green shirt raises a mallet over their long red mane. Someone else holds a sign reading "FUCK YOUR BORDERS!" Similarly, in *Bigger Than Any Border*, five people of color loom above and straddle a small red wall with the words "Bigger than any BORDER" scrawled across it. A gender nonbinary person in a yellow shirt holds a cane. A woman wears a

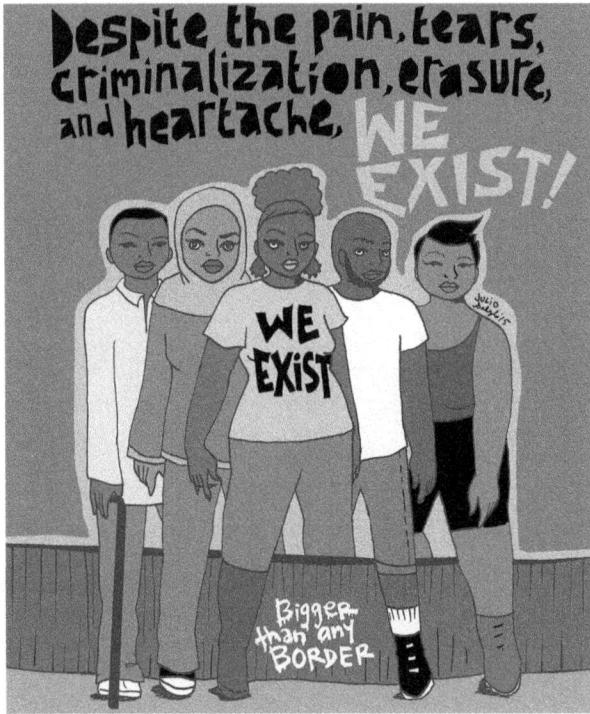

Figure 12. Julio Salgado, *Bigger Than Any Border* (2015). Used with permission from Julio Salgado.

light blue hijab. In the center, a dark woman with a blue afro puff wears a T-shirt with the words "WE EXIST" emblazoned across it. Above her and her black and brown companions, Salgado has written, "Despite the pain, tears, criminalization, erasure, and heartache, WE EXIST!"

Just as the heteronormative gender binary organizes kinship, national borders organize our world by purporting to link people, territory, and the nation-state's sovereignty. A politics of no borders recognizes that borders are artificial and transitory. Nor do borders stop people from moving. Instead, as Bridget Anderson, Nandita Sharma, and Cynthia Wright remind us, a politics of no borders emphasizes that borders "place people in new types of power relations ... and ... impart particular kinds of subjectivities," such as *citizen, refugee, migrant,* and *illegal alien.*[62] Not unlike intersectionality, a no borders politics envisions new relationships and new forms of belonging, signaling "a new sort of liberatory project, one with new ideas of 'society' and one aimed at creating new social actors not identified with nationalist projects (projects that are deeply racialized, gendered, sexualized, and productive of class relations)."[63] Racialized, gendered, sexualized, and classed, the undocuqueer is a social actor with the capacity to forge alliances across differences. Yet unlike the figure of the probationary citizen (in other words, the citizen in waiting), this subject refuses to identify with nationalist and, by extension, inherently exclusionary projects like citizenship. Therefore, the undocuqueer cannot be absorbed by the nation-state. "In order for politics to change," Salgado has maintained, "first we need to shift culture."[64] His art works for that shift by envisioning new subjects, new relationships, and new collectives—in short, a new world "that is not yet here."[65]

THE OAXACALIFORNIX

Just as the "illegal alien" cannot be an "immigrant" in the nation of immigrants that is also a nation of laws, the indigenous immigrant cannot be an "immigrant" in the settler colonial society. Critical Latinx indigeneities scholar María Josefina Saldaña Portillo argues that "the settler logic that defines the United States as an immigrant nation" demands that "to be a true American one must be an (European) immigrant, rather than Indigenous."[66] Settlers qua immigrants move from their country of origin to the settler nation qua host country. In contrast, "Indians" are imagined as temporally and physically immobile. They "can never be modern," Portillo notes, nor are they "properly Indian" if "they do not stay in their proper place."[67] Similarly, writer and scholar Lou Cornum observes, "Those we consider diasporic are often violently robbed of their indigeneity and those we consider indigenous are often on the move." To "bring the often disparate ideas of indigeneity and movement into closer proximity," Cornum self-identifies "as a diasporic Diné."[68]

"What happens to indigeneity when the indigenous subject is no longer in the location that has defined them?" Cornum asks.[69] Tlacolulokos's 2017 series of murals—*Gal rabenee ladxuu/Para orgullo de tu pueblo/ For the Pride of Your Hometown, Ra galumbanuu xhten guccran nii/Por el camino de los viejos/The Way of the Elders*, and *Ne guitenala'dxinu ca binii ma cusia'ndanu/Y el recuerdo de los olvidados/And in Memory of the Forgotten*—responds to Cornum's question. The series also dispels the myth that indigenous people are tethered to the past and to a single place. Comprised of eight thirteen-foot-tall, portable panels, *Gal rabenee ladxuu* was on display at the Los Angeles Public Library (LAPL) Central Library from September 16, 2017, until August 31, 2018. It was part of *Visualizing Language: Oaxaca in L.A.*, a series of events that "consider[ed] the relationship between [Los Angeles] and the Zapotec communities of Oaxaca and California through the visual arts, education, social activism and literature."[70] *Visualizing Language* was organized by the LAPL and the Library Foundation of Los Angeles in conjunction with Pacific Standard Time: L.A./L.A., the Getty Foundation's 2017–18 series of exhibitions exploring "Latin America and Latino art in dialogue with Los Angeles."[71] Like Hong's interruption of Obama's speech and Salgado's undocuqueer illustrations, Tlacolulokos's acrylic on canvas murals articulate a politics of presence and visibility by drawing attention to Los Angeles's burgeoning Zapotec community. Moreover, they bring into focus Oaxacalifornia, a hybrid space linking Oaxaca and California.[72]

Gal rabenee ladxuu "puts the indigenous migrant experience in the forefront," according to its curator, Amanda de la Garza Mata.[73] While Darío Canul and Cosijoesa Cernas, the self-taught duo comprising the visual arts collective, Tlacolulokos, self-identify as "brown," "Indian," and "from the South," they are not immigrants.[74] Nor are they based in Los Angeles. Instead, they live and work in their hometown of Tlacolula de Matamoros, a Zapotec community of around twenty-five thousand people.[75] Tlacolula is about five hundred kilometers southeast of Mexico City in Oaxaca, one of Mexico's poorest states and home to a sizable and diverse indigenous population. In 2015, Mexico's National Institute of Statistics and Geography reported nearly 480,000 speakers of Zapotec, of which there are some fifty-five language varieties.[76] The tripartite title of Tlacolulokos's series of murals at the Central Library is in three varieties: Teotitlán, Quialana, and Juchitán.[77]

When Canul and Cernas officially established Tlacolulokos in 2010, they "vowed to . . . 'cause a stir through our work.'"[78] Indeed, their collective's name combines Tlacolula and *lokos*, the latter word meaning "crazy" or, in Chicanx Spanish, "crazy dudes," as in *vatos locos*. The influence of urban Chicanxs is apparent in their visual art, which includes painting, photography, video, screen printing, and tattoos. By depicting young indigenous Oaxacans sporting traditional attire and jewelry, along with Doc Martens, Locs sunglasses, and tattoos inspired by both Mesoamerican motifs and urban, Chicanx style, their murals have pushed back against what one observer has described as the "kitschy art pieces" featuring servile or premodern indigenous Oaxacans popular among tourists and international art collectors.[79] As the artists themselves have put it, "We don't paint happy Indians."[80]

Before arriving in Los Angeles in 2016 for a month-long residency hosted by the Library Foundation, Canul and Cernas were already familiar with that city, a primary destination for indigenous Oaxacan immigrants since the establishment of the Bracero Program in the 1940s. Los Angeles now boasts the largest population of indigenous Oaxacans outside of Oaxaca; the majority (by some estimates, 250,000) are Zapotec.[81] It is also home to "the largest urban Indian population in the country," as well as diasporic indigenous peoples of Oceania and Latin America.[82] Despite the misperception that Indians are stuck in a static ancestral homeland and/or on a remote, rural reservation, migration among Zapotecs is so deep-seated and prevalent that scholars and cultural critics have identified it as a "central component of the community's experience."[83] In fact, in some regions of Oaxaca, more than

Figure 13. Tlacolulokos, *Recuerda que el mundo es mío/Remember That the World Is Mine* (2017). Photo by Catherine S. Ramírez.

half the population has emigrated, a consequence of neoliberal poli-cies across the hemisphere.[84] Canul and Cernas "make Oaxacalifornia visible," thereby acknowledging and producing a "visual diaspora."[85] For instance, in *Recuerda que el mundo es mío/Remember That the World Is Mine*, they incorporate the "LA" from the Los Angeles Dodgers logo in "Tlacolula," thereby merging these two places (see figure 13).

In 2016 the Library Foundation commissioned Tlacolulokos "to cre-ate a series of murals that document what it means to be Indigenous and migrant in both Los Angeles and Oaxaca, Mexico, in the 21st cen-tury."[86] The new and temporary murals were installed in the Grand Rotunda, a nave-like space on the second floor of the Central Library's Goodhue Building, an art deco structure completed in 1926. They were placed alongside the American illustrator Dean Cornwell's 1933 series of murals *Four Great Eras of California History*.

Comprised of twelve oil on linen panels, *Four Great Eras* narrates a history of California in four parts: *The Founding of the Pueblo de los Angeles*,

Figure 14. Grand Rotunda, with murals by Dean Cornwell and Tlacolulokos, Central Library, Los Angeles Public Library (August 2018). Photo by Catherine S. Ramírez.

The Landing of Cabrillo, The Building of the Missions, and *The American-ization of California.*[87] In the first three parts, docile Indians bow before conquistadors and toil with picks and shovels as Franciscan friars contemplate their plans for a mission. In the fourth and final part, the Indians' primitive tools have been replaced by a locomotive, clipper ship, and covered wagon, "the three modes of transport that brought settlers to California."[88] Likewise, the friars and Indians have been replaced by gun-toting frontiersmen, 49ers, businessmen in top hats, ladies in hoop skirts, musicians wearing vaguely southern European costumes, and two dancers, one of whom has a large Spanish comb in her brown hair. Except for a Native American man donning a feather headdress in the style of Plains Indians and a "squaw" holding an infant in a "papoose," everyone in *Americanization* is white.[89] (See figure 14.) Irrespective of their differences, all are from someplace else.

Four Great Eras reproduces the trope of the vanishing Indian and celebrates settler colonialism; it romanticizes the expropriation of indigenous land and labor and the genocide that took place in California after Juan Rodríguez Cabrillo arrived in 1542. Before it erases California's indigenous peoples from the face of the state, the series enunciates what journalist, editor, and lawyer Carey McWilliams called California's Spanish fantasy. In this fantasy, "the Indians were devoted to the Franciscans ... their true friends," while the Indians' lay colonizers, classy *dons* and pretty *señoritas*, "lived out days of beautiful indolence."[90] The Native Americans and Spaniards' mestizx offspring—Mexicans and Mexican Americans—and the indigenous peoples of the present have no role to play in the Spanish fantasy. Indeed, they disrupt it.

Enter Tlacolulokos, Zapotec artists charged with dialogizing Cornwell's murals. In order to "to create two dialogues," *Gal rabenee ladxuu* was placed directly beneath *Four Great Eras*.[91] As painters, Canul and Cernas "us[e] the same language" as their predecessor, but the juxtaposition of the two sets of murals is striking.[92] For example, Cornwell employed a muted palette of "pinks, yellows, greens and blues," while Canul and Cernas used bold, deep colors, like cobalt and charcoal.[93] The crimson and gold geometric pattern unifying all eight panels of *Gal rabenee ladxuu* is that of the floor of a colonial-era church in Tlacolula, a visualization of what literary and cultural critic Walter Mignolo has termed "the colonial matrix of power" linking Tlacolula and Los Angeles.[94]

Above all, *Gal rabenee ladxuu* diverges from *Four Great Eras* because it protagonizes indigenous people. Before they produced their murals for the Central Library, Canul and Cernas stated that they wanted to give "those people," whom they identified as "people like us," "a voice" and to make "invisible communities" visible.[95] By emphasizing indigenous voice and visibility, these Zapotec artists not only articulate a politics of presence and visibility; they also practice Native survivance, "an active sense of presence over absence, deracination, and oblivion" and "an active resistance and repudiation of dominance, obtrusive themes of tragedy, nihilism, and victimry."[96]

That said, *Gal rabenee ladxuu* does not shy away from these themes. Instead, it confronts them in order to expose "the complexity of

Figure 15. Tlacolulokos, *Sonríe ahora, llora después/Smile Now, Cry Later* (2017). Photo by Catherine S. Ramírez.

Oaxacalifornia."[97] For example, some of the series' characters, including the boy in the panel *Sonríe ahora, llora después/Smile Now, Cry Later*, have a teardrop tattooed beneath one eye (see figure 15). Among Chicanxs, this tattoo can signify time spent in prison. Like the maxim, "Smile now, cry later," it is usually associated with gang life, not with children. However, here it "represents the difficulties of migrant children and the conflicts they encounter."[98] In the context of the Trump administration's policy of separating migrant children from their parents and incarcerating them, the boy's teardrop takes on an even more pointed meaning, one that merges the tattoo's original association with prison and the plight of thousands of migrant children in the twenty-first century.

In Cornwell's murals, children and women are minor characters. Women are most visible in the fourth and final major panel, *Americanization*, as bearers of civilization, progress, and a proto-multiculturalism. In contrast, young women figure prominently in *Gal rabenee ladxuu*. In every panel in which they appear, they wear traditional clothing and jewelry, symbols of the past and tradition. At the same time, all of the young women have tattoos, and many wield the trappings of consumer culture. For example, the panel *A donde quiera que vayas/Wherever You May Go* features two young women and a girl beneath the word, "OAXA-CALIFORNIA," in lettering reminiscent of the iconic Hollywood sign (see figure 16). All three models wear traditional Oaxacan clothing and jewelry, and all bear tattoos comprised of pre-Columbian motifs and Mexican and Chicanx iconography. For example, the woman on the panel's left side sports a tattoo of Jesus wearing the crown of thorns on her right forearm. The woman on the panel's right side has "LA" tattooed in the style of the Dodgers' logo on the back of her right hand. The letters "SBQ," perhaps for San Bartolomé Quialana, a town near Tlacolula, appear on her index, middle, and ring fingers in Old English script, a stylized form of writing associated with Chicanx street art and gangs. On her left forearm is a tattoo in the style of the Coca-Cola logo. It reads "Cali-Cheu," "Where Are You Going?" in Zapotec, a nod, perhaps, to *Where Do We Come From? What Are We? Where Are We Going?*, Paul Gauguin's famous 1897–98 oil painting of female Tahitians in multiple stages of life, from infancy to old age.[99]

Aside from the fact that they, too, are indigenous, the models in *A donde quiera que vayas* do not resemble the models in *Where Do We Come From?* However, the former's composition loosely mirrors that of the latter. Furthermore, *A donde quiera que vayas* offers multiple responses to the questions posed by the title of Gauguin's painting. For example, the young woman on the left is resting her left hand atop a black dress embroidered with marigolds and calla lilies, a design from the Isthmus

Figure 16. Tlacolulokos, *A donde quiera que vayas/Wherever You May Go* (2017). Photo by Catherine S. Ramírez.

of Oaxaca. However, the fingers of her hand form a "W," a hand sign commonly associated with gangs that also denotes the Oaxacan enclave on Los Angeles's Westside. As if she is taking a selfie, she peers into a mobile device, a technology that "tell[s] us who we are, who we would like to be, and how we would like others to see us."[100] The girl in the center of the panel plays a trumpet, a European import that indigenous Oaxacans have incorporated in their music, while sitting atop a pile of books that includes *Dios y el Estado*, by the Russian anarchist Mikhail Bakunin, a title by Foucault, and José Vasconcelos's *La Raza Cósmica*. Vasconcelos, the minister of public education in Mexico during the 1920s, was a proponent of *mestizaje* (racial mixing) as a means of eliminating indigenous peoples and whitening Mexico's population. The girl wears a traditional blouse from San Bartolomé Quialana, dark slacks, and a pair of Skechers. The third model sits cross-legged and directs her gaze downward. Her Adidas Superstars loom large in the panel's foreground. An illustration of syncretism and a study in contrasts, *A donde quiera que vayas* shows how immigrant indigenous women and their diasporic daughters come to embody cultural identity and the tension between past and present, tradition and modernity, small town and big city, and Oaxaca and California.

The models' traditional clothing and jewelry; mass-produced sneakers; and indigenous, Mexican, and Chicanx tattoos are not the only signs of who Zapotec Angelenos are, who they would like to be, and how they would like others to see them. A human skull wearing a conquistador's helmet sits prominently in the panel's lower left corner. Both the skull and the helmet have been shot through with arrows. Affixed to the helmet by one arrow is a portrait of Toypurina, a Tongva (also known as Gabrielino) medicine woman who was born in the Los Angeles Basin in 1760. On October 25, 1785, she helped lead an unsuccessful revolt against Mission San Gabriel Arcángel after its clergy prohibited certain Tongvan customs and ceremonies. She was caught, tried, found guilty, and exiled to San Carlos Borromeo de Carmelo, the most distant mission from San Gabriel at the time. Eventually she converted to Christianity, married a Spaniard, and had three children with him. She died in 1799 and is buried at Mission San Juan Bautista, hundreds of miles from her birthplace.[101]

Toypurina is "a symbol of Gabrielino resistance to the missions and an icon of California Indian women's resistance to colonial oppression."[102] She is also a migrant and, as a convert, the wife of a colonizer, and the mother of mestizxs, an assimilated subject. In short, she is a powerful and fraught identificatory site for Zapotecs in twenty-first-century Los Angeles. The inclusion of her image in *A donde quiera que vayas* draws a connection between Zapotec Angelenos and some of Southern California's original inhabitants, as well as between Tlacolulokos and the various Chicanx visual artists who have made Toypurina the subject of their work (e.g., Judith F. Baca).[103] In addition to pointing to overlapping indigeneities and generating solidarity, Toypurina's portrait exposes what critical Latinx indigeneities scholar Maylei Blackwell calls "layers of coloniality"—that is, "the maintenance of colonial hierarchies," Spanish, Mexican, and US, "in current relations of power, discourses and institutions."[104]

In this context, the inclusion of Toypurina's image may be read as *kuleana*, the responsibility, authority, and right indigenous immigrants have to other indigenous peoples and the occupied lands they live and work on.[105] It may be an example of what literary critic Sheila Marie Contreras has identified as indigenism, the celebration of past and distant Indians, rather than a reckoning with present and proximate indigenous peoples.[106] And/or it is another iteration of US multiculturalism, the logic of which reduces indigenous peoples to another "minority" group. This is a dangerous conflation, Trask warns, since under international law, minorities may warrant protection but "do not have the right to self-determination."[107]

Altogether, *Gal rabenee ladxuu* speaks to "how indigenous migrants interact with settler colonial projects," like multiculturalism.[108] When the Library Foundation, in conjunction with the LAPL and the Getty Foundation, commissioned the murals from Tlacolulokos, rather than from a collective of, say, indigenous artists based in Southern California, it absorbed the former group into a venerable US institution, thereby making a poignant statement about the place, real and imagined, of indigenous Oaxacans in Los Angeles's civic and artistic institutions.[109] By incorporating them in the space of the Central Library, the Library Commission folded indigenous Oaxacans into Los Angeles's heterogeneous populace and transformed them from arrivants, people forced into a settler society through the violence of European and Anglo-American global expansion, into immigrants, newcomers whose contributions to society are recognized and valued. In short, Oaxacalifornixs were assimilated.

In their critique of *Gal rabenee ladxuu*, Lourdes Gutiérrez Nájera and Korinta Maldonado argue that even though "Indigenous Mexicans and Native peoples in the United States share experiences as targets of discrimination and exclusionary practices," indigenous Mexicans are not "exempt from perpetuating contemporary settler logics."[110] The same can be and has been said of other arrivants to this country.[111] As I show in chapter 2, the Puerto Rican arrivants who attended the Carlisle Indian Industrial School in the late nineteenth and early twentieth centuries perpetuated settler logics by actively distancing themselves from and disparaging their Native American classmates. While there are myriad reasons for migration—among them war, famine, dispossession, religious persecution, forced labor, joblessness, and environmental degradation—my concern in this book is not so much why people move, but if and how they are received where they land—assimilation, in other words.

In fact, Tlacolulokos's murals were received very well in Los Angeles. They attracted nearly 100,000 visitors to the Central Library.[112] They were so popular that they remained on display until August 31, 2018, six months after they were originally set to come down. From the library, they traveled to Lille, France, for an exhibition about Mexican culture, and then on to the Museum of Latin American Art in Long Beach, California.[113] Although they do not take into account the full sweep of *Visualizing Language*, a series of events and a collection of texts of which Tlacolulokos's mural series was but one component, Gutiérrez Nájera and Maldonado's assertion that *Gal rabenee ladxuu* testifies to the institutionalization and, by extension, the assimilation of indigenous Oaxacans in Los Angeles is compelling.

In an unexpected turn of events and a painful twist of irony, Canul and Cernas were unable to attend the closing party for Visualizing Language at the Central Library on August 26, 2018. Six months earlier, while traveling with tourist visas, they were refused entry to the United States at San Francisco International Airport after they told US customs agents that they were in the Bay Area for a *chambe*, a gig.[114] After spending a harrowing night in what amounted to detention, the two artists were, in effect, deported. In addition, their visas were revoked for five years on the grounds that they had attempted to

enter the United States with tourist visas, not work ones.[115] While Tlacolulokos's murals could be absorbed by the logic of US multiculturalism and travel the globe, the *tlacolulenses* themselves would be rendered
"illegal," denied entry, and banished from the United States.

A LEXICON OF THE NOT-YET-POSSIBLE

In his series of drawings, *The Undocumented Alphabet*, artist and writer
Alberto Ledesma describes the label, "undocumented," as a "more
polite" and "more optimistic" euphemism for "illegal."[116] In fact, mainstream US news outlets began replacing "illegal" with "undocumented"
in 2003.[117] More recently, "unauthorized" has gained traction in the
media, academia, and policy circles. Some see "unauthorized" as a more
accurate adjective since many undocumented immigrants have some
form, if not an abundance, of documentation.[118] Like "illegal," "undocumented," and "unauthorized," "dissident Dreamer," "undocuqueer," and
"Oaxacalifornix" testify to social relations and struggles over rights,
resources, and recognition. These neologisms simultaneously produce,
engage, shape, and reflect subjects, social actors, and their relationships
to the state, institutions, social movements, history, and other social
groups. Inherently contradictory, "dissident Dreamer" unites opposites,
while the portmanteaux "undocuqueer" and "Oaxacalifornia" articulate intersectionality and interstitiality.

The questions underpinning most of this book have been: *How have
certain social groups been assimilated? Specifically, how are they assimilated as
racialized and subordinated subjects?* In this chapter I ask: *Who has* not *been
assimilated, and why not?* I find answers to my questions in the figures
of the dissident Dreamer, the undocuqueer, and the Oaxacalifornix.
Their exclusion exposes the limits of the nation-state and arguments
for inclusion predicated on deservingness; traditional, state-bound
citizenship; and the logic of multiculturalism. These not-yet-possible
subjects also expose what Muñoz calls the "prison house" of the "here
and now" and point us to "a then and there . . . other ways of being in

the world, and ultimately new worlds."[119] As an undated manifesto by undocumented youth in Chicago proclaims, "We are not only fighting for inclusion in this society. We are working to create a new society that we will help to shape from the beginning—a society that understands the importance of every person, documented or not."[120] By envisioning and enacting new subjects, the artists and activists I study in this chapter help bring that new society into being.

Epilogue

Notes from the Interregnum

In the oft-quoted opening to *The Uprooted: The Epic Story of the Great Migrations That Made the American People*, Oscar Handlin, a pioneer in the field of immigration history, proclaims, "Once I thought to write a history of the immigrants in America. Then I discovered that the immigrants were American history."[1] When I set out to write this book, I thought that I would write a history of assimilation in the United States. Then I discovered that the people long regarded as unassimilable or not part of the story of assimilation *were* that story.

In this book I define "assimilation" as a relational process whereby the boundary between unequal groups and between inside and outside blurs, disappears, or, paradoxically, is reinforced. I refer to the incorporation of members of social groups as subordinate and abject subjects as the "paradox of assimilation." In short, assimilation is the process whereby certain social actors and groups are transformed into insiders, while others are rendered outsiders on the inside.

In the United States, assimilation is widely regarded as an outcome of immigration. It is the process by which immigrants turn into and are turned into Americans. Assimilation qua Americanization has been defined in relation to racialization, the process whereby racial categories are produced and understood as part of a social hierarchy. This book decouples immigration and assimilation and probes the gap between assimilation and citizenship in order to show how certain social groups that are not immigrants or that are not considered real or legitimate immigrants have been assimilated as racialized and subordinate subjects—namely, as denizens, probationary citizens, alien citizens, and failed citizens. I argue that not only is assimilation a result of immigration; assimilation qua racialization is also a consequence of US imperialism, slavery, and an immigration apparatus that ranks mobile subjects and produces and maintains illegality. Assimilation is a key element of the US nation-making project. As a tool for distinguishing insiders from outsiders, it is, above all, a relationship of power.

While many insightful theories of assimilation emphasize similarity and difference between groups (e.g., between natives and newcomers), I remain more interested in what assimilation tells us about power and inequality and about rights, resources, and recognition. To be sure, my definition of assimilation is not how assimilation, as a cultural and social process, is generally understood in the United States. Generally speaking, assimilation is understood as a process of becoming more alike—the "action of making or becoming like," to quote the *Oxford English Dictionary* (OED)—and/or as a process of absorption.[2] When I tell people that I am writing a book about assimilation, the responses I usually get signal that my interlocutors assume that my book is about acculturation—about, say, a Spanish-speaking Mexican who migrates to the United States, naturalizes as a US citizen, and names her US-born and therefore US-citizen daughter Catherine Sue, or about a fourth-generation Mexican American whose first language is English and who struggles to learn Spanish and to roll her Rs, even though and especially because her surname is *Ramírez*, an inheritance from her Chicano father. Acculturation, which the OED defines as the "[a]doption of or adaptation to a different culture, esp. that of a colonizing, conquering, or majority group," is certainly part of the story of assimilation and part of this book, but it is not my primary concern.[3] For the purposes of this book, I am more interested in whether or how people are received—what migration scholars call "context of reception" and "mode of incorporation"—than why people move or are moved. Furthermore, by introducing the paradox of assimilation, I aim to dispel the widespread and pernicious perception that assimilation is the exclusive domain of European immigrants; their white, US-citizen descendants; and the mobile subjects who have the power and privilege to move with the state's authorization.

Tom Brokaw's ill-founded and desultory remarks regarding Latinxs and assimilation underscore the importance of expanding and complicating understandings of assimilation. The retired news anchor appeared on the NBC weekly news program *Meet the Press* on January 27, 2019, two days after a thirty-five-day federal government shutdown (at the time, the longest in US history) had come to an end. President Donald Trump had shut down the federal government after Congress refused to set aside $5.7 billion for a wall at the US-Mexico border. Attributing the demand for Trump's wall and, by extension, blame for Trump's shutdown to Latinx inassimilability, Brokaw chided, "Hispanics should work harder at assimilation. . . . You know, they ought not to be just codified in their communities but make sure that all their kids are learning to speak English."[4] In fact, according to nonpartisan think tanks like the Migration Policy Institute and the Pew Research Center, most Latinxs are monolingual English by the third generation, a pattern found in my own Mexican American family and other immigrant groups in the United States.[5] Still, some people can be deemed so fundamentally alien—unassimilable, in other words—that even an *éminence grise* can publicly justify the call for a thirty-foot-tall, multi-billion-dollar wall to keep those people out.

Assimilation, based on the OED's and my own definitions, warrants our attention because it is connected to ideas about belonging and deservingness. Whether they are native born or newcomers, people who are not considered real or legitimate Americans and/or who are branded aliens do not enjoy the state's full protection or largesse. Instead, they are targets of state violence and are subjected to heightened state surveillance, especially if they live on a reservation, are in prison or detention, or are applying for or hold DACA or Temporary Protected Status (TPS). As mentioned previously, DACA is a temporary and revocable status that grants certain young undocumented immigrants permission to work and a stay of deportation. Similarly, TPS, a program that was established in 1990, allows nationals from certain countries afflicted by ongoing armed conflict or natural disaster to live and work in the United States for a limited time. In exchange, DACA and TPS participants must hand over to DHS the very information that it can then use to deport them. This includes residential address and identifying physical characteristics (height, weight, eye color, and hair color).[6] DACA and TPS participants, especially those who have spent many years if not most of their lives in the United States, have been assimilated as denizens and probationary citizens. They have more rights than immigrants with less authorization, but DACA and TPS participants are not and may never be legal permanent residents or US citizens. What is more, they are highly deportable. In September 2017 the Trump administration announced that it would end DACA. Two months later it announced the termination of TPS for Haitian and Nicaraguan immigrants. And in January 2018 Salvadoran immigrants learned that they, too, would be losing TPS. Although the efforts to undo DACA and TPS have been stalled by legal challenges, the future of both programs remains uncertain.[7]

DACA and TPS participants are part of a long line of denizens and probationary citizens in the United States. All have undergone and continue to undergo a trial in which they are expected to comport themselves in a particular manner. To prove their worthiness for inclusion in the polity, they must stress their loyalty to the nation, their contributions to society (especially to the market), and their familiarity with the dominant culture. In the nineteenth century, Native Americans were expected to cut themselves off from their homes and families and to shed language, culture, customs, and beliefs—an entire worldview and way of life—to show white Americans that they could be US citizens, too. In 1895, a moment of mounting anti-black violence, Booker T. Washington assured his white compatriots that African Americans were loyal, valuable, docile, and familiar. During the Cold War, the Japanese American model minority was upheld as proof of US egalitarianism and meritocracy. Disturbingly similar cases have been made by and for undocumented immigrants in the twenty-first century.

Yet pleas for the acceptability and admissibility—indeed, the very humanity—of the undocumented have fallen on deaf ears. Trump has disparaged immigrants from Mexico and Central America in particular as "rapists," "thugs," and "animals."[8] In contrast, he has described neo-Nazis, white supremacists, and white nationalists as "very fine people."[9] All the while, his administration has worked to undo the modern US immigration system and to halt immigration, especially from poor countries. Trump's wall has yet to be completed, but the pandemic of 2020 has effectively closed the border.

As I write this epilogue, an estimated 373,677 people have died of COVID-19, the novel coronavirus. Over 100,000 of those deaths have been in the United States.[10] Accounting for more than 20,000 COVID-19 deaths, black Americans are dying at almost three times the rate of white Americans.[11] Meanwhile, protests against police violence against African Americans are raging in cities around the world. The outcry was sparked by a video of Derek Chauvin, a white Minneapolis police officer, pinning George Floyd, an unarmed, handcuffed, forty-six-year-old African American man, to the ground by kneeling on his neck. On May 25, 2020, Chauvin and three other officers arrested Floyd because they suspected him of having used a counterfeit $20 bill to buy cigarettes at a nearby grocery store. For six minutes, Floyd writhed on the pavement and pleaded for his life as Chauvin pressed his knee into his neck. Then Floyd fell silent and became still. Nearly three minutes later, Chauvin released him. Unresponsive, Floyd was taken to a hospital and pronounced dead.[12]

Protestors are so outraged that not even a highly contagious and deadly virus or Trump's threats to have them shot and set upon by "vicious dogs" have stopped them from taking to the streets.[13] In Minneapolis, Datelle Straub, Avery Lewis, and Titan Harness-Reed joined the protest on May 30, 2020. Seniors at Patrick Henry High School, the three African Americans wore their graduation robes and carried their diplomas. Reminiscent of the countless young, undocumented activists who donned caps and gowns as they pushed for the DREAM Act, Straub explained, "Because of COVID we couldn't walk the stage, so we decided to put our robes on to show that there is black excellence in our community." In fact, the robes provided the teenagers with little protection from the police. A group of law enforcement officers brandishing guns accosted them. Straub recounted seeing the red target dots from the officers' guns dance on their robes as he lifted his diploma above his head.[14] Whether the struggle is for black lives or the DREAM Act, a graduation robe, evidence of accomplishment and a symbol of promise, is not enough to convince the state of a black person's or an immigrant's worthiness.

Both Floyd's murder and the pandemic have cast light on what and who matter in society. Alongside Floyd's murder, the grim tally of black deaths due to COVID-19 gives new urgency to the slogan "Black Lives Matter." People of color and immigrants, documented and undocumented alike, work on the front lines of the pandemic—for example, in health care, transportation, retail, manufacturing, custodial services, and food production and service.[15] Suddenly, workers and economic migrants who were dismissed as "unskilled" or classified as "temporary" (disposable, in other words) are recognized as essential. Even DHS has declared farmworkers, the majority of whom are undocumented, "Essential Critical Infrastructure Workers."[16] Yet despite this acknowledgment—and despite having paid taxes and having pitched in to the unemployment insurance fund—undocumented immigrants were not included in the Coronavirus Aid, Relief, and Economic Security Act, the $2 trillion relief package Trump signed into law on March 18, 2020.[17] Essential *and* excluded, these undocumented workers testify to the paradox of assimilation.

The Trump administration has done little to conceal the fact that the United States needs immigrant labor (economic migrants, in other words) but does not want the immigrants themselves, especially if they are poor and dark. The administration's practices and policies not only spurn international human rights conventions; they also reject the claim that the United States is a nation of immigrants. Indeed, when the original mission statement of USCIS was revised in February 2018, language regarding the "nation of immigrants" was removed. Whereas the original statement from 2005 avows, "USCIS secures America's promise as a nation of immigrants," the revision reads, "U.S. Citizenship and Immigration Services administers the nation's lawful immigration system, safeguarding its integrity and promise by efficiently and fairly adjudicating requests for immigration benefits while protecting Americans, securing the homeland and honoring our values."[18] In the Trump homeland, the paradox of assimilation *is* immigration policy.

Without a doubt, I am finishing this book during a moment of heightened hypocrisy, uncertainty, fear, and chaos. I write in the midst of what Italian journalist, labor organizer, philosopher, and communist Antonio Gramsci called the interregnum, the moment when "the old is dying and the new cannot be born."[19] By disrupting the normal, the quotidian, and the taken for granted, the pandemic and the calls for justice for George Floyd and other victims and survivors of police violence offer a glimpse of a different world, a world to come. I do not know in what kind of world you, my reader, will read these words. Will that world consist of citizen-consumers and noncitizen workers whose labor is considered essential, but whose bodies are treated as disposable? Will we find ourselves back in a world in which cops, the embodiment of the state, kill black and brown people with impunity? Will we continue to use similarity as a gauge for acceptance and see difference as a threat or a marker of inferiority? Or will we build a world in which we truly cherish the contributions of all members of society, irrespective of race, citizenship status, or occupation? In which the value of a human life is not determined by color, contribution, or cash? In which the notion of merit is a relic?

NOTES

CHAPTER ONE

1. "The Rush at Castle Garden," *New York Times*, May 15, 1880, 4, www.nytimes
.com/1880/05/15/archives/the-rush-at-castle-garden.html.

2. Zach Montellaro, "Latinos for Trump Founder Warns of 'Taco Trucks on
Every Corner,'" *Politico*, September 1, 2016, www.politico.com/story/2016/09/latinos
-for-trump-founder-taco-trucks-marco-gutierrez-227667.

3. Advertisement, *Rural New-Yorker* 57 (November 5, 1898), 761, https://books
.google.com/books?id=YqBIAQAAMAAJ&lpg=PA761&ots=RxVFpMoaTD&dq=J
.%20Fenimore%20Cooper%20Dr%20Pierce%20Golden%20Medical%20discovery
&pg=PA760#v=onepage&q=J.%20Fenimore%20Cooper%20Dr%20Pierce
%20Golden%20Medical%20discovery&f=false.

4. Advertisement, *Rural New-Yorker.*

5. I have gleaned information about Dr. Pierce's Golden Medical Discovery
and Pleasant Pellets from Dr. Pierce's Alternative Extract or Golden Medical Discovery, Smithsonian Institution, National Museum of American History, http://
americanhistory.si.edu/collections/search/object/nmah_715454; and Internet
Archive, "Here's Why You Should Use Dr. Pierce's Golden Medical Discovery," 6,
https://archive.org/details/DPGMD/page/n6.

6. *Oxford English Dictionary*, s.v. "assimilation," www-oed-com.oca.ucsc.edu/view
/Entry/11934?redirectedFrom=assimilation#eid.

7. Richmond Mayo-Smith, "Assimilation of Nationalities in the United States, I,"
Political Science Quarterly 9, no. 3 (September 1894): 431.

8. Sarah E. Simons, "Social Assimilation, I," *American Journal of Sociology* 6, no. 6 (May 1901): 790.

9. Simons, "Social Assimilation, I," 790. Regarding Mayo-Smith's and Simons's early writings on assimilation, see Peter Kivisto, "What Is the Canonical Theory of Assimilation?," *Journal of the History of the Behavioral Sciences* 40, no. 2 (2004): 149–163.

10. Stanford M. Lyman, "Robert E. Park Reconsidered: The Early Writings," *American Sociologist* 21, no. 4 (1990): 342.

11. Robert E. Park, "Racial Assimilation in Secondary Groups with Particular Reference to the Negro," *American Journal of Sociology* 19, no. 5 (1914): 611.

12. Raymond Williams, *Keywords: A Vocabulary of Culture and Society, Revised Edition* (New York: Oxford University Press, 1983), 59.

13. Francis Paul Prucha, ed., *Documents of United States Indian Policy (Third Edition)* (Lincoln: University of Nebraska Press, 2000), 33.

14. I take *citizenize* from the Richard Henry Pratt Papers (WA MSS S-1174), Series III, box 19, folder 679, Beinecke Rare Book and Manuscript Library, Yale University Library (hereafter cited in notes as Pratt Papers).

15. Quoted in Donald F. Lindsey, *Indians at Hampton Institute, 1877–1923* (Urbana: University of Illinois Press, 1995), 25. The label "backward races" was commonly applied to non-Europeans in the nineteenth and early twentieth centuries. See Robert Francis Engs, *Educating the Disenfranchised and Disinherited: Samuel Chapman Armstrong and Hampton Institute, 1839–1893* (Knoxville: University of Tennessee Press, 1999), esp. chapter 1.

16. Fourteenth Amendment, Amendments to the Constitution of the United States of America, https://web.archive.org/web/20050918042603/http://www.gpoaccess.gov/constitution/pdf/con001.pdf.

17. Transcript of the Dawes Act (1887), www.ourdocuments.gov/print_friendly.php?flash=false&page=transcript&doc=50&title=Transcript+of+Dawes+Act+%281887%29.

18. Transcript of the Burke Act (1906), https://public.csusm.edu/nadp/a1906.htm.

19. Richard Henry Pratt, "The Advantages of Mingling Indians with Whites," in *Americanizing the American Indians: Writings by the "Friends of the Indian," 1880–1900*, ed. Francis Paul Prucha (Cambridge, MA: Harvard University Press, 1973), 261. See also Pratt Papers, Series III, box 19, folder 653.

20. Stewart G. Cole and Mildred Wiese Cole, *Minorities and the American Promise: The Conflict of Principle and Practice* (New York: Harper & Brothers 1954), 46.

21. Angela S. García, *Legal Passing: Navigating Undocumented Life and Local Immigration Law* (Berkeley: University of California Press, 2019), 9.

22. Russell A. Kazal, "Revisiting Assimilation: The Rise, Fall, and Reappraisal of a Concept in American Ethnic History," *American Historical Review* 100, no. 2 (1995): 437.

23. Samuel P. Huntington, "The Hispanic Challenge," *Foreign Policy* 141 (March–April 2004): 32. See also Samuel P. Huntington, *Who Are We? The Challenges to America's National Identity* (New York: Simon & Schuster, 2004).

24. Horace M. Kallen, *Culture and Democracy in the United States* (New Brunswick, NJ: Transaction Publishers, 1998), 80.

25. For an estimate of the number of immigrants to the United States during and around the Great Wave, see Faye Hipsman and Doris Meisner, "Immigration in the United States: New Economic, Social, Political Landscapes with Legislative Reform on the Horizon," Migration Policy Institute, April 16, 2013, www.migrationpolicy .org/article/immigration-united-states-new-economic-social-political-landscapes -legislative-reform

26. Sidney Ratner, "Horace M. Kallen and Cultural Pluralism," *Modern Judaism* 4, no. 2 (1984): 187.

27. Kallen, *Culture and Democracy in the United States*, 116.

28. Richard Alba and Victor Nee, *Remaking the American Mainstream: Assimilation and Contemporary Immigration* (Cambridge, MA: Harvard University Press, 2003), 9.

29. Michael Omi and Howard Winant, *Racial Formation in the United States, Third Edition* (New York: Routledge, 2014), 21. For an overview of the ethnicity paradigm, see chapter 1 of *Racial Formation in the United States*. See also Kathleen Neils Conzen et al., "The Invention of Ethnicity: A Perspective from the U.S.A.," *Journal of American Ethnic History* 12, no. 1 (1992): 3–41.

30. Mary C. Waters, *Ethnic Options: Choosing Identities in America* (Berkeley: University of California Press, 1990), 5.

31. George M. Fredrickson, *The Comparative Imagination: On the History of Racism, Nationalism, and Social Movements* (Berkeley: University of California Press, 2000), 84 ("common ancestry"); Conzen et al., "Invention of Ethnicity," 4–5 ("a process of construction or invention"); and Alba and Nee, *Remaking the American Mainstream*, 11 ("a social boundary").

32. Omi and Winant, *Racial Formation in the United States*, 110.

33. Regarding symbolic ethnicity, see Herbert Gans, "Symbolic Ethnicity: The Future of Ethnic Groups and Cultures in America," *Ethnic and Racial Studies* 2, no. 1 (1979): 1–20.

34. Ramón Grosfoguel, *Colonial Subjects: Puerto Ricans in a Global Perspective* (Berkeley: University of California Press, 2003), 129; and Herbert J. Gans, "Ethnic Invention and Acculturation, a Bumpy Line Approach," *Journal of American Ethnic History* 12, no. 1 (1992): 42–52.

35. See, for example, Milton M. Gordon, *Assimilation in American Life: The Role of Race, Religion, and National Origins* (New York: Oxford University Press, 1964); Robert E. Park, "Racial Assimilation in Secondary Groups with Particular Reference to the Negro," *American Journal of Sociology* 19, no. 5 (1914): 606–623; Robert E. Park and Ernest W. Burgess, *Introduction to the Science of Sociology* (Chicago: University of Chicago Press, 1924); William Isaac Thomas and Florian Znaniecki, *The Polish Peasant in Europe and America: Monograph of an Immigrant Group* (Chicago: University of Chicago Press, 1919); and W. Lloyd Warner and Leo Srole, *The Social Systems of American Ethnic Groups* (New Haven, CT: Yale University Press, 1945).

36. Robert E. Park, "Assimilation, Social," in *Encyclopaedia of the Social Sciences*, vol. 2, ed. Edwin R. A. Seligman (New York: Macmillan Company, 1930), 281.

37. Park, "Assimilation, Social," 282.

38. See, for example, the essays collected in Robert Ezra Park, *Race and Culture* (New York: The Free Press, 1950).

39. I discuss the exclusion of African Americans from theories of assimilation in chapter 3. Sociologist Moon-Kie Jung attributes this exclusion in part to the split in sociology between the sociology of race "(e.g., split labor market theory, internal colonialism)" and the sociology of immigration. See Moon-Kie Jung, "The Racial Unconscious of Assimilation Theory," *Du Bois Review* 6, no. 2 (2009): 383.

40. See, for example, Daniel Patrick Moynihan, "The Negro Family: The Case for National Action," Office of Planning and Research, United States Department of Labor, March 1965, https://web.stanford.edu/~mrosenfe/Moynihan's%20The %20Negro%20Family.pdf; and William Julius Wilson, *The Truly Disadvantaged: The Inner City, the Underclass, and Public Policy* (Chicago: University of Chicago Press, 1987).

41. See, for example, Nathan Glazer and Daniel P. Moynihan, *Beyond the Melting Pot* (Cambridge, MA: The MIT Press, 1963); Bob Blauner, *Racial Oppression in America* (New York: Harper & Row, 1972); Eduardo Bonilla-Silva, *Racism without Racists: Color-blind Racism and the Persistence of Racial Inequality in the United States* (Lanham, MD: Rowman & Littlefield, 2003); and Edward Telles and Vilma Ortiz, *Generations of Exclusion: Mexican Americans, Assimilation, and Race* (New York: Russell Sage Foundation, 2008).

42. Omi and Winant, *Racial Formation in the United States*, 109.

43. Notable works in critical whiteness studies include Karen Brodkin, *How Jews Became White Folks and What That Says about Race in America* (New Brunswick, NJ: Rutgers University Press, 1999); Thomas A. Gugliemo, *White on Arrival: Italians, Race, Color, and Power in Chicago, 1890–1945* (New York: Oxford University Press, 2003); Noel Ignatiev, *How the Irish Became White* (New York: Routledge, 1995); Matthew Frye Jacobson, *Whiteness of a Different Color: European Immigrants and the Alchemy of Race*

(Cambridge, MA: Harvard University Press, 1998); David R. Roediger, *The Wages of Whiteness: Race and the Making of the American Working Class* (London: Verso, 1999); David R. Roediger, *Working toward Whiteness: How America's Immigrants Became White* (New York: Basic Books, 2005); Michael Paul Rogin, *Blackface, White Noise: Jewish Immigrants in the Hollywood Melting Pot* (Berkeley: University of California Press, 1996); and Matt Wray, *Not Quite White: White Trash and the Boundaries of Whiteness* (Durham, NC: Duke University Press, 2006).

44. Alba and Nee, *Remaking the American Mainstream*, 119.

45. Omi and Winant, *Racial Formation in the United States*, 46.

46. Charles Hirschman, "America's Melting Pot Reconsidered," *Annual Review of Sociology* 9 (1983): 397 ("to shed their social and cultural heritage"); and Richard Alba and Victor Nee, "Rethinking Assimilation Theory for a New Era of Immigration," *International Migration Review* 31, no. 4 (1997): 826–827 ("fallen into disrepute").

47. Nathan Glazer, "Is Assimilation Dead?" *Annals of the American Academy of Political and Social Science* 530 (1993): 122–136.

48. Jung, "Racial Unconscious of Assimilation Theory," 376.

49. Alba and Nee, *Remaking the American Mainstream*, 101.

50. Tanya Golash-Boza, "Dropping the Hyphen? Becoming Latino(a)-American through Racialized Assimilation," *Social Forces* 85, no. 1 (2006): 28.

51. Alejandro Portes and Rubén G. Rumbaut, *Legacies: The Story of the Immigrant Second Generation* (Berkeley and New York: University of California Press and Russell Sage Foundation, 2001), 45.

52. Alejandro Portes and Min Zhou, "The New Second Generation: Segmented Assimilation and Its Variants," *Annals of the American Academy of Political and Social Science* 530, no. 1 (1993): 96. Regarding segmented assimilation, see also Herbert Gans, "Second Generation Decline: Scenarios for the Economic and Ethnic Futures of the Post-1965 American Immigrants," *Ethnic and Racial Studies* 15, no. 2 (1992): 173–192; Jung, "Racial Unconscious of Assimilation Theory"; Rubén G. Rumbaut and Alejandro Portes, *Ethnicities: Children of Immigrants in America* (Berkeley: University of California Press and Russell Sage Foundation, 2001); and Min Zhou, "Segmented Assimilation: Issues, Controversies, and Recent Research on the New Second Generation," *International Migration Review* 31, no. 4 (1997): 975–1008.

53. Ruben G. Rumbaut, "Assimilation of Immigrants," in *International Encyclopedia of the Social and Behavioral Sciences*, Vol. 2, ed. Neil J. Smelser and Paul B. Baltes (New York: Elsevier, 2001), 845.

54. Aristide R. Zolberg and Long Litt Woon, "Why Islam Is Like Spanish: Cultural Incorporation in Europe and the United States," *Politics & Society* 27, no. 5 (1999): 8. See also Jung, "Racial Unconscious of Assimilation Theory," 389; Roger

Waldinger, "The Bounded Community: Turning Foreigners into Americans in Twenty-first Century L.A.," *Ethnic and Racial Studies* 30, no. 3 (2007): 341–374; and Roger Waldinger, "Transforming Foreigners into Americans," in *The New Americans: A Guide to Immigration since 1965*, ed. Mary C. Waters and Reed Ueda (Cambridge, MA: Harvard University Press, 2007), 137–148.

55. Portes and Rumbaut, *Legacies*, 44.

56. The observation that Puerto Rican is not hyphenated is from Grosfoguel, *Colonial Subjects*, 141.

57. Cecilia Menjívar, "Liminal Legality: Salvadoran and Guatemalan Immigrants' Lives in the United States," *American Journal of Sociology* 111, no. 4 (2006): 1002. See also Alejandro Portes and Joseph Böröcz, "Contemporary Immigration: Theoretical Perspectives on Its Determinants and Modes of Incorporation," *International Migration Review* 23, no. 3 (1989): 606–630; and Alejandro Portes and Rubén G. Rumbaut, *Immigrant America: A Portrait* (Berkeley: University of California Press, 1990).

58. Bridget Anderson, *Us and Them: The Dangerous Politics of Immigration Control* (Oxford: Oxford University Press, 2013), 4.

59. First introduced in Congress in 2001, the DREAM Act would have granted conditional residency and, upon meeting further qualifications, legal permanent residency to certain young undocumented immigrants.

60. Regarding the politics of disavowal, see Lisa Marie Cacho, *Social Death: Racialized Rightlessness and the Criminalization of the Unprotected* (New York: New York University Press, 2012); Christina B. Hanhardt, *Safe Space: Gay Neighborhood History and the Politics of Violence* (Durham, NC: Duke University Press, 2013); and Nayan Shah, *Contagious Divides: Epidemics and Race in San Francisco's Chinatown* (Berkeley: University of California Press, 2001).

61. Mae M. Ngai, "Birthright Citizenship and the Alien Citizen," *Fordham Law Review* 75, no. 5 (2007): 2521. See also Mae M. Ngai, *Impossible Subjects: Illegal Aliens and the Making of Modern America* (Princeton, NJ: Princeton University Press, 2005), 2.

62. According to sociologists Tamotsu Shibutani and Kian M. Kwan, assimilation involves a "transformation of perspectives. . . . [A] newcomer in a community comes to assume the outlook shared by his new associates and to redefine himself from this standpoint. Such transformations take place in many contexts—the son of a sharecropper who works his way through college by playing football and eventually becomes a cardiac specialist, or the first offender who becomes acclimated to the values of the underworld. The initial step consists of recognizing differences between oneself and the others and experiencing a sense of uneasiness." See Tamotsu Shibutani and Kian M. Kwan, *Ethnic Stratification: A Comparative Approach* (New York: Macmillan, 1965), 504.

63. Guy Standing, *A Precariat Charter: From Denizens to Citizens* (London: Bloomsbury Academic, 2014), 8.

64. Rachel Ida Buff, "Denizenship as Transnational Practice," in *Public Culture: Diversity, Democracy, and Community in the United States,* ed. Marguerite S. Shaffer (Philadelphia: University of Pennsylvania Press, 2012), 263–272; Susan Bibler Coutin, *Legalizing Moves: Salvadoran Immigrants' Struggle for U.S. Residency* (Ann Arbor: University of Michigan Press, 2000); and Cecilia Menjívar, "Liminal Legality: Salvadoran and Guatemalan Immigrants' Lives in the United States," *American Journal of Sociology* III, no. 4 (2006): 999–1037.

65. Buff, "Denizenship as Transnational Practice," 267. Regarding denizenship, see Nicholas De Genova, "Denizens All: The Otherness of Citizenship," in *Citizenship and Its Others,* ed. Bridget Anderson and Vanessa Hughes (New York: Palgrave Macmillan, 2015), 191–202; Tomas Hammar, *Democracy and the Nation State: Aliens, Denizens, and Citizens in a World of International Migration* (Brookfield, VT: Avebury/Gower Publishing), 1990; Marcel Paret, "Precarious Class Formations in the United States and South Africa," *International Labor and Working-Class History* 89 (2016): 84–106; Guy Standing, *The Precariat: The New Dangerous Class* (London: Bloomsbury Academic, 2011); and Neil Walker, "Denizenship and the Deterritorialization in the EU," *EUI Working Paper LAW,* no. 2008/8 (2008): 1–12.

66. Omi and Winant refer to the imposition of the "new" immigrant model onto non-Europeans as "the immigrant analogy," "the immigration model," and "the immigration framework." See Omi and Winant, *Racial Formation in the United States,* 29–30. In a similar vein, historian Michael B. Katz is critical of scholars who cast "blacks as the last of the immigrants" and policies that link African Americans' "advancement to patience, not government intervention." See Michael B. Katz, *The Undeserving Poor: America's Enduring Confrontation with Poverty* (New York: Oxford University Press, 2013), 27. And sociologists Mary C. Waters and Tomás R. Jiménez acknowledge that "both popular and scholarly notions of what constitutes success for post-1965 immigrants to the United States are either implicitly or explicitly comparative with the experiences of immigrants who came in the last mass immigration between 1880 and 1920" and that "many of the methods and theories we use to assess immigrant assimilation are also derived from the study of these earlier immigrants." See Mary C. Waters and Tomás R. Jiménez, "Assessing Immigrant Assimilation: New Empirical and Theoretical Challenges," *Annual Review of Sociology* 31 (2005): 106.

67. Molina shows that a "relational treatment of race recognizes that the construction of race is a mutually constitutive process and demonstrates how race is socially constructed, hence fighting against essentialist notions. Furthermore, it attends to how, when, where, and to what extent groups intersect." See Natalia

Molina, "Examining Chicana/o History through a Relational Lens," *Pacific Historical Review* 82, no. 4 (2013): 522. See also Daniel Martinez HoSang and Natalia Molina, "Introduction: Toward a Relational Consciousness of Race," in *Relational Formations of Race: Theory, Method, and Practice*, ed. Natalia Molina, Daniel Martinez HoSang, and Ramón A. Gutiérrez (Berkeley: University of California Press, 2019), 1–18; and Natalia Molina, "The Power of Racial Scripts: What the History of Mexican Immigration to the United States Teaches Us about Relational Notions of Race," *Latino Studies* 8, no. 2 (2010): 156–175. For theorizations of assimilation as a boundary crossing, see Richard Alba, "Bright vs. Blurred Boundaries: Second-generation Assimilation and Exclusion in France, Germany, and the United States," *Ethnic and Racial Studies* 28, no. 1 (2005): 20–49; Alba and Nee, *Remaking the American Mainstream*; Fredrik Barth, *Ethnic Groups and Boundaries: The Social Organization of Culture Difference* (Oslo: Universitetsforlaget, 1969); Conzen, et al., The Invention of Ethnicity"; Tomás R. Jiménez, *The Other Side of Assimilation: How Immigrants Are Changing American Life* (Berkeley: University of California Press, 2017); and Zolberg and Woon, "Why Islam Is Like Spanish."

68. Alba, "Bright vs. Blurred Boundaries," 22.

69. Julia Kristeva, *Powers of Horror: An Essay on Abjection* (New York: Columbia University Press, 1982), 4.

70. My definition of differential inclusion is indebted to that of sociologist Yen Le Espiritu: "I define *differential inclusion* as the process whereby a group of people is deemed integral to the nation's economy, culture, identity, and power—but integral only or precisely because of their designated subordinate standing." Yen Le Espiritu, *Home Bound: Filipino American Lives Across Cultures, Communities, and Countries* (Berkeley: University of California Press, 2003), 47. See also see Sandro Mezzadra et al., "Differential Inclusion/Exclusion," in "New Keywords: Migration and Borders," ed. Nicholas De Genova, Sandro Mezzadra, and John Pickles, special issue, *Cultural Studies* 29, no. 1 (2015): 25–26.

71. *Cherokee Nation v. Georgia*, Legal Information Institute, www.law.cornell.edu /supremecourt/text/30/1.

72. *Dred Scott v. Sandford*, Wikisource, https://en.wikisource.org/wiki/Dred_Scott _v._Sandford.

73. *Downes v. Bidwell*, Library of Congress, https://cdn.loc.gov/service/ll/usrep /usrep182/usrep182244/usrep182244.pdf.

74. William Petersen, "Success Story: Japanese-American Style," *New York Times Magazine*, January 9, 1966, 20–21, 33, 36, 38, 40–41, 43; and "Success Story of One Minority in the U.S.," *US News & World Report*, December 26, 1966, 73–78.

75. Keith Osajima, "Asian Americans as the Model Minority: An Analysis of the Popular Press Image in the 1960s and 1980s," in *A Companion to Asian American Studies*, ed. Kent A. Ono (Malden, MA: Blackwell Publishing, 2005), 217.

76. Lisa Sun-Hee Park, "Assimilation," in *Keywords for Asian American Studies*, ed. Cathy J. Schlund-Vials, K. Scott Wong, and Linda Trinh Vo (New York: New York University Press, 2015), 17.

77. Alicia Schmidt Camacho, *Migrant Imaginaries: Latino Cultural Politics in the U.S.-Mexico Borderlands* (New York: New York University Press, 2008), 206.

78. Regarding genealogy, see Michel Foucault, "Nietzsche, Genealogy, History," in Michel Foucault, *Language, Counter-memory, Practice: Selected Essays and Interviews*, ed. Donald F. Bouchard, trans. Donald F. Bouchard and Sherry Simon (Ithaca, NY: Cornell University Press, 1977), 139–164.

79. Omi and Winant, *Racial Formation in the United States*, 45 (emphasis in original).

80. Omi and Winant, *Racial Formation in the United States*, 45.

81. "New nativism," a term I take from sociologist Robin Dale Jacobson, refers to the nativism that erupted in the United States in the 1990s, as exemplified by California's Proposition 187. See Robin Dale Jacobson, *The New Nativism: Proposition 187 and the Debate over Immigration* (Minneapolis: University of Minnesota Press, 2008).

82. Patrick Wolfe, "Land, Labor, and Difference: Elementary Structures of Race," *American Historical Review* 106, no. 3 (2001): 866–905. Patrick Wolfe, "Settler Colonialism and the Elimination of the Native," *Journal of Genocide Research* 8, no. 4 (2006): 387–409.

83. Immigration Act of 197 (An act to regulate the immigration of aliens to, and the residence of aliens in, the United States), http://library.uwb.edu/Static/USimmigration/39%20stat%20874.pdf.

84. Harry Franqui-Rivera, "National Mythologies: U.S. Citizenship for the People of Puerto Rico and Military Service," *Centro* 10, no. 21 (2013): 14.

85. Franqui-Rivera, "National Mythologies," 10. See also Harry Franqui-Rivera, *Soldiers of the Nation: Military Service and Modern Puerto Rico, 1868–1952* (Lincoln: University of Nebraska Press, 2018); and Nicholas De Genova and Ana Y. Ramos-Zayas, *Latino Crossings: Mexicans, Puerto Ricans, and the Politics of Race and Citizenship* (New York: Routledge, 2003), esp. chapter 1.

86. De Genova and Ramos-Zayas, *Latino Crossings*, 3.

87. De Genova and Ramos-Zayas, , *Latino Crossings*, 4.

88. Transcript of Chinese Exclusion Act (1882), www.ourdocuments.gov/doc.php?flash=false&doc=47&page=transcript.

89. Ngai, *Impossible Subjects*, 7.

90. United Nations, Universal Declaration of Human Rights, Article 13, www.un .org/en/universal-declaration-human-rights/.

91. Bonnie Honig, *Democracy and the Foreigner* (Princeton, NJ: Princeton University Press, 2001), 78.

92. Oscar Handlin, *The Uprooted: The Epic Story of the Great Migrations That Made the American People* (Boston: Little Brown, 1951), 3.

93. Nonimmigrant, U.S. Citizenship and Immigration Services, www.uscis.gov /tools/glossary/nonimmigrant.

94. It is difficult to count undocumented immigrants, even those who once were undocumented and who are now naturalized US citizens. Naturalized US citizens who used to be undocumented are less likely to reveal their former status in light of the establishment in June 2018 of a US Citizenship and Immigration Services task force charged with tracking down, denaturalizing, and deporting people suspected of having lied on their applications for US citizenship. See Amy Taxin, "U.S. Launches Bid to Find Citizenship Cheaters," Associated Press, June 11, 2018, https://apnews.com/1da389a535684a5f9d0da74081c242f3. See also Mark Hugo Lopez and Ana Gonzalez-Barrera, "If They Could, How Many Unauthorized Immigrants Would Become U.S. Citizens?," Pew Research Center Factank, June 27, 2013, www .pewresearch.org/fact-tank/2013/06/27/if-they-could-how-many-unauthorized -immigrants-would-become-u-s-citizens/.

95. Sébastien Chauvin and Blanca Garcés-Mascareñas, "Beyond Informal Citizenship: The New Moral Economy of Migrant Illegality," *International Political Sociology* 6 (2012): 243.

96. "Rush at Castle Garden."

97. "Rush at Castle Garden."

98. Advertisement, *Rural New-Yorker.*

99. American historian Frederick Jackson Turner declared the frontier closed in "The Significance of the Frontier in American History," a paper he presented to the American Historical Association at the Chicago World's Fair in 1893. Frederick Jackson Turner, *The Frontier in American History* (New York: Henry Holt, 1921).

100. Frederick Hoxie, *A Final Promise: The Campaign to Assimilate the Indians, 1880– 1920* (Lincoln: University of Nebraska Press, 1984), 96.

101. Patty Limerick, "The Myth of the Vanishing Indian," *Denver Post*, October 16, 2015, www.denverpost.com/2015/10/16/limerick-the-myth-of-the-vanishing-indian/.

102. Mehreen Kasana, "Who Is Marco Gutierrez? The Latinos for Trump Founder Will Speak at MOAR," Bustle, September 16, 2017, www.bustle.com/p/who -is-marco-gutierrez-the-latinos-for-trump-founder-will-speak-at-moar-2366790.

103. Kasana, "Who Is Marco Gutierrez?"

104. Sarah Ravani and Trisha Thadani, "For Immigrant Trump Voter, Tensions Reach Boiling Point at Home," *San Francisco Chronicle*, March 26, 2017, www.sfchronicle.com/bayarea/article/For-immigrant-Trump-voters-tensions-reach-11029064.php; Sam Sanders, "#Meme of the Week: Taco Trucks on Every Corner," NPR, September 2, 2016, www.npr.org/2016/09/02/492390405/-memeoftheweek-taco-trucks-on-every-corner; and Elise Foley and Rebecca Shapiro, "Protestors Build Big, Beautiful Wall of Taco Trucks outside Trump's Las Vegas Hotel," *Huffpost*, October 19, 2016, www.huffingtonpost.com/entry/taco-trucks-trump-las-vegas_us_5806e250e4b0180a36e760e3.

105. Evelyn Rupert, "Clinton: A Taco Truck on Every Corner Sounds Delicious," *The Hill*, September 15, 2016, https://thehill.com/blogs/blog-briefing-room/news/296251-clinton-a-taco-truck-on-every-corner-sounds-delicious.

106. Miriam Jordan, "Making President Trump's Bed: A Housekeeper without Papers," *New York Times*, December 6, 2018, www.nytimes.com/2018/12/06/us/trump-bedminster-golf-undocumented-workers.html.

CHAPTER TWO

1. Records of the Carlisle Indian Industrial School, National Archives and Records Administration, Group 75, box 29, folder 1374.

2. The precise number of Puerto Rican students who passed through Carlisle is not entirely clear. Genevieve Bell tallies fifty-nine to sixty; Pablo Navarro-Rivera, sixty. See Genevieve Bell, "Telling Stories out of School: Remembering the Carlisle Indian Industrial School, 1879–1918" (PhD diss., Stanford University, 1998), vii, 290, 369, 397; Pablo Navarro-Rivera, "Acculturation under Duress: The Puerto Rican Experience at the Carlisle Indian Industrial School, 1898–1918," *Centro Journal* 18, no. 1 (2006): 239; and Pablo Navarro-Rivera, "The Imperial Enterprise and Educational Policies in Colonial Puerto Rico," in *Colonial Crucible: Empire in the Making of the Modern American State*, ed. Alfred W. McCoy and Francisco A. Scarano (Madison: University of Wisconsin Press, 2009), 163–174. Records for fifty Puerto Rican students are available via the Carlisle Indian Digital Resource Center, http://carlisleindian.dickinson.edu/.

3. Navarro-Rivera, "Acculturation under Duress," 238.

4. Bell, "Telling Stories out of School," 397.

5. "Our Porto Ricans" is from page 3 of the Carlisle student newspaper, *The Arrow* 1, no. 1 (August 25, 1904), Pratt Papers, Series III, box 20, folder 771.

6. William McNeill, *Polyethnicity and National Unity in World History* (Toronto: University of Toronto, 1986); and Patrick Wolfe, "Land, Labor, and Difference: Elementary Structures of Race," *American Historical Review* 106, no. 3 (2001): 866–905.

7. I take my understanding of the relational from Natalia Molina, "Examining Chicana/o History through a Relational Lens," *Pacific Historical Review* 82, no. 4 (2013): 520–541. See also Daniel Martinez HoSang and Natalia Molina, "Introduction: Toward a Relational Consciousness of Race," in *Relational Formations of Race: Theory, Method, and Practice*, ed. Natalia Molina, Daniel Martinez HoSang, and Ramón A. Gutiérrez (Berkeley: University of California Press, 2019), 1–18; and Natalia Molina, "The Power of Racial Scripts: What the History of Mexican Immigration to the United States Teaches Us about Relational Notions of Race," *Latino Studies* 8, no. 2 (2010): 156–175.

8. Min Zhou, "Segmented Assimilation: Issues, Controversies, and Recent Research on the New Second Generation," *International Migration Review* 31, no. 4 (1997): 975.

9. "Backward races" is from chapter 1 of Robert Francis Engs, *Educating the Disenfranchised and Disinherited: Samuel Chapman Armstrong and Hampton Institute, 1839–1893* (Knoxville: University of Tennessee Press, 1999).

10. Yen Le Espiritu, *Home Bound: Filipino American Lives Across Cultures, Communities, and Countries* (Berkeley: University of California Press, 2003), 47; Sandro Mezzadra et al., "Differential Inclusion/Exclusion," in "New Keywords: Migration and Borders," ed. Nicholas De Genova, Sandro Mezzadra, and John Pickles, special issue, *Cultural Studies* 29, no. 1 (2015): 25–26. See also Lisa Marie Cacho's concept of "differential devaluation" in *Social Death: Racialized Rightlessness and the Criminalization of the Unprotected* (New York: New York University Press, 2012), 18.

11. My reading of Dalrymple's illustration is indebted to anthropologist Nicholas De Genova's insightful discussion of the "originary triangulation of whiteness with the subordination of *both* blacks and Indians" in the United States. See Nicholas De Genova, "Latino and Asian Racial Formations at the Frontiers of U.S. Nationalism," in *Racial Transformations: Latinos and Asians Remaking the United States*, ed. Nicholas De Genova (Durham, NC: Duke University Press, 2006), 1.

12. Hallmarks of the Indian New Deal included John Colliers's leadership at the Bureau of Indian Affairs from 1933 until 1945 and the Indian Reorganization Act of 1934. Also known as the Wheeler-Howard Act, the Indian Reorganization Act reversed many of the policies and practices of the allotment and assimilation era by seeking to "conserve and develop Indian lands and resources; to extend to Indians the right to form business and other organizations; to establish a credit system for Indians; [and] to grant certain rights of home rule to Indians." See Wheeler-Howard Act, June 18, 1934, http://aghca.org/wp-content/uploads/2012/07/indianreorganizationact.pdf. See also Vine Deloria, *The Indian Reorganization Act: Congresses and Bills* (Norman: University of Oklahoma Press, 2002).

13. Gabriella Treglia, "Using Citizenship to Retain Identity: The Native American Dance Bans of the Later Assimilation Era, 1900–1930," *Journal of American Studies* 47, no. 3 (2012): 777–800.

14. Philip J. Deloria, *Playing Indian* (New Haven, CT: Yale University Press, 1998), 4.

15. Frederick Hoxie, *A Final Promise: The Campaign to Assimilate the Indians, 1880–1920* (Lincoln: University of Nebraska Press, 1984), 53–54.

16. Transcript of the Dawes Act (1887), www.ourdocuments.gov/print_friendly .php?flash=false&page=transcript&doc=50&title=Transcript+of+Dawes+Act+ %281887%29.

17. Transcript of the Burke Act (1906), https://public.csusm.edu/nadp/a1906.htm.

18. Henry L. Dawes, "Solving the Indian Problem," in *Americanizing the American Indians: Writings by the "Friends of the Indian," 1880–1900*, ed. Francis Paul Prucha (Cambridge, MA: Harvard University Press, 1973), 29 (emphasis in original).

19. Dawes, "Solving the Indian Problem," 30.

20. Janet A. McDonnell, *The Dispossession of the American Indian, 1887–1934* (Bloomington: Indiana University Press, 1991).

21. Francis Paul Prucha, ed., *Americanizing the American Indians: Writings by the "Friends of the Indian," 1880–1900* (Cambridge, MA: Harvard University Press, 1973), 77.

22. Quoted in Francis Paul Prucha, *American Indian Policy in the Formative Years: The Indian Trade and Intercourse Acts, 1790–1834* (Cambridge, MA: Harvard University Press, 1962), 220–221.

23. "Humanitarians" is from Prucha, *Americanizing the American Indians*, 7. "Capable persons of good moral character" and "the habits and arts of civilization" are from the Civilization Fund Act of 1819, in Francis Paul Prucha, ed., *Documents of United States Indian Policy (Third Edition)* (Lincoln: University of Nebraska Press, 2000), 33.

24. Pratt Papers, Series III, box 19, folder 659.

25. According to Bell and Linda F. Witmer, eight thousand to eighty-five hundred students from seventy-five nations attended Carlisle. See Bell, "Telling Stories out of School," vi, and the dust jacket of Linda F. Witmer, *The Indian Industrial School, Carlisle, Pennsylvania, 1879–1918* (Carlisle, PA: Cumberland County Historical Society, 1993).

26. Witmer, *Indian Industrial School*, 35.

27. Richard Henry Pratt, "The Advantages of Mingling Indians with Whites," in *Americanizing the American Indians: Writings by the "Friends of the Indian," 1880–1900*, ed. Francis Paul Prucha (Cambridge, MA: Harvard University Press, 1973), 261. A version of Pratt's 1892 speech may also be found in Pratt Papers, Series III, box 19, folder

653. Regarding the saying, "The only good Indian is a dead Indian," see Wolfgang Mieder, "'The Only Good Indian Is a Dead Indian': History and Meaning of a Proverbial Stereotype," *Journal of American Folklore* 106, no. 419 (1993): 38–60.

28. Pratt, "Advantages of Mingling Indians with Whites," 268.

29. Helen Ludlow, *Ten Years' Work for Indians at the Hampton Normal and Agricultural Institute at Hampton, Virginia, 1878–1888* (Hampton, VA: The Hampton Normal and Agricultural Institute, 1888), 45.

30. Witmer, *Indian Industrial School*, 114.

31. Pratt Papers, Series III, box 19, folder 659.

32. For an astute analysis of Carlisle's before-and-after portraits, see Hayes Peter Mauro, *The Art of Americanization at the Carlisle Indian School* (Albuquerque: University of New Mexico Press, 2011).

33. Richard H. Pratt to Rutherford B. Hayes, March 9, 1880, quoted in David Wallace Adams, *Education for Extinction: American Indians and the Boarding School Experience, 1875–1928* (Lawrence: University of Kansas Press, 1995), 55.

34. Witmer, *Indian Industrial School*, 1–2.

35. Richard Henry Pratt, *Battlefield and Classroom: Four Decades with the American Indian, 1867–1904* (New Haven, CT: Yale University Press, 1964), 7.

36. Adams, *Education for Extinction*, 39.

37. Pratt, *Battlefield and Classroom*, 175. See also Adams, *Education for Extinction*, 42.

38. Adams, *Education for Extinction*, 41–43.

39. Adams, *Education for Extinction*, 45.

40. Quoted in Edith Armstrong Talbot, *Samuel Chapman Armstrong: A Biographical Study* (New York: Negro Universities Press, 1969), 157.

41. Jeanne Zeidler, foreword to *To Lead and to Serve: American Indian Education at Hampton Institute, 1878–1923*, ed. Mary Lou Hultgren and Paulette Fairbanks Molin (Virginia Beach: Virginia Foundation for the Humanities and Public Policy, 1989), 6; and Brenda J. Child, *Boarding School Seasons: American Indian Families, 1900–1940* (Lincoln: University of Nebraska Press, 1998), 6.

42. Ludlow, *Ten Years' Work*, iv–v.

43. "Co-education of Races," *Southern Workman* 28, no. 1 (January 1899): 2, Publications Collection, Hampton University Archives.

44. According to Engs, Hampton received $167 per Native American student per year from the federal government when it began its Indian program. See Engs, *Educating the Disenfranchised*, 118. See also Donald F. Lindsey, *Indians at Hampton Institute, 1877–1923* (Urbana: University of Illinois Press, 1995), 247–271.

45. José-Manuel Navarro, *Creating Tropical Yankees: Social Science Textbooks and Ideological Control in Puerto Rico, 1898–1908* (New York: Routledge, 2002), 115–117; and

Lee D. Baker, "Research, Reform, and Racial Uplift: The Mission of the Hampton Folk-Lore Society, 1893–1899," in *Excluded Ancestors, Inventible Traditions: Essays toward a More Inclusive History of Anthropology*, ed. Richard Handler (Madison: University of Wisconsin Press, 2000), 46.

46. Ludlow, *Ten Years' Work*, vi.

47. Regarding Puerto Rican students at Hampton, Tuskegee, and Carlisle, see Sonia Migdalia Rosa, "Puerto Ricans at Carlisle Indian School," in *The Praeger Handbook of Latino Education in the US*, Vol. 2, ed. Lourdes Diaz Soto (Westport, CT: Praeger, 2007), 387–388; and Navarro-Rivera, "Acculturation under Duress." Regarding Cubans at Tuskegee, see Frank Andre Guridy, *Forging Diaspora: Afro-Cubans and African Americans in a World of Empire and Jim Crow* (Chapel Hill: University of North Carolina Press, 2010).

48. Adams, *Education for Extinction*, 45.

49. Jim Crow was the de jure and de facto system of racial segregation in the United States from the late nineteenth century until 1965, when the Voting Rights Act ended legally sanctioned state barriers to voting in federal, state, and local elections.

50. Samuel Chapman Armstrong Collection, Sawyer Library, Williams College, Series I, box 1, folder 36 (hereafter cited in notes as Armstrong Collection).

51. Adams, *Education for Extinction*, 46.

52. Pratt Papers, Series III, box 20, folder 696.

53. Moon-Kie Jung, "The Racial Unconscious of Assimilation Theory," *Du Bois Review* 6, no. 2 (2009): 387 ("contagious social ills"); and Engs, *Educating the Disenfranchised*, 123–124 ("degraded negroes").

54. Pratt Papers, Series III, box 20, folder 696; and Child, *Boarding School Seasons*, 6.

55. "Co-education of Races," 2.

56. Ludlow, *Ten Years' Work*, 14.

57. Helen W. Ludlow, "Hampton's Indian Students at Home," in *Hampton Institute, 1868 to 1885: Its Work for Two Races*, ed. M. F. Armstrong, Helen W. Ludlow, and Elaine Goodale (Hampton, VA: Normal School Press Print, 1885), 15–19.

58. Caroline Andrus (Hampton teacher) to Addie Stevens Bouchier (former student), September 6, 1923, quoted in Lindsey, *Indians at Hampton Institute*, 261.

59. Wolfe, "Land, Labor, and Difference," 867.

60. Wolfe, "Land, Labor, and Difference," 884.

61. "Co-education of Races," 2.

62. Pratt Papers, Series III, box 19, folder 669 ("tremendous advantage"); and Pratt, "Advantages of Mingling Indians with Whites," 263 ("the Negro race").

63. Pratt Papers, Series III, box 19, folder 669 ("vast numbers"); and Pratt, "Advantages of Mingling Indians with Whites," 263 ("increase their value").

64. Pratt Papers, Series III, box 19, folder 669.

65. Quoted in Lindsey, *Indians at Hampton Institute*, 25.

66. Aihwa Ong, "Cultural Citizenship as Subject-Making: Immigrants Negotiate Racial and Cultural Boundaries in the United States," *Current Anthropology* 37, no. 5 (December 1996): 740.

67. Juan Santano Student File, Carlisle Indian Digital Resource Center, http://carlisleindian.dickinson.edu/student_files/juan-santano-student-file.

68. Richard Henry Pratt to Dr. M.G. Brumbaugh, October 8, 1900, Records of the Carlisle Indian Industrial School, NARA, Group 75, box 1, folder 1323. See also Navarro-Rivera, "Acculturation under Duress," 238.

69. Bell, "Telling Stories out of School," 369.

70. Navarro-Rivera, "Imperial Enterprise and Educational Policies in Colonial Puerto Rico," 164–169. See also Navarro-Rivera, "Acculturation under Duress"; and Rosa, "Puerto Ricans at Carlisle Indian School." Congress ended funding for Puerto Ricans to attend Carlisle in 1903. See Hoxie, *Final Promise*, 192.

71. Navarro-Rivera, "Imperial Enterprise and Educational Policies in Colonial Puerto Rico," 164–169. See also Guridy, *Forging Diaspora*, esp. chapter 1.

72. Rosa, "Puerto Ricans at Carlisle Indian School," 388.

73. Angela Rivera Tudó, "Los 'Indios' de Puerto Rico," *La Correspondencia de Puerto Rico*, January 3, 1931, 4. Regarding the elite status of many of Carlisle's Puerto Rican students, see Rosa, "Puerto Ricans at Carlisle Indian School."

74. Emilio de Arce Pagan Student File, Carlisle Indian Digital Resource Center, http://carlisleindian.dickinson.edu/student_files/emilio-de-arce-pagan-student-file.

75. Records of the Carlisle Indian Industrial School, NARA, Group 75, box 113, folder 4676.

76. Delores Nieves Student File, Carlisle Indian Digital Resource Center, http://carlisleindian.dickinson.edu/student_files/delores-nieves-student-file (Porto-Rican); and Records of the Carlisle Indian Industrial School, NARA, Group 75, box 29, folder 1374 ("Spanish").

77. Records of the Carlisle Indian Industrial School, NARA, Group 75, box 124, folder 4962.

78. Adela Barrelli Student File, Carlisle Indian Digital Resource Center, http://carlisleindian.dickinson.edu/student_files/adela-barrelli-student-file.

79. Providencia Martinez Student File, Carlisle Indian Digital Resource Center, http://carlisleindian.dickinson.edu/student_files/providencia-martinez-student-file.

80. Angela Rivera de Tudó, *Idioms and Other Expressions in English and Spanish, and Their Use with a University Supplement, and about 500 Proverbs in English and Spanish, and a List of Homophonous Words* (San Juan, PR: Casa Baldrich, 1940).

81. Tudó, "Los 'Indios' de Puerto Rico," 4.

82. Tudó, "Los 'Indios' de Puerto Rico," 4.

83. Juan José Osuna, "An Indian in Spite of Myself," *Summer School Review* 10, no. 5 (1932): 2.

84. Devon W. Carbado, "Racial Naturalization," *American Quarterly* 57, no. 3 (2005): 633.

85. Frantz Fanon, "The Fact of Blackness," in *Black Skin, White Masks*, trans. Charles Lam Markmann (New York: Grove Weidenfeld, 1967), 109.

86. Osuna, "Indian in Spite of Myself," 3.

87. Osuna, "Indian in Spite of Myself," 3.

88. Regarding Prado's complaint about having to work in a kitchen, see the letter by Father Feeser, January 3, 1917, St. Patrick's Rectory, Carlisle, Pennsylvania, in Records of the Carlisle Indian Industrial School, NARA, Group 75, box 124, folder 4962.

89. Luis Muñoz Rivera, "Una visita a Indian School," *Puerto Rico Herald* 1, no. 10, September 14, 1901.

90. Hoxie, *Final Promise*, 96.

91. Quoted in Hoxie, *Final Promise*, 163, 199.

92. Hoxie, *Final Promise*, 196. See also K. Tsianina Lomawaima and T. Tsianina Lomawaima, "Estelle Reel, Superintendent of Indian Schools, 1898–1910: Politics, Curriculum, and Land," *Journal of American Indian Education* 35, no. 3 (1996): 5–31.

93. "Co-education of Races," 3.

94. Hoxie, *Final Promise*, 187.

95. Osuna, "Indian in Spite of Myself," 3.

96. Osuna, "Indian in Spite of Myself," 4.

97. Navarro-Rivera, "Acculturation under Duress," 243. Bell estimates that of the approximately eighty-five hundred students who attended Carlisle, only six hundred graduated. See Bell, "Telling Stories out of School," vii.

98. Osuna, "Indian in Spite of Myself," 4.

99. Regarding Mexican American claims to whiteness, see Neil Foley, *The White Scourge: Mexicans, Blacks, and Poor Whites in Texas Cotton Culture* (Berkeley: University of California Press, 1999); Patrick D. Lukens, *A Quiet Victory for Latino Rights: FDR and the Controversy over "Whiteness"* (Tucson: University of Arizona Press, 2012); and Natalia Molina, "'In a Race All Their Own': The Quest to Make Mexicans Ineligible for U.S. Citizenship," *Pacific Historical Review* 79, no. 2 (2010): 167–201.

100. Transcript of the Indian Citizenship Act of 1924, http://legisworks.org/congress/68/publaw-175.pdf.

101. Armstrong Collection, Series I, box 1, folder 36.

102. "Foreign to the United States in a domestic sense" is from *Downes v. Bidwell*, the 1901 case in which the US Supreme Court ruled that Puerto Rico, Guam, and the Philippines were "'unincorporated territories,' belonging to—but not part of—the United States." See Christina Duffy Burnett and Burke Marshall, "Between the Foreign and the Domestic: The Doctrine of Territorial Incorporation, Invented and Reinvented," in *Foreign in a Domestic Sense: Puerto Rico, American Expansion, and the Constitution*, ed. Christina Duffy Burnett and Burke Marshall (Durham, NC: Duke University Press, 2001), 1.

103. Hazel W. Hertzberg, *The Search for an American Indian Identity: Modern Pan-Indian Movements* (Syracuse, NY: Syracuse University Press, 1971), viii.

104. Child, *Boarding School Seasons*, xiv.

105. Juan Flores, "Que Assimilated, Brother, Yo Soy Assimilao: The Structuring of Puerto Rican Identity in the U.S." *Journal of Ethnic Studies* 13, no. 3 (1985): 4.

CHAPTER THREE

1. Ben Wattenberg and Richard Scammon, *The Real Majority: An Extraordinary Examination of the American Electorate* (New York: Coward-McCann, 1970).

2. Theodore Roosevelt, "Address before the National Congress of Mothers, Washington, D.C., March 13, 1905," in *Presidential Addresses and State Papers of Theodore Roosevelt* (New York: Kauss Reprint, 1970), 3:282–291.

3. Regarding the Dillingham Commission's trip to Europe, see "U.S. Immigration Commission Back," *New York Times*, September 7, 1907, 11; and John M. Lund, "Boundaries of Restriction: The Dillingham Commission," *University of Vermont History Review* 6 (1994), www.uvm.edu/~hag/histreview/vol6/lund.html.

4. William P. Dillingham et al., *Abstracts of Reports of the Immigration Commission: With Conclusions and Recommendations, and Views of the Minority (in Two Volumes)* (Washington, DC: Government Printing Office, 1911), 1:45.

5. See, for example, Josh Dawsey, "Trump Derides Protections for Immigrants from 'Shithole' Countries," *Washington Post*, January 12, 2018, www.washingtonpost.com/politics/trump-attacks-protections-for-immigrants-from-shithole-countries-in-oval-office-meeting/2018/01/11/bfc0725c-f711-11e7-91af-31ac729add94_story.html?utm_term=.192454d370b2.

6. Ian Schwartz, "Jeff Sessions: 'What Good Does It Do to Bring in Somebody Who Is Illiterate in Their Own Country?,'" www.realclearpolitics.com/video/2018/01/16/jeff_sessions_what_good_does_it_do_to_bring_in_somebody_who_is_illiterate_in_their_own_country.html.

7. "White Nationalists Chant 'You Will Not Replace Us,'" BBC News, August 12, 2017, www.bbc.com/news/av/world-asia-40911744/white-us-nationalists -chant-you-will-not-replace-us; and David Neiwert, "When White National- ists Chant Weird Slogans, What Do They Mean?," Southern Poverty Law Center Hatewatch, October 10, 2017, www.splcenter.org/hatewatch/2017/10/10/when-white -nationalists-chant-their-weird-slogans-what-do-they-mean.

8. Ed Mazza, "Laura Ingraham Targets Even Legal Immigrants in Off-the-Rails Rant," *Huffpost*, August 9, 2018, www.huffingtonpost.com/entry/laura-ingraham -immigration-rant_us_5b6bbfd7e4b0bdd0620646fa.

9. Rebecca Shapiro, "Tom Brokaw: 'Hispanics Should Work Harder at Assim- ilation,'" *Huffpost*, January 27, 2019, www.huffingtonpost.com/entry/tom-brokaw -hispanics-should-work-harder-at-assimilation_us_5c4e2ed3e4b0287e5b8bd250.

10. Thomas Jefferson, *The Life and Selected Writings of Thomas Jefferson*, ed. Adri- enne Koch and William Peden (New York: Modern Library, 1944), 256.

11. Jefferson, *Life and Selected Writings*, 255.

12. Jefferson, *Life and Selected Writings*, 256.

13. Daniel Kanstroom, *Deportation Nation: Outsiders in American History* (Cam- bridge, MA: Harvard University Press, 2007).

14. Jefferson, *Life and Selected Writings*, 256.

15. "Negro problem" appears in W. E. B. Du Bois's 1903 essay "Of Our Spiritual Strivings." See W. E. B. Du Bois, *The Souls of Black Folk* (New York: Bantam Books, 1989), 9.

16. Jefferson, *Life and Selected Writings*, 255.

17. Afrofuturism encompasses literature, music/sound, visual art, and film, among other forms. See Mark Dery, "Black to the Future: Interviews with Samuel R. Delany, Greg Tate, and Tricia Rose," *South Atlantic Quarterly* 92, no. 4 (1993): 735–778; and Alondra Nelson, "Introduction: Future Texts," *Social Text* 20, no. 2 (2002): 1–15.

18. For a sharp analysis of Park's oversized role as an expert on race and race relations, see Aldon Morris, *The Scholar Denied: W.E.B. Du Bois and the Birth of Modern Sociology* (Berkeley: University of California Press, 2015).

19. Samuel Getachew, "21 Savage and the Way We See Black Immigrants," *New York Times*, February 2, 2019, www.nytimes.com/2019/02/09/opinion/21-savage-ice .html. Notable studies of black immigrants to the United States include Nancy Foner, *In a New Land: A Comparative View of Immigration* (New York: New York University Press, 2005); Nancy Foner, *Islands in the City: West Indian Migration to New York* (Berkeley: Uni- versity of California Press, 2001); Philip Kasinitz, *Caribbean New York: Black Immigrants and the Politics of Race* (Ithaca, NY: Cornell University Press, 1992); Alex Stepick, *Pride*

against Prejudice: Haitians in the United States (Boston: Allyn and Bacon, 1998); Mary C. Waters, *Black Identities: West Indian Immigrant Dreams and American Realities* (New York: Russell Sage Foundation, 1999); and Flore Zéphir, *Haitian Immigrants in Black America: A Sociological and Sociolinguistic Portrait* (Westport, CT: Bergin & Garvey, 1996).

20. Moon-Kie Jung, "The Racial Unconscious of Assimilation Theory," *Du Bois Review* 6, no. 2 (2009): 384.

21. Milton M. Gordon, *Assimilation in American Life: The Role of Race, Religion, and National Origins* (New York: Oxford University Press, 1964), 77.

22. Gordon, *Assimilation in American Life,* 113.

23. Nathan Glazer, "Is Assimilation Dead?," *Annals of the American Academy of Political and Social Science* 530 (1993): 122.

24. Yen Le Espiritu, *Home Bound: Filipino American Lives Across Cultures, Communities, and Countries* (Berkeley: University of California Press, 2003), 47; Sandro Mezzadra et al., "Differential Inclusion/Exclusion," in "New Keywords: Migration and Borders," ed. Nicholas De Genova, Sandro Mezzadra, and John Pickles, special issue, *Cultural Studies* 29, no. 1 (2015): 25–26.

25. Susan Roth Breitzer, "Race, Immigration, and Contested Americanness: Black Nativism and the American Labor Movement, 1880–1930," *Race/Ethnicity* 4, no. 2 (2011): 269–283; David J. Hellwig, "Black Leaders and United States Immigration Policy, 1917–1929," *Journal of Negro History* 66, no. 2 (1981): 110–127; and David J. Hellwig, "Strangers in Their Own Land: Patterns of Black Nativism, 1830–1930," *American Studies* 23, no. 1 (1982): 85–98. For a concise, albeit tendentious, compilation of quotes about immigrants and immigration by notable African Americans, see Robert Malloy, "'Cast Down Your Bucket Where You Are': Black Americans on Immigration," Center for Immigration Studies, https://cis.org/Report/Cast-Down -Your-Bucket-Where-You-Are-Black-Americans-Immigration?&utm_source= email&utm_medium=social-media&utm_campaign=addtoany. See also Southern Poverty Law Center, Center for Immigration Studies, n.d., www.splcenter.org /fighting-hate/extremist-files/group/center-immigration-studies.

26. "Fifty Years of Freedom: A Suggestion," Robert Ezra Park Collection, box 15, folder 10, Special Collections Research Center, University of Chicago.

27. "Fifty Years of Freedom."

28. Dickson D. Bruce Jr., "Booker T. Washington's *The Man Farthest Down* and the Transformation of Race," *Mississippi Quarterly* 28, no. 2 (1995): 239–253; Louis R. Harlan, *Booker T. Washington: The Wizard of Tuskegee* (New York: Oxford University Press, 1983), 291; and Gary Totten, "Southernizing Travel in the Black Atlantic: Booker T. Washington's 'The Man Farthest Down,'" *MELUS* 32, no. 2 (2007): 107–131.

29. Regarding Washington's October 7, 1910 luncheon with the Anti-Slavery and Aborigines Protection Society, see "News Item in the London *Times*," in *The Booker T. Washington Papers*, ed. Louis R. Harlan and Raymond W. Smock et al., vol. 10, *1909–11* (Urbana: University of Illinois Press, 1981), 401–404. Regarding his October 3, 1910 dinner with the Danish royal family, see "A News Item in the New York *Evening Post*," in Harlan and Smock et al., *Washington Papers*, vol. 10, *1909–11*, 391–392. And regarding his stay at Skibo Castle, Carnegie's estate in Scotland, see Booker T. Washington "to Emmet Jay Scott," September 2, 1910, in Harlan and Smock et al., *Washington Papers*, vol. 10, *1909–11*, 382.

30. Booker T. Washington and Robert E. Park, *The Man Farthest Down: A Record of Observation and Study in Europe* (Garden City, NY: Doubleday, Page, 1912), 16. Regarding Park's graduate work in Germany, see Winifred Raushenbush, *Robert E. Park: Biography of a Sociologist* (Durham, NC: Duke University Press, 1979).

31. Robert Francis Engs, *Educating the Disenfranchised and Disinherited: Samuel Chapman Armstrong and Hampton Institute, 1839–1893* (Knoxville: University of Tennessee Press, 1999).

32. Robert Ezra Park, "Politics and 'The Man Farthest Down,'" in *The Collected Papers of Robert Ezra Park*, vols. 1, 2 and 3, ed. Everett Cherington Hughes et al. (New York: Arno Press, 1974), 167.

33. Park, "Politics and 'The Man Farthest Down,'" 167.

34. Park, "Politics and 'The Man Farthest Down,'" 167.

35. Washington and Park, *Man Farthest Down*, 14.

36. Robert Ezra Park, "An Autobiographical Note," in *Race and Culture: The Collected Papers of Robert Ezra Park*, vol. 1, ed. Everett Cherrington Hughes et al. (Glencoe, IL: Free Press, 1950), vii.

37. Park, "Autobiographical Note," vii.

38. Robert Ezra Park to Booker T. Washington, January 28, 1907, Robert Ezra Park Collection, box 19, folder 9, Special Collections Research Center, University of Chicago.

39. Robert E. Park, "Racial Assimilation in Secondary Groups with Particular Reference to the Negro," *American Journal of Sociology* 19, no. 5 (1914): 612.

40. Park, "Autobiographical Note," vii–viii.

41. Washington and Park, *Man Farthest Down*, 17.

42. Washington and Park, *Man Farthest Down*, 16–17.

43. Robert Ezra Park to Booker T. Washington, April 26, 1911, Robert Ezra Park Collection, box 15, folder 10, Special Collections Research Center, University of Chicago.

44. Booker T. Washington, "1895 Atlanta Compromise Speech," in *The Booker T. Washington Papers*, vol. 3, ed. Louis R. Harlan (Urbana: University of Illinois Press, 1974), 583–587.

45. Washington, "1895 Atlanta Compromise Speech," 583–587.

46. Washington, "1895 Atlanta Compromise Speech," 583–587.

47. Washington, "1895 Atlanta Compromise Speech," 583–587.

48. Regarding African American antipathy to immigrants in the late nineteenth and early twentieth centuries, see Breitzer, "Race, Immigration, and Contested Americanness"; Hellwig, "Black Leaders and United States Immigration Policy"; and Hellwig, "Strangers in Their Own Land."

49. Hellwig, "Strangers in Their Own Land," 89. See also Jennifer L. Hochschild, *Facing up to the American Dream: Race, Class, and the Soul of the Nation* (Princeton, NJ: Princeton University Press, 1995); Matthew Frye Jacobson, *Whiteness of a Different Color: European Immigrants and the Alchemy of Race* (Cambridge, MA: Harvard University Press, 1998); Aihwa Ong, "Cultural Citizenship as Subject-Making: Immigrants Negotiate Racial and Cultural Boundaries in the United States," *Current Anthropology* 47, no. 5 (1996): 737–762; David R. Roediger, *The Wages of Whiteness: Race and the Making of the American Working Class* (London: Verso, 1999); and David R. Roediger, *Working toward Whiteness: How America's Immigrants Became White* (New York: Basic Books, 2005).

50. Toni Morrison, "On the Backs of Blacks," *Time* 142, no. 21 (December 2, 1993): 57.

51. Washington and Park, *Man Farthest Down*, 17 ("man farthest down") and 20 ("European people").

52. Washington and Park, *Man Farthest Down*, 3 ("our country each year"), 4–5 ("born and reared"), and 8 ("scale of civilization").

53. Washington and Park, *Man Farthest Down*, 4.

54. Washington and Park, *Man Farthest Down*, 25.

55. Washington and Park, *Man Farthest Down*, 84–85.

56. "Sunday Evening Talk," *Tuskegee Student*, October 29, 1910, Robert Ezra Park Collection, box 1, folder 5, Special Collections Research Center, University of Chicago.

57. Washington and Park, *Man Farthest Down*, 91.

58. "Fifty Years of Freedom."

59. "Fifty Years of Freedom."

60. Washington and Park, *Man Farthest Down*, 81.

61. Washington and Park, *Man Farthest Down*, 160.

62. Washington and Park, *Man Farthest Down*, 113.

63. "To Dr. Park," Robert Ezra Park Collection, box 1, folder 5, Special Collections Research Center, University of Chicago.

64. "Fifty Years of Freedom" ("under-races"); and "To Dr. Park" ("here in the South")

65. William Edward Burghardt Du Bois et al., "An Open Letter to the People of Great Britain and Europe," in Harlan and Smock et al., *Washington Papers*, vol. 10, *1909–11*, 422.

66. Du Bois et al., "An Open Letter to the People of Great Britain," 422.

67. Park quoted in Harlan, *Booker T. Washington*, 292.

68. Washington and Park, *Man Farthest Down*, 26.

69. Washington and Park, *Man Farthest Down*, 146.

70. Washington and Park, *Man Farthest Down*, 146.

71. Robert E. Park, "Assimilation, Social," in *Encyclopaedia of the Social Sciences*, vol. 2, ed. Edwin R. A. Seligman (New York: Macmillan, 1930), 282.

72. Park, "Assimilation, Social," 281.

73. Park, "Assimilation, Social," 282.

74. Park, "Assimilation, Social," 282 ("distinctive racial mark"); and Robert E. Park and Ernest W. Burgess, *Introduction to the Science of Sociology* (Chicago: University of Chicago Press, 1924), 761 ("racial uniform").

75. Park and Burgess, *Introduction to the Science of Sociology*, 760–761.

76. See, for example, Du Bois, *Souls of Black Folk*; Daniel Patrick Moynihan, "The Negro Family: The Case for National Action," Office of Planning and Research, United States Department of Labor, March 1965, https://web.stanford.edu/~mrosenfe/Moynihan's%20The%20Negro%20Family.pdf; and William Julius Wilson, *The Truly Disadvantaged: The Inner City, the Underclass, and Public Policy* (Chicago: University of Chicago Press, 1987).

77. Quoted in Michael B. Katz, *The Undeserving Poor: America's Enduring Confrontation with Poverty* (Oxford: Oxford University Press, 2013), 17.

78. George S. Schuyler, *Black No More: Being an Account of the Strange and Wonderful Workings of Science in the Land of the Free, A.D. 1933–1940* (Boston: Northeastern University Press, 1989), 27.

79. Schuyler, *Black No More*, 109.

80. Madame C. J. Walker, née Sara Breedlove (1867–1919), was an African American businesswoman, philanthropist, and activist who amassed a fortune manufacturing and selling beauty and hair products for black women. She is widely regarded as the first black, female, self-made millionaire.

81. Schuyler, *Black No More*, 156.

82. Schuyler, *Black No More*, 218.

83. Schuyler, *Black No More*, 219.

84. Schuyler, *Black No More*, 221.

85. Schuyler, *Black No More*, 222.

86. Schuyler, *Black No More*, 222.

87. Schuyler, *Black No More*, 193.

88. Breitzer "Race, Immigration, and Contested Americanness," 271.

89. Elaine K. Ginsberg, "Introduction: The Politics of Passing," in *Passing and the Fictions of Identity*, ed. Elaine K. Ginsberg (Durham, NC: Duke University Press, 1996), 2.

90. Rachel Dolezal (also known as Nkechi Amare Diallo) resigned as president of the NAACP chapter in Spokane, Washington, in 2015 after her parents accused her of fraud and exposed her as white. See Decca Aitkenhead, "Rachel Dolezal: 'I'm Not Going to Stoop and Apologise and Grovel,'" *Guardian*, February 25, 2017, www .theguardian.com/us-news/2017/feb/25/rachel-dolezal-not-going-stoop-apologise -grovel. Ginsberg. "Introduction," 2.

91. Schuyler, *Black No More*, 39.

92. Schuyler, *Black No More*, 46–47.

93. Schuyler, *Black No More*, 48.

94. Harryette Mullen, "Optic White: Blackness and the Production of Whiteness," *Diacritics* 24, nos. 2/3 (1994): 77.

95. Cheryl I. Harris, "Whiteness as Property," *Harvard Law Review* 106, no. 8 (1993): 1707–1791; and George Lipsitz, *The Possessive Investment in Whiteness: How White People Profit from Identity Politics* (Philadelphia: Temple University Press, 1998).

96. Library of Congress, "A Century of Lawmaking for a New Nation: U.S. Congressional Documents and Debates, 1774–1875," *Statutes at Large*, 1st Cong., 2d Sess., http://rs6.loc.gov/cgi-bin/ampage?collId=llsl&fileName=001/llsl001.db& recNum=226.

97. Park, "Racial Assimilation in Secondary Groups," 613.

98. Dery, "Black to the Future," 190–191.

99. Schuyler, *Black No More*, 34.

100. See, for example, Nicholas De Genova, "Denizens All: The Otherness of Citizenship," in *Citizenship and Its Others*, ed. Bridget Anderson and Vanessa Hughes (New York: Palgrave Macmillan, 2015), 191–202; Tomas Hammar, *Democracy and the Nation State, Aliens, Denizens, and Citizens in a World of International Migration* (Brookfield, VT: Avebury/Gower Publishing, 1990); Marcel Paret, "Precarious Class Formations in the United States and South Africa," *International Labor and Working-Class History* 89 (2016): 84–106; Guy Standing, *A Precariat Charter: From Denizens to Citizens* (London: Bloomsbury Academic, 2014); Guy Standing, *The Precariat: The New Dangerous Class* (London: Bloomsbury Academic, 2011); and Neil Walker, "Denizenship and the Deterritorialization in the EU," *EUI Working Paper LAW*, no. 2008/8 (2008): 1–12.

101. Kirsten Silva Gruesz, "'Poor Eliza' on the Border," *J19* 6, no. 1 (2018): 183.

102. Frederick Douglass, *Narrative of the Life of Frederick Douglass* (New York: Signet, 2005); Ericka Lee, *At America's Gates: Chinese Immigration during the Exclusion Era, 1882–1943* (Chapel Hill: University of North Carolina Press, 2003); and Sarah B. Horton, "From 'Deportability' to 'Denounce-ability': New Forms of Labor Subordination in an Era of Governing Immigration through Crime," *Political and Legal Anthropology Review* 39, no. 2 (2016): 312–326.

103. "Less illegal" is from Sébastien Chauvin and Blanca Garcés-Mascareñas, "Becoming Less Illegal: Deservingness Frames and Undocumented Migrant Incorporation," *Race & Ethnicity* 8, no. 4 (2014): 422–432.

104. Park and Burgess, *Introduction to the Science of Sociology*, 735 ("other persons or groups"); and Tamotsu Shibutani and Kian M. Kwan, *Ethnic Stratification: A Comparative Approach* (New York: Macmillan, 1965), 504 ("his new associates").

105. Regarding the acculturation of young, undocumented, primarily Mexican immigrants in the United States, see Shannon Gleeson and Roberto G. Gonzales, "When Do Papers Matter? An Institutional Analysis of Undocumented Life in the United States," *International Migration* 50, no. 4 (2012): 1–19; and Roberto G. Gonzales, "Learning to Be Illegal: Undocumented Youth and Shifting Legal Contexts in the Transition to Adulthood," *American Sociological Review* 76, no. 4 (2011): 602–619.

106. I take the label "undocumented American" from the work of Jose Antonio Vargas. See Jose Antonio Vargas, "Not Legal, Not Leaving," *Time* 179, no. 25 (June 25, 2012): 1; Jose Antonio Vargas, dir., *Documented: A Film by an Undocumented American* (New York: Apo Anak Productions, 2013); and Jose Antonio Vargas, *Dear America: Notes of an Undocumented Citizen* (New York: Dey Street Books, 2018).

107. Adrian J. Bailey et al., "(Re)producing Salvadoran Transnational Geographies," *Annals of the Association of American Geographers* 92, no. 1 (2002): 125–144.

108. Lou Cornum, "The Space NDN's Star Map," *New Inquiry*, January 26, 2015, https://thenewinquiry.com/the-space-ndns-star-map/.

109. "Method of asepsis" is from Michel Foucault, *Power/Knowledge: Selected Interviews and Other Writings, 1972–1977*, ed. Colin Gordon, trans. Colin Gordon et al. (New York: Pantheon Books, 1980), 55.

110. Kelly Weill, "The Jewish Group Taking on ICE—and the 'Concentration Camp' Taboo," *Daily Beast*, July 13, 2019, www.thedailybeast.com/never-again-action -takes-on-ice-and-the-concentration-camp-taboo?source=email&via=desktop.

111. Amanda Sakuma, "Undocumented Immigrants Tell Trump They Are #HereToStay," NBC News, November 9, 2016, www.nbcnews.com/storyline /2016-election-day/undocumented-immigrants-tell-trump-they-re-heretostay -n681206.

CHAPTER FOUR

1. Sono Okamura, "The Nisei Discover a Larger America," *Mademoiselle*, April 1947, 345, Miné Okubo Collection (collection number 2007.62), Japanese American National Museum, box 2, folder 3.

2. Okamura, "The Nisei Discover a Larger America," 217.

3. Okamura, "The Nisei Discover a Larger America," 342.

4. Okamura, "The Nisei Discover a Larger America," 342.

5. Okamura, "The Nisei Discover a Larger America," 344 ("little Tokyos"), and 217 and 341 ("social and economic life").

6. Okamura, "The Nisei Discover a Larger America," 342.

7. Okamura, "The Nisei Discover a Larger America," 345.

8. Larissa Martinez, "America Can Be Great Again without the Construction of a Wall Built on Hatred and Prejudice, McKinney-Boyd High School-2016," https://speakola.com/grad/larissa-martinez-mckinney-boyd-high-2016.

9. Martinez, "America Can Be Great Again."

10. Martinez, "America Can Be Great Again"; and Aline Barros and Gesell Tobias, "Undocumented Valedictorian: I'm Cheating No One Out of College," VOA, June 25, 2016, www.voanews.com/usa/undocumented-valedictorian-im-cheating-no-one-out-college.

11. Martinez, "America Can Be Great Again."

12. Politico, "2016 Texas Presidential Election Results," www.politico.com/2016-election/results/map/president/texas/.

13. See, for example, Willa Frej, "Undocumented Valedictorian Takes Down Trump in Epic Speech," *Huffpost*, June 10, 2016, www.huffpost.com/entry/undocumented-valedictorian-takes-down-trump-in-epic-speech_n_575aaca2e4b0ced23ca7bda0.

14. Kristin Weisell, "At Graduation McKinney Boyd Valedictorian Reveals Undocumented Immigrant Status," 11/21 CBS DFW, https://dfw.cbslocal.com/2016/06/09/at-graduation-mckinney-boyd-valedictorian-reveals-undocumented-immigrant-status/.

15. Mae M. Ngai, "Birthright Citizenship and the Alien Citizen," *Fordham Law Review* 75, no. 5 (2007): 2521. See also Mae M. Ngai, *Impossible Subjects: Illegal Aliens and the Making of Modern America* (Princeton, NJ: Princeton University Press, 2005), 2.

16. Sébastien Chauvin and Blanca Garcés-Mascareñas, "Beyond Informal Citizenship: The New Moral Economy of Migrant Illegality," *International Political Sociology* 6 (2012): 243.

17. Donald F. Lindsey, *Indians at Hampton Institute, 1877–1923* (Urbana: University of Illinois Press, 1995), 25 ("assimilation under duress"); and Ngai, *Impossible Subjects*, 177

("benevolent"); and Mae M. Ngai, "'An Ironic Testimony to the Value of American Democracy': Assimilationism and the World War II Internment of Japanese Americans," in *Contested Democracy: Freedom, Race, and Power in American History*, ed. Manisha Sinha and Penny Von Eschen (New York: Columbia University Press, 2007), 238 ("coercive assimilation").

18. Ngai, *Impossible Subjects*, 177.

19. My understanding of neoliberal subjectivity draws from Salman Türken et al.'s "Making Sense of Neoliberal Subjectivity: A Discourse Analysis of Media Language on Self-Development," *Globalizations* 13, no. 1 (2016): 32–46.

20. Walter J. Nicholls, *The DREAMers: How the Undocumented Youth Movement Transformed the Immigrant Rights Debate* (Stanford, CA: Stanford University Press, 2013), 50.

21. Jennifer L. Hochschild, *Facing Up to the American Dream: Race, Class, and the Soul of the Nation* (Princeton, NJ: Princeton University Press, 1995), 6.

22. David Kamp, "Rethinking the American Dream," *Vanity Fair*, March 5, 2009, www.vanityfair.com/culture/2009/04/american-dream200904; and Robert J. Shiller, "The Transformation of the 'American Dream,'" *New York Times*, August 4, 2017, www.nytimes.com/2017/08/04/upshot/the-transformation-of-the-american-dream.html.

23. James Truslow Adams, *The Epic of America* (Boston: Little, Brown, 1934), 416 ("a dream of merely material plenty"), and 415 ("circumstances of birth or position").

24. Adams, *Epic of America*, 416.

25. Hochschild, *Facing Up to the American Dream*, 15.

26. See, for example, Ian Haney-López, *White by Law: The Legal Construction of Race* (New York: New York University Press, 2006); Cheryl I. Harris, "Whiteness as Property," *Harvard Law Review* 106, no. 8 (1993): 1707–1721; George Lipsitz, *The Possessive Investment in Whiteness: How White People Profit from Identity Politics* (Philadelphia: Temple University Press, 2018); Charles J. McClain, "Tortuous Path, Elusive Goal: The Asian Quest for American Citizenship," *Asian Law Journal* 2, no. 3 (1995): 33–60; and Natalia Molina, "'In a Race All Their Own': The Quest to Make Mexicans Ineligible for U.S. Citizenship," *Pacific Historical Review* 79, no. 2 (2010): 167–201.

27. Hector Amaya, *Citizenship Excess: Latinas/os, Media, and the Nation* (New York: New York University Press, 2013), 2.

28. Regarding laws prohibiting Asians from owning, leasing, or renting land, see Sucheng Chan, *Asian Americans: An Interpretive History* (Boston: Twayne, 1991); and Ronald T. Takaki, *Strangers from a Different Shore: A History of Asian Americans* (Boston: Little Brown, 1989). Regarding Japanese Americans' economic losses during World War II, see Sandra C. Taylor, "Evacuation and Economic Loss: Questions

and Perspectives," in *Japanese Americans: From Relocation to Redress*, ed. Roger Daniels, Sandra C. Taylor, and Harry H. L. Kitano (Seattle: University of Washington Press, 1991), 163–167; Gary Y. Okihiro and David Drummond, "The Concentration Camps and Japanese Economic Losses in California Agriculture, 1900–1942," in *Japanese Americans: From Relocation to Redress*, ed. Roger Daniels, Sandra C. Taylor, and Harry H. L. Kitano (Seattle: University of Washington Press, 1991), 168–175; and "Sold, Damaged, Stolen, Gone: Japanese American Property Loss during World War II," *Densho Blog*, April 4, 2017, https://densho.org/sold-damaged-stolen-gone -japanese-american-property-loss-wwii/.

29. Henry L. Dawes, "Solving the Indian Problem," in *Americanizing the American Indians: Writings by the "Friends of the Indian," 1880–1900*, ed. Francis Paul Prucha (Cambridge, MA: Harvard University Press, 1973), 30.

30. Miriam Jordan, "They Achieved the American Dream: Will the Supreme Court Let Them Keep It?," *New York Times*, November 7, 2019, www.nytimes.com /interactive/2019/11/07/us/dreamers-daca-supreme-court.html?action=click& module=Top%20Stories&pgtype=Homepage.

31. Jordan, "They Achieved the American Dream."

32. Jordan, "They Achieved the American Dream."

33. Kamp, "Rethinking the American Dream."

34. Michael B. Katz, *The Undeserving Poor: America's Enduring Confrontation with Poverty* (Oxford: Oxford University Press, 2013), 6–7.

35. Michael Harrington, *The Other America: Poverty in the United States* (New York: Macmillan, 1962), 6–7.

36. John Kenneth Galbraith, *The Affluent Society: Fortieth Anniversary Edition* (Boston: Houghton Mifflin, 1998), 1–2.

37. David M. Potter, *The People of Plenty: Economic Abundance and the American Character* (Chicago: University of Chicago Press, 1954), 208.

38. Katz, *Undeserving Poor*, 11.

39. Bridget Anderson, "Exclusion, Failure and the Politics of Citizenship," *RCIS Working Paper* 1 (2014): 4.

40. Harrington, *Other America*, 10.

41. Harrington, *Other America*, 20. Regarding precarity, see Pierre Bourdieu, *Acts of Resistance: Against the New Myths of Our Time* (Cambridge, UK: Polity Press, 1998); Judith Butler, "Performativity, Precarity and Sexual Politics," *AIBR* 4, no. 3 (2009): i–xiii; and Guy Standing, *The Precariat: The New Dangerous Class* (London: Bloomsbury Academic, 2011).

42. Harrington, *Other America*, 13, 158.

43. Harrington, *Other America*, 17, 159.

44. Harrington, *Other America*, 17.

45. Oscar Lewis, "The Culture of Poverty," *Scientific American* 215, no. 4 (1966): 19.

46. Jessi Streib et al., "Life, Death, and Resurrections: The Culture of Poverty Perspective," in *The Oxford Handbook of the Social Science of Poverty*, ed. David Brady and Linda M. Burton (New York: Oxford University Press, 2016), 248.

47. Lewis, "Culture of Poverty," 19 ("generation along family lines"); and Streib et al., "Life, Death, and Resurrections," 249 ("structural conditions change").

48. Linda Gordon, *Pitied but Not Entitled: Single Mothers and the History of Welfare, 1890–1935* (New York: Free Press, 1994), 12. See also Lipsitz, *Possessive Investment in Whiteness*; Gwendolyn Mink, *The Wages of Motherhood: Inequality in the Welfare State, 1917–1942* (Ithaca, NY: Cornell University Press, 1995); and Jill Quadango, *The Color of Welfare: How Racism Undermined the War on Poverty* (New York: Oxford University Press, 1994).

49. Katz, *Undeserving Poor*, 9–17; Alice O'Connor, *Poverty Knowledge: Social Science, Social Policy, and the Poor in Twentieth-Century U.S. History* (Princeton, NJ: Princeton University Press, 2001), 102–107; and Streib et al., "Life, Death, and Resurrections," 249.

50. William Petersen, "Success Story, Japanese-American Style," *New York Times Magazine*, January 9, 1966, 21.

51. Oscar Lewis, *Five Families: Mexican Case Studies in the Culture of Poverty Five Families: Mexican Case Studies in the Culture of Poverty* (New York: Basic Books, 1959); and Oscar Lewis, *La Vida: A Puerto Rican Family in the Culture of Poverty—San Juan and New York* (New York: Random House, 1965).

52. Katz, *Undeserving Poor*, 18.

53. Daniel Patrick Moynihan, "The Negro Family: The Case for National Action," Office of Planning and Research, United States Department of Labor (March 1965), https://web.stanford.edu/~mrosenfe/Moynihan's%20The%20Negro%20Family.pdf, n.p.

54. Moynihan, *The Negro Family*, 29.

55. Petersen, "Success Story, Japanese-American Style," 21.

56. Petersen, "Success Story, Japanese-American Style," 40 ("white-collar"), and 21 ("including native-born whites").

57. "Success Story of One Minority Group in U.S.," *U.S. News & World Report*, December 26, 1966, 73–78. See also Keith Osajima, "Asian Americans as the Model Minority: An Analysis of the Popular Image in the 1960s and 1980s," in *A Companion Guide to Asian American Studies*, ed. Kent A. Ono (Malden, MA: Blackwell Publishing, 2005), 215–225; and Ellen D. Wu, *The Color of Success: Asian Americans and the Origins of the Model Minority* (Princeton, NJ: Princeton University Press, 2013), 2 (emphasis in original).

58. Petersen, "Success Story, Japanese-American Style," 21.

59. Petersen, "Success Story, Japanese-American Style," 41.

60. Petersen, "Success Story, Japanese-American Style," 21.

61. Petersen, "Success Story, Japanese-American Style," 38.

62. Petersen, "Success Story, Japanese-American Style," 40.

63. Petersen, "Success Story, Japanese-American Style," 43.

64. Regarding segmented assimilation, see Herbert Gans, "Second Generation Decline: Scenarios for the Economic and Ethnic Futures of the Post-1965 American Immigrants," *Ethnic and Racial Studies* 15, no. 2 (1992): 173–192; Alejandro Portes and Rubén G. Rumbaut, *Legacies: The Story of the Immigrant Second Generation* (Berkeley and New York: University of California Press and Russell Sage Foundation, 2001); Alejandro Portes and Min Zhou, "The New Second Generation: Segmented Assimilation and Its Variants," *Annals of the American Academy of Political and Social Science* 530, no. 1 (1993): 74–96; Rubén G. Rumbaut and Alejandro Portes, *Ethnicities: Children of Immigrants in America* (Berkeley: University of California Press; New York: Russell Sage Foundation, 2001); and Min Zhou, "Segmented Assimilation: Issues, Controversies, and Recent Research on the New Second Generation," *International Migration Review* 31, no. 4 (1997): 975–1008.

65. Petersen, "Success Story, Japanese-American Style," 40.

66. Petersen, "Success Story, Japanese-American Style," 43.

67. Lisa Sun-Hee Park, "Continuing Significance of the Model Minority Myth: The Second Generation," *Social Justice* 35, no. 2 (2008): 135–136.

68. Frank H. Wu, *Yellow: Race in America beyond Black and White* (New York: Basic Books, 2002), 54.

69. Petersen, "Success Story, Japanese-American Style," 36.

70. Karen Tei Yamashita, "John Okada's *No-No Boy* Is a Test of American Character," *Atlantic*, May 21, 2019, www.theatlantic.com/entertainment/archive/2019/05/karen-tei-yamashita-john-okadas-no-no-boy/588466/.

71. Yamashita, "John Okada's *No-No Boy*"; and Alexandra Alter, "Dispute Arises over 'No-No Boy,' a Classic of Asian-American Literature with a Complex History," *New York Times*, June 6, 2019, www.nytimes.com/2019/06/06/books/no-no-boy-penguin.html.

72. I have gleaned information about Okada's life from Frank Abe, *John Okada: The Life and Rediscovered Work of the Author of "No-No Boy"* (Seattle: University of Washington Press, 2018).

73. *Densho Encyclopedia*, s.v. "loyalty questionnaire," https://encyclopedia.densho.org/Loyalty_questionnaire/.

74. John Okada, *No-No Boy* (Seattle: University of Washington Press, 1976), 3–4.

75. Okada, *No-No Boy*, 5. Saint Lucy, patron saint of the blind, is said to have had her eyes torn out or to have torn out her own eyes prior to her execution in the third century CE.

76. Okada, *No-No Boy*, 1.

77. Okada, *No-No Boy*, 4.

78. Okada, *No-No Boy*, 73.

79. Okada, *No-No Boy*, 12.

80. Okada, *No-No Boy*, 1.

81. Michi Weglyn, *Years of Infamy: The Untold Story of America's Concentration Camps* (New York: William Morrow, 1976), 21.

82. Okada, *No-No Boy*, 91.

83. Okada, *No-No Boy*, 16.

84. Okada, *No-No Boy*, 16.

85. Okada, *No-No Boy*, 60.

86. Okada, *No-No Boy*, 154.

87. Gayle K. Fujita Sato, "Momotaro's Exile: John Okada's *No-No Boy*," in *Reading the Literatures of Asian America*, ed. Shirley Geok-lin Lim and Amy Ling (Philadelphia: Temple University Press, 1992), 252.

88. Okada, *No-No Boy*, 10 ("dried and toughened"), and 83 ("like a white woman's").

89. Okada, *No-No Boy*, 96.

90. Okada, *No-No Boy*, 150.

91. Okada, *No-No Boy*, 150.

92. Okada, *No-No Boy*, 151.

93. Okada, *No-No Boy*, 153–154.

94. Okada, *No-No Boy*, 154.

95. Daniel Y. Kim, "Once More, with Feeling: Cold War Masculinity and the Sentiment of Patriotism in John Okada's *No-No Boy*," *Criticism* 47, no. 1 (2005): 67.

96. Okada, *No-No Boy*, 59 ("leaving six children"), and 118 ("big television set").

97. Okada, *No-No Boy*, 60.

98. Viet Thanh Nguyen, *Race and Resistance: Literature and Politics in Asian America* (New York: Oxford University Press, 2002), 73.

99. Okada, *No-No Boy*, 14.

100. Okada, *No-No Boy*, 188.

101. Okada, *No-No Boy*, 185.

102. Okada, *No-No Boy*, 196.

103. Okada, *No-No Boy*, 209.

104. Stan Yogi, "'You Had to Be One or the Other': Oppositions and Reconciliation in John Okada's *No-No Boy*," *MELUS* 21, no. 2 (1996): 72.

105. Okada, *No-No Boy*, 211.

106. Sato, "Momotaro's Exile," 241.

107. Jinqi Ling, "Race, Power, and Cultural Politics in John Okada's *No-No Boy*," *American Literature* 67, no. 2 (1995): 360. See also Kim, "Once More, with Feeling"; Nguyen, *Race and Resistance*; and Helen Heran Jun, *Race for Citizenship: Black Orientalism and Asian Uplift from Pre-Emancipation to Neoliberal America* (New York: New York University Press, 2011), esp. chapter 3.

108. Ling, "Race, Power, and Cultural Politics," 360–361. For a reading of Jade Snow Wong's 1950 memoir, *Fifth Chinese Daughter*, as an example of "Chinese American cultural diplomacy," see Wu, *The Color of Success*, esp. chapter 4. See also Jade Snow Wong, *Fifth Chinese Daughter* (New York: Harper & Row, 1950).

109. Patricia P. Chu, *Assimilating Asians: Gendered Strategies of Authorship in Asian America* (Durham, NC: Duke University Press, 2000), 57; Stephen H. Sumida, "Japanese American Moral Dilemmas in John Okada's *No-No Boy* and Milton Murayama's *All I Asking for Is My Body*," in *Frontiers of Asian American Studies: Writing, Research, and Commentary*, ed. Gail M. Nomura, Russell Endo, Stephen H. Sumida, and Russell C. Leong (Pullman: Washington State University Press, 1989), 222–233.

110. Ling, "Race, Power, and Cultural Politics," 363.

111. Okada, *No-No Boy*, 249 ("cut ... in two"); and Yogi, "'You Had to Be One or the Other,'" 73 ("his shattered life").

112. Okada, *No-No Boy*, 251.

113. Alberto Ledesma, *Diary of a Reluctant Dreamer: Undocumented Vignettes from a Pre-American Life* (Columbus, OH: Mad Creek Books, 2017), 1.

114. Ledesma, *Diary of a Reluctant Dreamer*, 1.

115. Ledesma, *Diary of a Reluctant Dreamer*, 4.

116. Ledesma, *Diary of a Reluctant Dreamer*, 57.

117. Alex Dueben, "Smash Pages Q&A: Alberto Ledesma on 'Diary of a Reluctant Dreamer,'" Smash Pages, September 18, 2017, http://smashpages.net/2017/09/18/smash-pages-qa-alberto-ledesma-on-diary-of-a-reluctant-dreamer/.

118. Ledesma, *Diary of a Reluctant Dreamer*, 65.

119. Ledesma, *Diary of a Reluctant Dreamer*, 65.

120. William Boelhower, "The Brave New World of Immigrant Autobiography," *MELUS* 9, no. 2 (1982): 18.

121. Ledesma, *Diary of a Reluctant Dreamer*, 67.

122. Ledesma, *Diary of a Reluctant Dreamer*, 110.

123. Ledesma, *Diary of a Reluctant Dreamer*, 67.

124. Ledesma, *Diary of a Reluctant Dreamer*, 41.

125. Ledesma, *Diary of a Reluctant Dreamer*, 62.

126. Ledesma, *Diary of a Reluctant Dreamer*, 63.

127. Ledesma, *Diary of a Reluctant Dreamer*, 63.

128. Ledesma, *Diary of a Reluctant Dreamer*, 63.

129. Ledesma, *Diary of a Reluctant Dreamer*, 64.

130. Ledesma, *Diary of a Reluctant Dreamer*, 9.

131. Ledesma, *Diary of a Reluctant Dreamer*, 9.

132. Muzaffar Chishti, Doris Meissner, and Claire Bergeron, "At Its 25th Anniversary, IRCA's Legacy Lives On," Migration Policy Institute, November 16, 2011, www.migrationpolicy.org/article/its-25th-anniversary-ircas-legacy-lives.

133. Alberto Ledesma, "Illustrating My Immigrant Experience," TEDx Ohlone College Newark, May 23, 2018, www.youtube.com/watch?v=B_5pounNiTo.

134. Ledesma, *Diary of a Reluctant Dreamer*, 44.

135. Ledesma, *Diary of a Reluctant Dreamer*, 35. Ledesma credits Aurora Chang with coining the term "hyperdocumented."

136. United Nations High Commissioner for Refugees, "Master Glossary of Terms," n.d., www.refworld.org/docid/42ce7d444.html.

137. Walter J. Nicholls and Tara Fiorito, "Dreamers Unbound: Immigrant Youth Mobilizing," *New Labor Forum* 21, no. 1 (2014): 87.

138. Dina Nayeri, *The Ungrateful Refugee: What Immigrants Never Tell You* (New York: Catapult, 2019), 8.

139. Ledesma, *Diary of a Reluctant Dreamer*, 93.

140. Ledesma, *Diary of a Reluctant Dreamer*, 93.

141. Karl Marx and Frederick Engels, *Manifesto of the Communist Party*, February 1848, 18, www.marxists.org/archive/marx/works/download/pdf/Manifesto.pdf.

142. Ledesma, *Diary of a Reluctant Dreamer*, 85.

143. Ledesma, *Diary of a Reluctant Dreamer*, 114.

144. Ledesma, *Diary of a Reluctant Dreamer*, 91.

145. Regarding Cuccinelli's ancestry, see Noah Lanard, "Cuccinelli's Family Tree Suggests His New Immigration Rule Might Have Blocked His Ancestors," *Mother Jones*, August 14, 2019, www.motherjones.com/politics/2019/08/cuccinellis-family-tree -suggests-his-new-immigration-rule-might-have-blocked-his-ancestors/.

146. US Citizenship and Immigration Services, "Public Charge," n.d., www.uscis .gov/greencard/public-charge.

147. Department of Homeland Security, "Inadmissibility on Public Charge Grounds," *Federal Register*, August 14, 2019, www.federalregister.gov/documents/2019 /08/14/2019-17142/inadmissibility-on-public-charge-grounds.

148. Chris Dolmetsch and Edvard Pettersson, "Judge Says Trump's Immigrant Wealth Test Is 'Repugnant,' Blocks Its Enforcement," *Boston Globe*, October 11,

2019, www.bostonglobe.com/news/nation/2019/10/11/judge-says-trump-immigrant
-wealth-test-repugnant/pecnue4UQPJ5jcZcp7t5IO/story.html.

149. Adam Liptak, "Supreme Court Allows Trump's Wealth Test for Green
Cards," *New York Times,* January 27, 2020, www.nytimes.com/2020/01/27/us/supreme
-court-trump-green-cards.html.

150. US Citizenship and Immigration Services, "Public Charge Fact Sheet," n.d.,
www.uscis.gov/news/fact-sheets/public-charge-fact-sheet.

151. See Civil Liberties Act of 1988, H.R. 442, www.congress.gov/bill/100th
-congress/house-bill/442.

CHAPTER FIVE

1. Jörg Brüggemann, *Tourists vs. Refugees,* n.d., www.joergbrueggemann.com
/tourists-vs-refugees/. See also Jörg Brüggemann, "Distant Shores: Tourists and
Refugees on Kos—in Pictures," *Guardian,* September 4, 2015, www.theguardian
.com/world/gallery/2015/sep/04/distant-shores-tourists-and-refugees-on-kos-in
-pictures; and Patrick Kingsley, "Kos: The Greek Island Where Refugees and Tourists Share the Same Beaches," *Guardian,* September 5, 2015, www.theguardian.com
/world/2015/sep/05/refugees-and-holidaymakers-in-kos-patrick-kingsley.

2. Jon Wiener, "'Call Me a Refugee, Not an Immigrant': Viet Thanh Nguyen,"
Nation, June 11, 2018, www.thenation.com/article/call-refugee-not-immigrant-viet
-thanh-nguyen/.

3. United Nations High Commissioner for Refugees, "What Is a Refugee?," n.d.,
www.unrefugees.org/refugee-facts/what-is-a-refugee/.

4. David Scott FitzGerald, "The Sociology of International Migration," in
Migration Theory: Talking across Disciplines, 3rd ed., ed. Caroline B. Brettell and James
F. Hollifield (New York: Routledge, 2014), 124 ("a special category of protection");
and Thomas Nail, *The Figure of the Migrant* (Stanford, CA: Stanford University Press,
2015), 4 ("regime of social circulation").

5. Kirsten Silva Gruesz, "'Poor Eliza' on the Border," *J19: The Journal of
Nineteenth-Century Americanists* 6, no. 1 (2018): 183.

6. *Oxford Living Dictionaries,* s.v. "tourist," https://en.oxforddictionaries.com
/definition/tourist.

7. Mimi Sheller and John Urry, "The New Mobilities Paradigm," *Environment
and Planning* 38 (2006): 207–226.

8. Nail, *Figure of the Migrant,* 3.

9. Haunani-Kay Trask, "Settlers of Color and 'Immigrant' Hegemony: 'Locals'
in Hawai'i," in *Asian Settler Colonialism: From Local Governance to the Habits of Everyday*

Life in Hawai'i, ed. Jonathan Y. Okamura and Candace Fujikane (Honolulu: University of Hawaii Press, 2008), 46.

10. Aileen Moreton-Robinson, "I Still Call Australia Home: Indigenous Belonging and Place in a White Postcolonizing Society," in *Uprootings/Regroundings: Questions of Home and Migration*, ed. Sara Ahmed, Claudia Castañeda, Anne-Marie Fortier, and Mimi Sheller (Oxford: Berg, 2003), 24.

11. Jodi A. Byrd, *The Transit of Empire: Indigenous Critique of Colonialism* (Minneapolis: University of Minnesota Press, 2011), xix. Byrd takes the term "arrivant" from Edward Brathwaite's collection of poems *The Arrivants: A New World Trilogy* (Oxford: Oxford University Press, 1967) ("arrivant"); US Department of State, Bureau of Consular Affairs, "Directory of Visa Categories," n.d., https://travel.state.gov/content /travel/en/us-visas/visa-information-resources/all-visa-categories.html ("non-immigrant"); International Organization for Migration, "Key Migration Terms," n.d., www.iom.int/key-migration-terms ("migrant"); and Bridget Anderson, "Exclusion, Failure, and the Politics of Citizenship," *RCIS Working Paper* 1 (2014): 3 ("one of the global poor").

12. See, for example, United Nations High Commissioner for Refugees, "Master Glossary of Terms," June 2006, www.refworld.org/docid/42ce7d444.html; European Commission, Migration and Home Affairs, "Economic Migrant," n.d., https:// ec.europa.eu/home-affairs/what-we-do/networks/european_migration_network /glossary_search/economic-migrant_en; and UN High Commissioner for Human Rights, "International Convention on the Protection of the Rights of All Migrant Workers and Members of Their Families," December 18, 1990, www.ohchr.org/en /professionalinterest/pages/cmw.aspx.

13. Sociologist Ramón Grosfoguel defines context of reception as "the state policies toward a specific migrant group, the reaction/perceptions of public opinion, and the presence or absence of an ethnic community" in the host society. See Ramón Grosfoguel, *Colonial Subjects: Puerto Ricans in a Global Perspective* (Berkeley: University of California Press, 2003), 130.

14. Nail, *Figure of the Migrant*, 4.

15. I take "dissident Dreamer" from Sujatha Fernandes, *Curated Stories: The Uses and Misuses of Storytelling* (New York: Oxford University Press, 2017). "Bad Dreamer" and "reluctant Dreamer" are from Alberto Ledesma, *Diary of a Reluctant Dreamer* (Columbus, OH: Mad Creek Books, 2017); "unbounded Dreamer" is from Walter J. Nicholls and Tara Fiorito, "Dreamers Unbound: Immigrant Youth Mobilizing," *New Labor Forum* 24, no. 1 (2014): 86–92.

16. Regarding the politics of presence and visibility in immigrant and queer migrant politics, see Karma R. Chávez, *Queer Migration Politics: Activist Rhetoric and*

Coalitional Possibilities (Urbana: University of Illinois Press, 2013); Jesus Cisneros and Julia Gutierrez, "'What Does It Mean to Be Undocuqueer?' Exploring (Il)legibility within the Intersection of Gender, Sexuality, and Immigration Status," *QED* 5, no. 1 (2018): 84–102; Nicholas De Genova, "Migrant 'Illegality' and Deportability in Everyday Life," *Annual Review of Anthropology* 31 (2002): 419–447; Nicholas De Genova, "The Queer Politics of Migration: Reflections on 'Illegality' and Incorrigibility," *Studies in Social Justice* 4, no. 2 (2010): 101–126; Carrie Hart, "The Activism of Julio Salgado's *I Am Undocuqueer!* Series," *Working Papers on Language and Diversity in Education* 1, no. 1 (2015): 1–14; Eithne Luibhéid, "Sexuality, Migration, and the Shifting Line between Legal and Illegal Status," *GLQ* 14, nos. 2–3 (2008): 289–315; Rebecca Schreiber, *The Undocumented Everyday: Migrant Lives and the Politics of Visibility* (Minneapolis: University of Minnesota, 2018); Imogen Tyler and Katarzyna Marciniak, "Immigrant Protest: An Introduction," *Citizenship Studies* 17, no. 2 (2013): 143–156; and Melissa Autumn White, "Documenting the Undocumented: Toward a Queer Politics of No Borders," *Sexualities* 17, no. 8 (2014): 976–997.

17. José Esteban Muñoz, *Cruising Utopia: The Then and There of Queer Futurity* (New York: New York University Press, 2009), 1.

18. Muñoz, *Cruising Utopia*, 27.

19. Muñoz, *Cruising Utopia*, 3.

20. Muñoz, *Cruising Utopia*, 1.

21. Mae M. Ngai, *Impossible Subjects: Illegal Aliens and the Making of Modern America* (Princeton, NJ: Princeton University Press, 2005).

22. Nicholls and Fiorito, "Dreamers Unbound," 87.

23. Nicholls and Fiorito, "Dreamers Unbound," 89.

24. Kimberle Crenshaw, "Demarginalizing the Intersection of Race and Sex: A Black Feminist Critique of Antidiscrimination Doctrine, Feminist Theory and Antiracist Politics," *University of Chicago Legal Forum* 1989, no. 1 (1989): 139.

25. Leslie McCall, "The Complexity of Intersectionality," *Signs* 30, no. 3 (2005): 1771.

26. Nicholls and Fiorito, "Dreamers Unbound," 89.

27. Nicholls and Fiorito, "Dreamers Unbound," 91.

28. Fernandes, *Curated Stories*, 123.

29. ASPIRE, "ASPIRE: The First Pan-Asian Undocumented Group in the USA," n.d., https://sfbay.aspireforjustice.org/.

30. Josh Richman, "Obama's Immigration Speech in Deep-Blue San Francisco Interrupted by Anti-deportation Hecklers," *San Jose Mercury News*, November 25, 2013, www.mercurynews.com/2013/11/25/obamas-immigration-speech-in-deep-blue-san-francisco-interrupted-by-anti-deportation-hecklers/.

31. Hong's life and political activism have been the subjects of newspaper stories, videos, and even a drawing by Alberto Ledesma, *Ju Hong Interrupts President Obama*, which can be seen in Jacqueline Villarrubia-Mendoza and Roberto Vélez-Vélez, "Iconoclastic Dreams: Interpreting Art in the DREAMers Movement," *Sociological Quarterly 58*, no. 3 (2017): 350–372. Regarding Hong's biography and activism, see Diana Arbas, "UC Berkeley Student Ju Hong: Undocumented and Unafraid," *Berkeleyside*, August 3, 2011, www.berkeleyside.com/2011/08/03/ju-hong-undocumented-and-unafraid; Shirin Jaafari, "Obama Heckler Talks about His Life as an Undocumented Immigrant," *PRI's The World*, November 29, 2013, www.pri.org/stories/2013-11-29/obama-heckler-talks-about-his-life-undocumented-immigrant; Haas Jr., "Ju Hong: Cal Dreamer Finds His Voice and Helps Others Do the Same," Perspectives: First Person Stories, May 2016, www.haasjr.org/perspectives/first-person-stories/ju-hong; Define American, "Ju Hong Shares His Story," published August 24, 2016, www.youtube.com/watch?v=wdh8nqL8bQM; UC Berkeley Newscenter, "Ju Hong: UC Berkeley Undocumented Student," published December 10, 2012, www.youtube.com/watch?v=UktXJIeBıtg; Matt O'Brien, "SF State Student Who Shouted at Obama Has History of Gutsy Protests," *San Jose Mercury News*, November 25, 2013, www.mercurynews.com/2013/11/25/s-f-state-student-who-shouted-at-obama-has-history-of-gutsy-protests/; Matt O'Brien, "San Francisco Shout Helped Set the Stage for Obama Immigration Action," *San Jose Mercury News*, November 20, 2014, www.mercurynews.com/2014/11/20/san-francisco-shout-helped-set-stage-for-obama-immigration-action-2/; Anna Oh, *Halmoni*, [2017], https://vimeo.com/213793631; and "UC Berkeley Student Senator Released after Arrest at Immigration Rally," *East Bay Times*, July 12, 2011, www.eastbaytimes.com/2011/07/12/uc-berkeley-student-senator-released-after-arrest-at-immigration-rally/.

32. The video and transcript of Hong and Obama's exchange can be found at Democracy Now!, "Plea to End Deportations Heard Nationwide as Activist Interrupts Obama Speech on Immigration," November 27, 2013, www.democracynow.org/2013/11/27/my_family_has_been_separated_for. See also CNN Politics, "Obama Responds to Hecklers at Speech," November 25, 2013, www.cnn.com/videos/politics/2013/11/25/sot-obama-gets-heckled-at-reform-speech.cnn/video/playlists/politicians-get-heckled/; Lisa Fernandez, "Ju Hong, UC Berkeley Graduate, Heckles President Obama on Deportation," NBC Bay Area, November 25, 2013, www.nbcbayarea.com/news/local/Ju-Hong-UC-Berkley-Graduate-Heckles-Obama-on-Deportation-233362861.html; Mlk best, "Immigrant from South Korea Interrupt [*sic*] Obama's Speech," published December 20, 2013, www.youtube.com/watch?v=YBw4Su5XCm8; NBC Bay Area, "President Obama Talks Immigration, Fundraises in San Francisco, Los Angeles," November 25, 2013, www.nbcbayarea.com/news

/local/President-Obama-to-Talk-Immigration-Fundraise-in-San-Francisco-Los -Angeles-233329131.html; and NBC News, "One Year Later, Obama's Immigration Heckler Feels Vindicated," www.nbcnews.com/news/asian-america/one-year-later -obamas-immigration-heckler-feels-vindicated-n258951.

33. ASPIRE, "The Aspire Team," http://sfbay.aspireforjustice.org/about-us-2 /our-people.

34. Valenciano's shirt can be seen at the 1:34 mark in NBC Bay Area, "President Obama Talks Immigration."

35. Mikhail Bakhtin, *Problems of Dostoyevsky's Poetics*, trans. Caryl Emerson (Minneapolis: University of Minnesota Press, 1984); and Mikhail Bakhtin, *The Dialogic Imagination: Four Essays*, ed. Michael Holquist, trans. Caryl Emerson and Michael Holquist (Austin: University of Texas Press, 1983).

36. ASPIRE, "API Undocumented Immigrants Respond to Obama's Speech on Immigration Reform," November 25, 2013, http://archive.constantcontact.com/fs123 /1103244704062/archive/1115787723119.html.

37. O'Brien, "SF State Student Who Shouted at Obama Has History of Gutsy Protests" ("props"); and ASPIRE, "API Undocumented Immigrants Respond to Obama's Speech on Immigration Reform" ("what you can do today").

38. Democracy Now!, "Plea to End Deportations Heard Nationwide"; and Jaafari, "Obama Heckler Talks about His Life as an Undocumented Immigrant."

39. Ju Hong, "President Obama, Stop Separating and Deporting Our Families," *Huffpost*, December 2, 2013, www.huffingtonpost.com/ju-hong/president-obama-stop -sepa_b_4371244.html.

40. "UC Berkeley Student Senator Released after Arrest at Immigration Rally."

41. O'Brien, "San Francisco Shout Helped Set the Stage for Obama Immigration Action."

42. NBC News, "One Year Later, Obama's Immigration Heckler Feels Vindicated."

43. US Department of Justice, "Attorney General Jeff Sessions Delivers Remarks on DACA," September 5, 2017, www.justice.gov/opa/speech/attorney-general -sessions-delivers-remarks-daca.

44. US Department of Justice, "Attorney General Sessions Delivers Remarks on DACA."

45. Julio Salgado and Faviana Rodriguez, "A Conversation with DREAMer Julio Salgado," CultureStrike, August 21, 2012, http://archive.culturestrike.org/julio -salgado-and-favianna-rodriguez-at-la-pena/.

46. White, "Documenting the Undocumented," 987.

47. Hinda Seif, "'Layers of Humanity': Interview with Undocuqueer Artivist Julio Salgado," *Latino Studies* 12, no. 2 (2014): 304.

48. Organized Communities against Deportations, "National Come Out of the Shadows Day!," February 17, 2010, http://organizedcommunities.org/national -coming-out-of-the-shadows-day/. See also Chávez, *Queer Migration Politics*, 84.

49. Jorge Gutierrez, "I Am Undocuqueer: New Strategies for Alliance Building for the LGBTQ and Immigrant Rights Movements," *Huffpost*, January 21, 2013, www.huffingtonpost.com/jorge-gutierrez/i-am-undocuqueer_b_2521339.html; Jorge Gutierrez, "'Coming Out' as Queer and Undocumented: A New Strategy for the Immigrant and LGBTQ Rights Movements," Syracuse Peace Council (June 2012), www.peacecouncil.net/pnl/june-2012-pnl-815/coming-out-as-queer-and -undocumented.

50. Mónica Novoa, "Julio Salgado: Creating Undocu-Love and Undocu-Queer Art," *Colorlines*, March 15, 2012, www.colorlines.com/content/julio-salgado-creating -undocu-love-and-undocu-queer-art; and Julio Salgado, "Queer, Undocumented and Unafraid," *Huffpost*, October 13, 2011, www.huffingtonpost.com/julio-salgado /queer-undocumented_b_1007869.html.

51. Seif, "'Layers of Humanity,'" 302; and Hart, "Activism of Julio Salgado's *I Am Undocuqeer!* Series," 5.

52. Julio Salgado, "I Am Undocuqueer," http://juliosalgadoart.com/post /15803758188/i-am-undocuqueer-is-an-art-project-in.

53. Salgado, "I Am Undocuqueer."

54. Salgado has identified Douglas as an influence. See Julio Salgado, "Emory Douglas on SB1070," CultureStrike, July 19, 2012, http://archive.culturestrike.org /emory-douglas-on-sb1070/; and Seif, "'Layers of Humanity,'" 304.

55. Erika L. Sánchez, "The UndocuQueer Movement Rises to Push for a Dream Act," NBC Latino, November 2, 2012, http://nbclatino.com/2012/11/02/the -undocuqueer-movement-rises-to-push-for-a-dream-act/#s:quip-7.

56. Regarding Salgado's *I Exist* series, see Rahulb, "Interview Highlights: Dreamers Adrift and the 'I Exist' Collection," MIT Center for Civic Media, April 8, 2012, https://civic.mit.edu/2012/4/8/interview-highlights-dreamers-adrift-and-the -i-exist-collection/.

57. Harrick Wu, "'Undocu-Queer' Artist Julio Salgado on Creative Resistance," KQED Arts, July 5, 2018, www.kqed.org/arts/13836333/undocu-queer-artist-julio -salgado-on-creative-resistance.

58. Navi, "Undocuqueer Artist Julio Salgado on Creating to Counter Crisis," Into, January 17, 2018, www.intomore.com/culture/undocuqueer-artist-julio-salgado -on-creating-to-counter-crisis/5e5563fb49f74a5e.

59. Wu, "'Undocu-Queer' Artist Julio Salgado on Creative Resistance."

60. Navi, "Undocuqueer Artist Julio Salgado on Creating to Counter Crisis."

61. Regina Napolitano, "Julio Salgado's 'Queer Butterfly' Featured in CAC's Art Series," *Daily Bruin*, January 8, 2014, https://dailybruin.com/2014/01/08/julio-salgados-queer-butterfly-featured-in-cacs-art-series/).

62. Bridget Anderson, Nandita Sharma, and Cynthia Wright, "Why No Borders?," *Refuge* 26, no. 2 (2009): 6.

63. Anderson, Sharma, and Wright, "Why No Borders?"

64. *Latinos Who Lunch*, episode 43: Julio Salgado, October 19, 2017, www.latinoswholunch.com/episodes/2017/10/19/julio-salgado.

65. Muñoz, *Cruising Utopia*, 26.

66. María Josefina Saldaña-Portillo, "Critical Latinx Indigeneities: A Paradigm Drift," *Latino Studies* 15, no. 2 (2017): 141.

67. Saldaña-Portillo, "Critical Latinx Indigeneities," 141 ("can never be modern"), and 153 ("their proper place").

68. Lou Cornum, "The Space NDN's Star Map," *New Inquiry*, January 26, 2015, https://thenewinquiry.com/the-space-ndns-star-map/.

69. Cornum, "The Space NDN's Star Map."

70. From *Gal rabenee ladxuu*, one of the labels in the Grand Rotunda during the exhibition of *Gal rabenee ladxuu*.

71. David Shook, ed., *Visualizando el lenguaje: Oaxaca en L.A./Visualizing Language: Oaxaca in L.A.* (Los Angeles: Library Foundation of Los Angeles and Phoneme Media, 2017), 3.

72. Michael Kearney is widely credited for first using the term "Oaxacalifornia" in an academic publication. Michael Kearney, "The Effects of Transnational Culture, Economy, and Migration on Mixtec Identity in Oaxacalifornia," in *The Bubbling Cauldron: Race, Ethnicity, and the Urban Crisis*, ed. Michael Peter Smith and Joe R. Feagin (Minneapolis: University of Minnesota Press, 1995), 226–243.

73. Deborah Vankin, "Oaxacalifornia Dreaming: L.A. Library Mural Project Looks at a Visual Language That Transcends Borders," *Los Angeles Times*, September 20, 2017, www.latimes.com/entertainment/arts/la-ca-cm-oaxacan-murals-central-library-20170920-htmlstory.html.

74. Yolanda Cruz, *Tlacolulokos!*, [2017], https://player.vimeo.com/video/236582214.

75. David Lee and Charles Roberts, "The Market at Tlacolula," *Focus on Geography* 47, no. 4 (2004): 29.

76. "Lenguas indígenas en México y hablantes (de 3 años y más) al 2015," http://cuentame.inegi.org.mx/hipertexto/todas_lenguas.htm; and Xóchitl Flores-Marcial, "A Perspective from the South: Tlacolula to L.A.," in *Visualizando el lenguaje: Oaxaca en L.A./Visualizing Language: Oaxaca in L.A.*, ed. David Shook (Los Angeles: Library Foundation of Los Angeles and Phoneme Media, 2017), 80.

77. The three varieties of Zapotec are listed on *Gal rabenee ladxuu*, one of the labels in the Grand Rotunda during the exhibition of *Gal rabenee ladxuu*.

78. Cruz, *Tlacolulokos!*; and Alicia Vargas, "The Voice of Indigenous Resistance in Oaxaca," Telesur, September 17, 2017, www.telesurtv.net/english/opinion/The -Voice-of-Indigenous-Resistance-in-Oaxacalifornia-20170914-0023.html.

79. Vargas, "Voice of Indigenous Resistance in Oaxaca."

80. Amanda de la Garza, "Rewriting Public Art: Oaxacalifornia and the Indigenous Murals by Tlacolulokos," in *Visualizando el lenguaje: Oaxaca en L.A./Visualizing Language: Oaxaca in L.A.*, ed. David Shook (Los Angeles: Library Foundation of Los Angeles and Phoneme Media, 2017), 34–35.

81. Los Angeles Public Library, "Visualizing Language: Oaxaca in L.A.," n.d., www.lapl.org/whats-on/exhibits/oaxaca.

82. M. Bianet Castellanos, "Rewriting the Mexican Immigrant Narrative: Situating Indigeneity in Maya Women's Stories," *Latino Studies* 15, no. 2 (2017): 220 ("population in the country"); and Maylei Blackwell, "Geographies of Indigeneity: Indigenous Migrant Women's Organizing and Translocal Politics of Place," *Latino Studies* 15, no. 2 (2017): 157. See also Renya Ramirez, *Native Hubs: Culture, Community, and Belonging in Silicon Valley and Beyond* (Durham, NC: Duke University Press, 2007) (Latin America).

83. De la Garza, "Rewriting Public Art," 35. See also Blackwell, "Geographies of Indigeneity"; M. Bianet Castellanos, *A Return to Servitude: Maya Migration and the Tourist Trade in Cancún* (Minneapolis: University of Minnesota Press, 2010); Jonathan Fox and Gaspar Rivera-Salgado, eds., *Indigenous Mexican Migrants in the United States* (La Jolla: University of California, San Diego, Center for Comparative Immigration Studies and Center for US-Mexican Studies, 2004); and Lynn Stephen, *Transborder Lives: Indigenous Oaxacans in Mexico, California, and Oregon* (Durham, NC: Duke University Press, 2007).

84. Lourdes Gutiérrez Nájera, M. Bianet Castellanos, and Arturo J. Aldama, "Introduction: Hemispheric *Encuentros* and Re-memberings," in *Comparative Indigeneities of the Américas: Toward a Hemispheric Approach*, ed. M. Bianet Castellanos, Lourdes Gutiérrez Nájera, and Arturo J. Aldama (Tucson: University of Arizona Press, 2012), 9.

85. Louise Steinman and Maureen Moore, "Telling Another Story: A Conversation between Louise Steinman and Maureen Moore," in *Visualizando el lenguaje: Oaxaca en L.A./Visualizing Language: Oaxaca in L.A.*, ed. David Shook (Los Angeles: Library Foundation of Los Angeles and Phoneme Media, 2017), 73; and de la Garza, "Rewriting Public Art," 36.

86. From *Gal rabenee ladxuu*, one of the labels in the Grand Rotunda during the exhibition of *Gal rabenee ladxuu*.

87. Los Angeles Public Library, "Painted Decoration: Goodhue Building," n.d., www.lapl.org/branches/central-library/art-architecture/painting; and Ed Fuentes, "Central Library Murals Are Also 80 Years Old," KCET History & Society, March 28, 2013, www.kcet.org/history-society/central-library-murals-are-also-80 -years-old.

88. "Painted Decoration."

89. "Painted Decoration."

90. Carey McWilliams, *Southern California Country: An Island on the Land* (New York: Duell, Sloane & Pearce, 1946), 22.

91. Cruz, *Tlacolulokos!*

92. Cruz, *Tlacolulokos!*

93. Fuentes, "Central Library Murals Are Also 80 Years Old."

94. Steinman and Moore, "Telling Another Story," 75; Vankin, "Oaxacalifornia Dreaming"; and Walter Mignolo, *The Darker Side of Western Modernity: Global Futures, Decolonial Options* (Durham, NC: Duke University Press, 2011), xxvii.

95. Cruz, *Tlacolulokos!*

96. Gerald Vizenor, "Aesthetics of Survivance: Literary Theory and Practice," in *Survivance: Narratives of Native Presence*, ed. Gerald Vizenor (Lincoln: University of Nebraska Press, 2008), 1 and 11.

97. Cruz, *Tlacolulokos!*

98. From *Smile Now, Cry Later*, one of the labels in the Grand Rotunda during the exhibition of *Gal rabenee ladxuu*.

99. Vankin, "Oaxacalifornia Dreaming." I am grateful to my colleague Stacy Kamehiro for bringing *Where Do We Come From? What Are We? Where Are We Going?* to my attention.

100. From *Migration: Oaxacalifornia*, one of the labels in the Grand Rotunda during the exhibition of *Gal rabenee ladxuu*.

101. Steven W. Hackel, "Sources of Rebellion: Indian Testimony and the Mission San Gabriel Uprising of 1785," *Ethnohistory* 50, no. 4 (2003): 643–669; Maria John, "Toypurina: A Legend Etched in the Landscape of Los Angeles," KCET, May 15, 2014, www.kcet.org/history-society/toypurina-a-legend-etched-in-the-landscape -of-los-angeles; and Cecilia Rasmussen, "Shaman and Freedom-Fighter Led Indians' Mission Revolt," *Los Angeles Times*, June 10, 2001, http://articles.latimes.com/2001 /jun/10/local/me-8853.

102. Hackel, "Sources of Rebellion," 649.

103. Regarding depictions of Toypurina in Los Angeles County, see John, "Toypurina."

104. Maylei Blackwell, "Indigeneity," in *Keywords for Latina/o Studies*, ed. Deborah R. Vargas, Nancy Raquel Mirabal, and Lawrence LaFountain-Stokes (New York: New York University Press, 2017), 100 ("layers of coloniality"); and Blackwell, "Geographies of Indigeneity," 174 ("institutions").

105. I take my definition of *kuleana* from Hokulani K. Aikau, "Indigeneity in the Diaspora: The Case of Native Hawaiians at Iosepa, Utah," *American Quarterly* 62, no. 3 (2010): 490, and Blackwell, "Geographies of Indigeneity," 104.

106. Sheila Marie Contreras, *Blood Lines: Myth, Indigenism and Chicana/o Literature* (Austin: University of Texas Press, 2008).

107. Trask, "Settlers of Color and 'Immigrant' Hegemony," 57. See also see Ann Curthoys, "An Uneasy Conversation: The Multicultural and the Indigenous," in *Race, Colour, and Identity in Australia and New Zealand*, ed. John Docker and Gerhard Fischer (Sydney: UNSW Press, 2000), 21–36.

108. Blackwell, "Geographies of Indigeneity," 159.

109. Louise Steinman, the Library Foundation of Los Angeles director of cultural programs, and Maureen Moore, the producer of *Visualizing Language: Oaxaca in L.A.*, credited Xóchitl Flores-Marcial with introducing them to the work of Tlacolulokos. Flores-Marcial, research consultant for *Visualzing Language*, was born in Tlacolula and grew up between Oaxaca and Los Angeles. See Steinman and Moore, "Telling Another Story," 73; and Flores-Marcial, "A Perspective from the South," 80.

110. Lourdes Gutiérrez Nájera and Korinta Maldonado, "Transnational Settler Colonial Formations and Global Capital: A Consideration of Indigenous Mexican Migrants," *American Quarterly* 69, no. 4 (2017): 812.

111. See, for example, Candace Fujikane, "Introduction: Asian Settler Colonialism in the U.S. Colony of Hawai'i," in *Asian Settler Colonialism: From Local Governance to the Habits of Everyday Life in Hawaii*, ed. Jonathan Y. Okamura and Candace Fujikane (Honolulu: University of Hawaii Press, 2008), 1–42.

112. Deborah Vankin, "Oaxacan Muralists' L.A. Works Give Voice to Indigenous Peoples—But the Artists Cannot Travel to the U.S. to View Them," *Los Angeles Times*, August 29, 2018, www.latimes.com/entertainment/arts/la-et-cm-tlacolulokos-visa-revoked-20180829-story.html.

113. Vankin, "Oaxacan Muralists' L.A. Works."

114. Daniel Hernandez, "These Oaxacan Muralists Brought Indigenous Flavor to the Central Library; Now They Are Deported," *L.A. Taco*, August 28, 2018, www.lataco.com/these-oaxacan-muralists-brought-indigenous-flavor-to-the-central-library-now-they-are-deported-an-exclusive/.

115. Hernandez, "These Oaxacan Muralists."

116. Ledesma, *Diary of a Reluctant Dreamer*, 93.

117. Robert Stribley, "The Way We Speak about Unauthorized Immigrants Matters," *Huffpost*, October 19, 2016, www.huffingtonpost.com/entry/the-language-of-illegal-immigration_us_58076b62e4b00483d3b5cdba.

118. Carola Suárez-Orozco et al., "Growing Up in the Shadows: The Developmental Implications of Unauthorized Status," *Harvard Educational Review* 81, no. 3 (2011): 438–472.

119. Muñoz, *Cruising Utopia*, 1.

120. Area Chicago, "Documents, Identities and Institutions," n.d., www.areachicago.org/documents-identities-and-institutions/.

EPILOGUE

1. Oscar Handlin, *The Uprooted: The Epic Story of the Great Migrations That Made the American People* (Boston: Little Brown, 1951), 3.

2. *Oxford English Dictionary*, s.v. "Assimilation," www-oed-com.oca.ucsc.edu/view/Entry/11934?redirectedFrom=assimilation#eid.

3. *Oxford English Dictionary*, "Acculturation," www-oed-com.oca.ucsc.edu/view/Entry/1259?redirectedFrom=acculturation#eid.

4. Rebecca Shapiro, "Tom Brokaw: 'Hispanics Should Work Harder at Assimilation,'" *Huffpost*, January 27, 2019, www.huffingtonpost.com/entry/tom-brokaw-hispanics-should-work-harder-at-assimilation_us_5c4e2ed3e4b0287e5b8bd250.

5. Richard Alba, "Bilingualism Persists, but English Still Dominates," Migration Policy Institute, February 1, 2005, www.migrationpolicy.org/article/bilingualism-persists-english-still-dominates; and Mark Hugo Lopez, Ana Gonzalez-Barrera, and Gustavo López, "Hispanic Identity Fades across Generations as Immigrant Connections Fall Away," Pew Research Center, December 20, 2017, www.pewhispanic.org/2017/12/20/hispanic-identity-fades-across-generations-as-immigrant-connections-fall-away/.

6. See US Citizenship and Immigration Services, I-821D, "Consideration of Deferred Action for Childhood Arrivals," www.uscis.gov/i-821d; and US Citizenship and Immigration Services, I-821, "Application for Temporary Protected Status," www.uscis.gov/i-821.

7. US Department of Justice, "Attorney General Jeff Sessions Issues Statement on DACA," September 5, 2017, www.justice.gov/opa/speech/attorney-general-sessions-delivers-remarks-daca; US Citizenship and Immigration Services, "Temporary Protected Status Designated Country: Haiti," n.d., www.uscis.gov/humanitarian

/temporary-protected-status/temporary-protected-status-designated-country
-haiti; US Citizenship and Immigration Services, "Temporary Protected Status
Designated Country: Nicaragua," n.d., www.uscis.gov/humanitarian/temporary
-protected-status/temporary-protected-status-designated-country-nicaragua;
and US Citizenship and Immigration Services, "Temporary Protected Status
Designated Country: El Salvador," n.d., www.uscis.gov/humanitarian/temporary
-protected-status/temporary-protected-status-designated-country-el-salvador.

8. Eugene Scott, "Trump's Most Insulting—and Violent—Language Is Often
Reserved for Immigrants," *Washington Post*, October 2, 2019, www.washingtonpost
.com/politics/2019/10/02/trumps-most-insulting-violent-language-is-often
-reserved-immigrants/.

9. Glenn Kessler, "The 'Very Fine People' at Charlottesville: Who Were They?,"
Washington Post, May 8, 2020, www.washingtonpost.com/politics/2020/05/08/very
-fine-people-charlottesville-who-were-they-2/.

10. Worldometer, COVID-19 Coronavirus Pandemic, May 31, 2020, www
.worldometers.info/coronavirus/.

11. APM Research Lab Staff, "The Color of Coronavirus: COVID-19 Deaths
by Race and Ethnicity in the U.S.," May 27, 2020, www.apmresearchlab.org/covid
/deaths-by-race; and Ed Pilkington, "Black Americans Dying of Covid-19 at Three
Times the Rate of White People," *Guardian*, May 20, 2020, www.theguardian.com
/world/2020/may/20/black-americans-death-rate-covid-19-coronavirus.

12. "George Floyd: What Happened in the Final Moments of His Life," BBC
News, May 30, 2020, www.bbc.com/news/world-us-canada-52861726.

13. Maggie Haberman, "Trump Threatens White House Protestors with 'Vicious
Dogs' and 'Ominous Weapons,'" *New York Times*, May 30, 2020, www.nytimes.com
/2020/05/30/us/politics/trump-threatens-protesters-dogs-weapons.html.

14. Nina Strochlic, "'We're Hurting, We're Hurting'—Grief and Outrage Converge in Minneapolis," *National Geographic*, May 30, 2020, www.nationalgeographic
.com/photography/2020/05/were-hurting-were-hurting-grief-and-outrage
-converge-in-minneapolis/#close.

15. Julia Gelatt, "Immigrant Workers: Vital to the U.S. COVID-19 Response,
Disproportionately Vulnerable," Migration Policy Institute Fact Sheet, March 2020,
www.migrationpolicy.org/research/immigrant-workers-us-covid-19-response.

16. US Department of Homeland Security, Memorandum on Identification of
Essential Critical Infrastructure Workers During COVID-19 Response, March 19,
2020, www.cisa.gov/sites/default/files/publications/CISA-Guidance-on-Essential
-Critical-Infrastructure-Workers-1-20-508c.pdf; and Miriam Jordan, "Farmworkers, Mostly Undocumented, Become 'Essential' During Pandemic," *New York*

Times, April 2, 2020, www.nytimes.com/2020/04/02/us/coronavirus-undocumented
-immigrant-farmworkers-agriculture.html.

17. Muzaffar Chishti and Jessica Bolter, "Vulnerable to COVID-19 and in Frontline Jobs, Immigrants Are Mostly Shut Out of U.S. Relief," Migration Policy Institute, April 24, 2020, www.migrationpolicy.org/article/covid19-immigrants-shut-out
-federal-relief.

18. Miriam Jordan, "Is America a 'Nation of Immigrants'? Immigration Agency
Says No," *New York Times*, February 22, 2018, www.nytimes.com/2018/02/22/us/uscis
-nation-of-immigrants.html.

19. Antonio Gramsci, *Selections from the Prison Notebooks of Antonio Gramsci*, ed. and
trans. Quentin Hoare and Geoffrey Nowell Smith (London: ElecBook, 1999), 556,
http://abahlali.org/files/gramsci.pdf.

BIBLIOGRAPHY

ARCHIVAL AND MANUSCRIPT COLLECTIONS

Carlisle Indian Digital Resource Center. http://carlisleindian.dickinson.edu/.

Miné Okubo Collection. Japanese American National Museum.

Publications Collection. Hampton University Archives, Hampton University.

Records of the Carlisle Indian Industrial School. National Archives and Records Administration, Washington, DC.

Richard Henry Pratt Papers. Beinecke Rare Book and Manuscript Library, Yale University.

Robert Ezra Park Collection. Special Collections Research Center, University of Chicago.

Samuel Chapman Armstrong Collection. Sawyer Library, Williams College.

DISSERTATIONS, FILMS, PUBLISHED ARTICLES AND BOOKS, THESES, AND WEBSITES

Abc, Frank. *John Okada: The Life and Rediscovered Work of the Author of "No-No Boy."* Seattle: University of Washington Press, 2018.

Adams, David Wallace. *Education for Extinction: American Indians and the Boarding School Experience, 1875–1928.* Lawrence: University of Kansas Press, 1995.

Adams, James Truslow. *The Epic of America.* Boston: Little, Brown, 1934.

Aikau, Hokulani K. "Indigeneity in the Diaspora: The Case of Native Hawaiians at Iosepa, Utah." *American Quarterly* 62, no. 3 (2010): 477–500.

Aitkenhead, Decca. "Rachel Dolezal: 'I'm Not Going to Stoop and Apologise and Grovel.'" *Guardian*, February 25, 2017. www.theguardian.com/us-news /2017/feb/25/rachel-dolezal-not-going-stoop-apologise-grovel.

Alba, Richard. "Bilingualism Persists, but English Still Dominates." Migration Policy Institute, February 1, 2005. www.migrationpolicy.org/article /bilingualism-persists-english-still-dominates.

———. "Bright vs. Blurred Boundaries: Second-generation Assimilation and Exclusion in France, Germany, and the United States." *Ethnic and Racial Studies* 28, no. 1 (2005): 20–49.

Alba, Richard, and Victor Nee. *Remaking the American Mainstream: Assimilation and Contemporary Immigration.* Cambridge, MA: Harvard University Press, 2003.

———. "Rethinking Assimilation Theory for a New Era of Immigration." *International Migration Review* 31, no. 4 (1997): 826–827.

Alter, Alexandra. "Dispute Arises over 'No-No Boy,' a Classic of Asian-American Literature with a Complex History." *New York Times*, June 6, 2019. www.nytimes.com/2019/06/06/books/no-no-boy-penguin.html.

Amaya, Hector. *Citizenship Excess: Latinas/os, Media, and the Nation.* New York: New York University Press, 2013.

Anderson, Bridget. "Exclusion, Failure and the Politics of Citizenship." *RCIS Working Paper* 1 (2014): 1–11.

———. "Immigration and the Worker Citizen." In *Citizenship and Its Others*, edited by Bridget Anderson and Vanessa Hughes, 41–57. New York: Palgrave Macmillan, 2015.

———. *Us and Them: The Dangerous Politics of Immigration Control.* Oxford: Oxford University Press, 2013.

Anderson, Bridget, Nandita Sharma, and Cynthia Wright, "Why No Borders?" *Refuge* 26, no. 2 (2009): 5–18.

APM Research Lab Staff. "The Color of Coronavirus: COVID-19 Deaths by Race and Ethnicity in the U.S." May 27, 2020, www.apmresearchlab.org /covid/deaths-by-race.

Arbas, Diana. "UC Berkeley Student Ju Hong: Undocumented and Unafraid." Berkeleyside, August 3, 2011. www.berkeleyside.com/2011/08/03/ju-hong -undocumented-and-unafraid.

Area Chicago. "Documents, Identities and Institutions." n.d. www.areachicago .org/documents-identities-and-institutions/.

ASPIRE. "API Undocumented Immigrants Respond to Obama's Speech on Immigration Reform." Last modified November 25, 2013. http://archive .constantcontact.com/fs123/1103244704062/archive/1115787723119.html.

―――. "ASPIRE: The First Pan-Asian Undocumented Group in the USA." n.d. https://sfbay.aspireforjustice.org/.

―――. "The Aspire Team." n.d. http://sfbay.aspireforjustice.org/about-us-2/our-people.

Bailey, Adrian J., Richard A. Wright, Alison Mountz, and Ines M. Miyares. "(Re)producing Salvadoran Transnational Geographies." *Annals of the Association of American Geographers* 92, no. 1 (2002): 125–144.

Baker, Lee D. "Research, Reform, and Racial Uplift: The Mission of the Hampton Folk-Lore Society, 1893–1899." In *Excluded Ancestors, Inventible Traditions: Essays toward a More Inclusive History of Anthropology*, edited by Richard Handler, 42–80. Madison: University of Wisconsin Press, 2000.

Bakhtin, Mikhail. *The Dialogic Imagination: Four Essays*. Edited by Michael Holquist. Translated by Caryl Emerson and Michael Holquist. Austin: University of Texas Press, 1983.

―――. *Problems of Dostoyevsky's Poetics*. Translated by Caryl Emerson. Minneapolis: University of Minnesota Press, 1984.

Barros, Aline, and Gesell Tobias. "Undocumented Valedictorian: I'm Cheating No One Out of College." VOA, June 25, 2016. www.voanews.com/usa/undocumented-valedictorian-im-cheating-no-one-out-college.

Barth, Fredrik. *Ethnic Groups and Boundaries: The Social Organization of Culture Difference*. Oslo: Universitetsforlaget, 1969.

Bell, Genevieve Bell. "Telling Stories out of School: Remembering the Carlisle Indian Industrial School, 1879–1918." PhD diss., Stanford University, 1998.

Blackwell, Maylei. "Geographies of Indigeneity: Indigenous Migrant Women's Organizing and Translocal Politics of Place." *Latino Studies* 15, no. 2 (2017): 156–181.

―――. "Indigeneity." In *Keywords for Latina/o Studies*, edited by Deborah R. Vargas, Nancy Raquel Mirabal, and Lawrence LaFountain-Stokes, 125–130. New York: New York University Press, 2017.

Blauner, Bob. *Racial Oppression in America*. New York: Harper & Row, 1972.

Boelhower, William. "The Brave New World of Immigrant Autobiography." *MELUS* 9, no. 2 (1982): 5–23.

Bonilla-Silva, Eduardo. *Racism without Racists: Color-Blind Racism and the Persistence of Racial Inequality in the United States*. Lanham, MD: Rowman & Littlefield, 2003.

Bourdieu, Pierre. *Acts of Resistance: Against the New Myths of Our Time*. Cambridge, UK: Polity Press, 1998.

Brathwaite, Edward. *The Arrivants: A New World Trilogy.* Oxford: Oxford University Press, 1967.

Breitzer, Susan Roth. "Race, Immigration, and Contested Americanness: Black Nativism and the American Labor Movement, 1880–1930," *Race/Ethnicity* 4, no. 2 (2011): 269–283.

Brodkin, Karen. *How Jews Became White Folks and What That Says about Race in America.* New Brunswick, NJ: Rutgers University Press, 1999.

Bruce, Dickson D., Jr. "Booker T. Washington's *The Man Farthest Down* and the Transformation of Race," *Mississippi Quarterly* 28, no. 2 (1995): 239–253.

Brüggemann, Jörg. "Distant Shores: Tourists and Refugees on Kos—in Pictures." *Guardian,* September 4, 2015. www.theguardian.com/world/gallery/2015/sep/04/distant-shores-tourists-and-refugees-on-kos-in-pictures.

———. "Tourists vs. Refugees." n.d. www.joergbrueggemann.com/tourists-vs-refugees/.

Buff, Rachel Ida. "Denizenship as Transnational Practice." In *Public Culture: Diversity, Democracy, and Community in the United States,* edited by Marguerite S. Shaffer, 263–272. Philadelphia: University of Pennsylvania Press, 2012.

Burnett, Christina Duffy, and Burke Marshall. "Between the Foreign and the Domestic: The Doctrine of Territorial Incorporation, Invented and Reinvented." In *Foreign in a Domestic Sense: Puerto Rico, American Expansion, and the Constitution,* edited by Christina Duffy Burnett and Burke Marshall, 1–36. Durham, NC: Duke University Press, 2001.

Butler, Judith. "Performativity, Precarity and Sexual Politics." *AIBR* 4, no. 3 (2009): i–xiii.

Byrd, Jodi A. *The Transit of Empire: Indigenous Critique of Colonialism.* Minneapolis: University of Minnesota Press, 2011.

Cacho, Lisa Marie. *Social Death: Racialized Rightlessness and the Criminalization of the Unprotected.* New York: New York University Press, 2012.

Camacho, Alicia Schmidt. *Migrant Imaginaries: Latino Cultural Politics in the U.S.-Mexico Borderlands.* New York: New York University Press, 2008.

Carbado, Devon W. "Racial Naturalization." *American Quarterly* 57, no. 3 (2005): 633–658.

Castellanos, M. Bianet. *A Return to Servitude: Maya Migration and the Tourist Trade in Cancún.* Minneapolis: University of Minnesota Press, 2010.

———. "Rewriting the Mexican Immigrant Narrative: Situating Indigeneity in Maya Women's Stories." *Latino Studies* 15, no. 2 (2017): 219–241.

Chan, Sucheng. *Asian Americans: An Interpretive History.* Boston: Twayne, 1991.

Chauvin, Sébastien, and Blanca Garcés-Mascareñas. "Becoming Less Illegal: Deservingness Frames and Undocumented Migrant Incorporation." *Race & Ethnicity* 8, no. 4 (2014): 422–432.

———. "Beyond Informal Citizenship: The New Moral Economy of Migrant Illegality." *International Political Sociology* 6 (2012): 241–259.

Chávez, Karma R. *Queer Migration Politics: Activist Rhetoric and Coalitional Possibilities.* Urbana: University of Illinois Press, 2013.

Cherokee Nation v. Georgia [1831]. Legal Information Institute. www.law.cornell .edu/supremecourt/text/30/1.

Child, Brenda J. *Boarding School Seasons: American Indian Families, 1900–1940.* Lincoln: University of Nebraska Press, 1998.

Chishti, Muzzafar, and Jessica Bolter. "Vulnerable to COVID-19 and in Frontline Jobs, Immigrants Are Mostly Shut Out of U.S. Relief." Migration Policy Institute, April 24, 2020. www.migrationpolicy.org/article/covid19 -immigrants-shut-out-federal-relief.

Chishti, Muzaffar, Doris Meissner, and Claire Bergeron. "At Its 25th Anniversary, IRCA's Legacy Lives On." Migration Policy Institute, November 16, 2011. www.migrationpolicy.org/article/its-25th-anniversary-ircas-legacy-lives.

Chu, Patricia P. *Assimilating Asians: Gendered Strategies of Authorship in Asian America.* Durham, NC: Duke University Press, 2000.

Cisneros, Jesus, and Julia Gutierrez. "'What Does It Mean to Be Undocuqueer?' Exploring (Il)legibility within the Intersection of Gender, Sexuality, and Immigration Status." *QED* 5, no. 1 (2018): 84–102.

Civil Liberties Act of 1988. www.congress.gov/bill/100th-congress/house-bill /442.

CNN Politics. "Obama Responds to Hecklers at Speech." November 25, 2013. www.cnn.com/videos/politics/2013/11/25/sot-obama-gets-heckled-at-reform -speech.cnn/video/playlists/politicians-get-heckled/.

Cole, Stewart G., and Mildred Wiese Cole. *Minorities and the American Promise: The Conflict of Principle and Practice* New York. Harper & Bros., 1954.

Contreras, Sheila Marie. *Blood Lines: Myth, Indigenism and Chicana/o Literature.* Austin: University of Texas Press, 2008.

Conzen, Kathleen Neils, David A. Gerber, Ewa Morawska, George E. Pozzetta, and Rudolph J. Veccoli. "The Invention of Ethnicity: A Perspective from the U.S.A." *Journal of American Ethnic History* 12, no. 1 (1992): 3–41.

Cornum, Lou. "The Space NDN's Star Map." *New Inquiry*, January 26, 2015. https://thenewinquiry.com/the-space-ndns-star-map/.

Coutin, Susan Bibler. *Legalizing Moves: Salvadoran Immigrants' Struggle for U.S. Residency.* Ann Arbor: University of Michigan Press, 2000.

Crenshaw, Kimberle. "Demarginalizing the Intersection of Race and Sex: A Black Feminist Critique of Antidiscrimination Doctrine, Feminist Theory and Antiracist Politics." *University of Chicago Legal Forum* 1989, no. 1 (1989): 139–168.

Cruz, Yolanda. *Tlacolulokos!* [2017]. https://player.vimeo.com/video/236582214.

Curthoys, Ann. "An Uneasy Conversation: The Multicultural and the Indigenous." In *Race, Colour, and Identity in Australia and New Zealand*, edited by John Docker and Gerhard Fischer, 21–36. Sydney: University of New South Wales Press, 2000.

Dawes, Henry L. "Solving the Indian Problem." In *Americanizing the American Indians: Writings by the "Friends of the Indian," 1880–1900*, edited by Francis Paul Prucha, 27–30. Cambridge, MA: Harvard University Press, 1973.

Dawsey, Josh. "Trump Derides Protections for Immigrants from 'Shithole' Countries," *Washington Post*, January 12, 2018. www.washingtonpost.com /politics/trump-attacks-protections-for-immigrants-from-shithole -countries-in-oval-office-meeting/2018/01/11/bfc0725c-f711-11e7-91af -31ac729add94_story.html?utm_term=.192454d370b2.

De Genova, Nicholas. "Denizens All: The Otherness of Citizenship." In *Citizenship and Its Others*, edited by Bridget Anderson and Vanessa Hughes, 191–202. New York: Palgrave Macmillan, 2015.

———. "Latino and Asian Racial Formations at the Frontiers of U.S. Nationalism." In *Racial Transformations: Latinos and Asians Remaking the United States*, edited by Nicholas De Genova, 1–20. Durham, NC: Duke University Press, 2006.

———. "Migrant 'Illegality' and Deportability in Everyday Life." *Annual Review of Anthropology* 31 (2002): 419–447.

———. "The Queer Politics of Migration: Reflections on 'Illegality' and Incorrigibility." *Studies in Social Justice* 4, no. 2 (2010): 101–126.

De Genova, Nicholas, and Ana Y. Ramos-Zayas. *Latino Crossings: Mexicans, Puerto Ricans, and the Politics of Race and Citizenship.* New York: Routledge, 2003.

de la Garza, Amanda. "Rewriting Public Art: Oaxacalifornia and the Indigenous Murals by Tlacolulokos." In *Visualizando el lenguaje: Oaxaca en L.A./ Visualizing Language: Oaxaca in L.A.*, edited by David Shook, 32–37. Los Angeles: Library Foundation of Los Angeles and Phoneme Media, 2017.

Define American. "Ju Hong Shares His Story." Published August 24, 2016. www.youtube.com/watch?v=wdh8nqL8bQM.

Deloria, Philip J. *Playing Indian.* New Haven, CT: Yale University Press, 1998.

Deloria, Vine. *The Indian Reorganization Act: Congresses and Bills.* Norman: University of Oklahoma Press, 2002.

Democracy Now! "Plea to End Deportations Heard Nationwide as Activist Interrupts Obama Speech on Immigration." November 27, 2013. www.democracynow.org/2013/11/27/my_family_has_been_separated_for.

Department of Homeland Security. "Inadmissibility on Public Charge Grounds." *Federal Register,* August 14, 2019. www.federalregister.gov/documents/2019/08/14/2019-17142/inadmissibility-on-public-charge-grounds.

Dery, Mark. "Black to the Future: Interviews with Samuel R. Delany, Greg Tate, and Tricia Rose." *South Atlantic Quarterly* 92, no. 4 (1993): 735–778.

Dillingham, William P., William S. Bennet, John L. Burnett, Benjamin F. Howell, Jeremiah W. Jenks, Asbury C. Latimer, Henry Cabot Lodge, et al. *Abstracts of Reports of the Immigration Commission: With Conclusions and Recommendations, and Views of the Minority (in Two Volumes).* Vol. 1. Washington, DC: Government Printing Office, 1911.

Dolmetsch, Chris, and Edvard Pettersson. "Judge Says Trump's Immigrant Wealth Test Is 'Repugnant,' Blocks Its Enforcement." *Boston Globe,* October 11, 2019. www.bostonglobe.com/news/nation/2019/10/11/judge-says-trump-immigrant-wealth-test-repugnant/pecnue4UQPJ5jcZcp7t5IO/story.html.

Douglass, Frederick. *Narrative of the Life of Frederick Douglass.* New York: Signet, 2005.

Downes v. Bidwell [1900]. Library of Congress. https://cdn.loc.gov/service/ll/usrep/usrep182/usrep182244/usrep182244.pdf.

Dred Scott v. Sandford [1857]. Wikisource. https://en.wikisource.org/wiki/Dred_Scott_v._Sandford.

Du Bois, W. E. B. *The Souls of Black Folk.* New York: Bantam Books, 1989.

Dueben, Alex. "Smash Pages Q&A: Alberto Ledesma on 'Diary of a Reluctant Dreamer.'" Smash Pages, September 18, 2017. http://smashpages.net/2017/09/18/smash-pages-qa-alberto-ledesma-on diary-of-a-reluctant-dreamer/.

East Bay Times. "UC Berkeley Student Senator Released after Arrest at Immigration Rally." July 12, 2011. www.eastbaytimes.com/2011/07/12/uc-berkeley-student-senator-released-after-arrest-at-immigration-rally/.

Engs, Robert Francis. *Educating the Disenfranchised and Disinherited: Samuel Chapman Armstrong and Hampton Institute, 1839–1893.* Knoxville: University of Tennessee Press, 1999.

Espiritu, Yen Le. *Home Bound: Filipino American Lives Across Cultures, Communities, and Countries.* Berkeley: University of California Press, 2003.

European Commission, Migration and Home Affairs. "Economic Migrant." n.d. https://ec.europa.eu/home-affairs/what-we-do/networks/european _migration_network/glossary_search/economic-migrant_en

Fanon, Frantz. "The Fact of Blackness." In *Black Skin, White Masks*, translated by Charles Lam Markmann, 109–140. New York: Grove Weidenfeld, 1967.

Fernandes, Sujatha. *Curated Stories: The Uses and Misuses of Storytelling*. New York: Oxford University Press, 2017.

Fernandez, Lisa. "Ju Hong, UC Berkeley Graduate, Heckles President Obama on Deportation," NBC Bay Area, November 25, 2013. www.nbcbayarea .com/news/local/Ju-Hong-UC-Berkley-Graduate-Heckles-Obama-on -Deportation-233362861.html.

FitzGerald, David Scott. "The Sociology of International Migration." In *Migration Theory: Talking across Disciplines*, 3rd ed., edited by Caroline B. Brettell and James F. Hollifield, 115–147. New York: Routledge, 2014.

Flores, Juan. "Que Assimilated, Brother, Yo Soy Assimilao: The Structuring of Puerto Rican Identity in the U.S." *Journal of Ethnic Studies* 13, no. 3 (1985): 1–16.

Flores-Marcial, Xóchitl. "A Perspective from the South: Tlacolula to L.A." In *Visualizando el lenguaje: Oaxaca en L.A./Visualizing Language: Oaxaca in L.A.*, edited by David Shook, 80–83. Los Angeles: Library Foundation of Los Angeles and Phoneme Media, 2017.

Foley, Elise, and Rebecca Shapiro. "Protestors Build Big, Beautiful Wall of Taco Trucks Outside Trump's Las Vegas Hotel." *Huffpost*, October 19, 2016. www.huffingtonpost.com/entry/taco-trucks-trump-las-vegas_us_5806 e250e4b0180a36e760e3.

Foley, Neil. *The White Scourge: Mexicans, Blacks, and Poor Whites in Texas Cotton Culture*. Berkeley: University of California Press, 1999.

Foner, Nancy. *In a New Land: A Comparative View of Immigration*. New York: New York University Press, 2005.

———. *Islands in the City: West Indian Migration to New York*. Berkeley: University of California Press, 2001.

Foucault, Michel. "Nietzsche, Genealogy, History." In Michel Foucault, *Language, Counter-memory, Practice: Selected Essays and Interviews*, edited by Donald F. Bouchard, 139–164. Translated by Donald F. Bouchard and Sherry Simon. Ithaca, NY: Cornell University Press, 1977.

———. *Power/Knowledge: Selected Interviews and Other Writings, 1972–1977*. Edited by Colin Gordon. Translated by Colin Gordon et al. New York: Pantheon Books, 1980.

Fourteenth Amendment. Amendments to the Constitution of the United States of America. https://web.archive.org/web/20050918042603/http://www.gpoaccess.gov/constitution/pdf/con001.pdf.

Fox, Jonathan, and Gaspar Rivera-Salgado, eds. *Indigenous Mexican Migrants in the United States.* La Jolla: University of California, San Diego, Center for Comparative Immigration Studies and Center for U.S.-Mexican Studies, 2004.

Franqui-Rivera, Harry. "National Mythologies: U.S. Citizenship for the People of Puerto Rico and Military Service." *Centro* 10, no. 21 (2013): 5–21.

———. *Soldiers of the Nation: Military Service and Modern Puerto Rico, 1868–1952.* Lincoln: University of Nebraska Press, 2018.

Fredrickson, George M. *The Comparative Imagination: On the History of Racism, Nationalism, and Social Movements.* Berkeley: University of California Press, 2000.

Frej, Willa. "Undocumented Valedictorian Takes Down Trump in Epic Speech." *Huffpost,* June 10, 2016. www.huffpost.com/entry/undocumented-valedictorian-takes-down-trump-in-epic-speech_n_575aaca2e4b0ced23ca7bda0.

Fuentes, Ed. "Central Library Murals Are Also 80 Years Old." KCET History & Society, March 28, 2013. www.kcet.org/history-society/central-library-murals-are-also-80-years-old.

Fujikane, Candace. "Introduction: Asian Settler Colonialism in the U.S. Colony of Hawai'i." In *Asian Settler Colonialism: From Local Governance to the Habits of Everyday Life in Hawaii,* edited by Jonathan Y. Okamura and Candace Fujikane, 1–42. Honolulu: University of Hawaii Press, 2008.

Galbraith, John Kenneth. *The Affluent Society: Fortieth Anniversary Edition.* Boston: Houghton Mifflin, 1998.

Gans, Herbert. "Second Generation Decline: Scenarios for the Economic and Ethnic Futures of the Post-1965 American Immigrants." *Ethnic and Racial Studies* 15, no. 2 (1992): 173–192.

———. "Symbolic Ethnicity: The Future of Ethnic Groups and Cultures in America." *Ethnic and Racial Studies* 2, no. 1 (1979). 1–20.

Gans, Herbert J. "Ethnic Invention and Acculturation, a Bumpy Line Approach." *Journal of American Ethnic History* 12, no. 1 (1992): 42–52.

García, Angela S. *Legal Passing: Navigating Undocumented Life and Local Immigration Law.* Berkeley: University of California Press, 2019.

Gelatt, Julia. "Immigrant Workers: Vital to the U.S. COVID-19 Response, Disproportionately Vulnerable." Migration Policy Institute Fact Sheet, March 2020. www.migrationpolicy.org/research/immigrant-workers-us-covid-19-response.

"George Floyd: What Happened in the Final Moments of His Life." BBC News, May 30, 2020. www.bbc.com/news/world-us-canada-52861726.

Getachew, Samuel. "21 Savage and the Way We See Black Immigrants." *New York Times*, February 2, 2019. www.nytimes.com/2019/02/09/opinion/21 -savage-ice.html.

Ginsberg, Elaine K. "Introduction: The Politics of Passing." In *Passing and the Fictions of Identity*, edited by Elaine K. Ginsberg, 1–18. Durham, NC: Duke University Press, 1996.

Glazer, Nathan. "Is Assimilation Dead?" *Annals of the American Academy of Political and Social Science* 530 (1993): 122–136.

Glazer, Nathan, and Daniel P. Moynihan. *Beyond the Melting Pot*. Cambridge, MA: MIT Press, 1963.

Gleeson, Shannon, and Roberto G. Gonzales. "When Do Papers Matter? An Institutional Analysis of Undocumented Life in the United States." *International Migration* 50, no. 4 (2012): 1–19.

Golash-Boza, Tanya. "Dropping the Hyphen? Becoming Latino(a)-American through Racialized Assimilation." *Social Forces* 85, no. 1 (2006): 27–55.

Gonzales, Roberto G. "Learning to Be Illegal: Undocumented Youth and Shifting Legal Contexts in the Transition to Adulthood." *American Sociological Review* 76, no. 4 (2011): 602–619.

Gordon, Linda. *Pitied but Not Entitled: Single Mothers and the History of Welfare, 1890–1935*. New York: Free Press, 1994.

Gordon, Milton M. *Assimilation in American Life: The Role of Race, Religion, and National Origins*. New York: Oxford University Press, 1964.

Gramsci, Antonio. *Selections from the Prison Notebooks of Antonio Gramsci*. Edited and translated by Quentin Hoare and Geoffrey Nowell Smith. London: ElecBook, 1999. http://abahlali.org/files/gramsci.pdf.

Grosfoguel, Ramón. *Colonial Subjects: Puerto Ricans in a Global Perspective*. Berkeley: University of California Press, 2003.

Gruesz, Kirsten Silva. "'Poor Eliza' on the Border." *J19* 6, no. 1 (2018): 182–189.

Gugliemo, Thomas A. *White on Arrival: Italians, Race, Color, and Power in Chicago, 1890–1945*. New York: Oxford University Press, 2003.

Guridy, Frank Andre. *Forging Diaspora: Afro-Cubans and African Americans in a World of Empire and Jim Crow*. Chapel Hill: University of North Carolina Press, 2010.

Gutierrez, Jorge. "'Coming Out' as Queer and Undocumented: A New Strategy for the Immigrant and LGBTQ Rights Movements." Syracuse Peace

Council, June 2012. www.peacecouncil.net/pnl/june-2012-pnl-815/coming -out-as-queer-and-undocumented.

———. "I Am Undocuqueer: New Strategies for Alliance Building for the LGBTQ and Immigrant Rights Movements." *Huffpost*, January 21, 2013. www.huffingtonpost.com/jorge-gutierrez/i-am-undocuqueer_b_2521339 .html.

Haas Jr. "Ju Hong: Cal Dreamer Finds His Voice and Helps Others Do the Same." Perspectives: First Person Stories, May 2016. www.haasjr.org /perspectives/first-person-stories/ju-hong.

Haberman, Maggie. "Trump Threatens White House Protestors with 'Vicious Dogs' and 'Ominous Weapons.'" *New York Times*, May 30, 2020. www.nytimes .com/2020/05/30/us/politics/trump-threatens-protesters-dogs-weapons .html.

Hackel, Steven W. "Sources of Rebellion: Indian Testimony and the Mission San Gabriel Uprising of 1785." *Ethnohistory* 50, no. 4 (2003): 643–669.

Hammar, Tomas. *Democracy and the Nation State, Aliens, Denizens, and Citizens in a World of International Migration*. Brookfield, VT: Avebury/Gower Publishing, 1990.

Handlin, Oscar. *The Uprooted: The Epic Story of the Great Migrations That Made the American People*. Boston: Little, Brown, 1951.

Haney-López, Ian. *White by Law: The Legal Construction of Race*. New York: New York University Press, 2006.

Hanhardt, Christina B. *Safe Space: Gay Neighborhood History and the Politics of Violence*. Durham, NC: Duke University Press, 2013.

Harlan, Louis R. *Booker T. Washington: The Wizard of Tuskegee*. New York: Oxford University Press, 1983.

———, ed. *The Booker T. Washington Papers*. Vol. 3. Urbana: University of Illinois Press, 1974.

Harlan, Louis R., Raymond W. Smock, Geraldine McTigue, and Nan E. Woodruff, eds. *The Booker T. Washington Papers*. Vol. 10, *1909–11*. Urbana: University of Illinois Press, 1981.

Harrington, Michael. *The Other America: Poverty in the United States*. New York: Macmillan, 1962.

Harris, Cheryl I. "Whiteness as Property." *Harvard Law Review* 106, no. 8 (1993): 1707–1791.

Hart, Carrie. "The Activism of Julio Salgado's *I Am Undocuqueer!* Series." *Working Papers on Language and Diversity in Education* 1, no. 1 (2015): 1–14.

Hellwig, David J. "Black Leaders and United States Immigration Policy, 1917–1929." *Journal of Negro History* 66, no. 2 (1981): 110–127.

———. "Strangers in Their Own Land: Patterns of Black Nativism, 1830–1930." *American Studies* 23, no. 1 (1982): 85–98.

Hernandez, Daniel. "These Oaxacan Muralists Brought Indigenous Flavor to the Central Library; Now They Are Deported." *L.A. Taco*, August 28, 2018. www.lataco.com/these-oaxacan-muralists-brought-indigenous-flavor-to-the-central-library-now-they-are-deported-an-exclusive/.

Hertzberg, Hazel W. *The Search for an American Indian Identity: Modern Pan-Indian Movements.* Syracuse, NY: Syracuse University Press, 1971.

Hipsman, Faye, and Doris Meisner. "Immigration in the United States: New Economic, Social, Political Landscapes with Legislative Reform on the Horizon." Migration Policy Institute, April 16, 2013. www.migrationpolicy.org/article/immigration-united-states-new-economic-social-political-landscapes-legislative-reform.

Hirschman, Charles. "America's Melting Pot Reconsidered." *Annual Review of Sociology* 9 (1983): 397–423.

Hochschild, Jennifer L. *Facing Up to the American Dream: Race, Class, and the Soul of the Nation.* Princeton, NJ: Princeton University Press, 1995.

Hong, Ju. "President Obama, Stop Separating and Deporting Our Families." *Huffpost*, December 2, 2013. www.huffingtonpost.com/ju-hong/president-obama-stop-sepa_b_4371244.html.

Honig, Bonnie. *Democracy and the Foreigner.* Princeton, NJ: Princeton University Press, 2001.

Horton, Sarah B. "From 'Deportability' to 'Denounce-ability': New Forms of Labor Subordination in an Era of Governing Immigration through Crime." *Political and Legal Anthropology Review* 39, no. 2 (2016): 312–326.

HoSang, Daniel Martinez, and Natalia Molina. "Introduction: Toward a Relational Consciousness of Race." In *Relational Formations of Race: Theory, Method, and Practice,* edited by Natalia Molina, Daniel Martinez HoSang, and Ramón A. Gutiérrez, 1–18. Berkeley: University of California Press, 2019.

Hoxie, Frederick. *A Final Promise: The Campaign to Assimilate the Indians, 1880–1920.* Lincoln: University of Nebraska Press, 1984.

Huntington, Samuel P. "The Hispanic Challenge." *Foreign Policy* 141 (March–April 2004): 30–44.

Huntington, Samuel P. *Who Are We? The Challenges to America's National Identity.* New York: Simon & Schuster, 2004.

Ignatiev, Noel. *How the Irish Became White.* New York: Routledge, 1995.

Immigration Act of 1907. (An act to regulate the immigration of aliens to, and the residence of aliens in, the United States). http://library.uwb.edu/Static /USimmigration/39%20stat%20874.pdf.

Indian Citizenship Act of 1924. http://legisworks.org/congress/68/publaw-175 .pdf.

International Organization for Migration. "Key Migration Terms." n.d. www .iom.int/key-migration-terms.

Jaafari, Shirin. "Obama Heckler Talks about His Life as an Undocumented Immigrant." *PRI's The World,* November 29, 2013. www.pri.org/stories/2013 -11-29/obama-heckler-talks-about-his-life-undocumented-immigrant.

Jacobson, Matthew Frye. *Whiteness of a Different Color: European Immigrants and the Alchemy of Race.* Cambridge, MA: Harvard University Press, 1998.

Jacobson, Robin Dale. *The New Nativism: Proposition 187 and the Debate over Immigration.* Minneapolis: University of Minnesota Press, 2008.

Jefferson, Thomas. *The Life and Selected Writings of Thomas Jefferson.* Edited by Adrienne Koch and William Peden. New York: Modern Library, 1944.

Jiménez, Tomás R. *The Other Side of Assimilation: How Immigrants Are Changing American Life.* Berkeley: University of California Press, 2017.

John, Maria. "Toypurina: A Legend Etched in the Landscape of Los Angeles." KCET, May 15, 2014. www.kcet.org/history-society/toypurina-a-legend -etched-in-the-landscape-of-los-angeles.

Jordan, Miriam. "Farmworkers, Mostly Undocumented, Become 'Essential' During Pandemic." *New York Times,* April 2, 2020. www.nytimes.com /2020/04/02/us/coronavirus-undocumented-immigrant-farmworkers -agriculture.html.

———. "Is America a 'Nation of Immigrants'? Immigration Agency Says No." *New York Times,* February 22, 2018. www.nytimes.com/2018/02/22/us/uscis -nation-of-immigrants.html.

———. "Making President Trump's Bed: A Housekeeper without Papers." *New York Times,* December 6, 2018. www.nytimes.com/2018/12/06/us/trump -bedminster-golf-undocumented-workers.html.

———. "They Achieved the American Dream. Will the Supreme Court Let Them Keep It?" *New York Times,* November 7, 2019. www.nytimes.com /interactive/2019/11/07/us/dreamers-daca-supreme-court.html?action= click&module=Top%20Stories&pgtype=Homepage.

Jun, Helen Heran. *Race for Citizenship: Black Orientalism and Asian Uplift from Pre-Emancipation to Neoliberal America.* New York: New York University Press, 2011.

Jung, Moon-Kie. "The Racial Unconscious of Assimilation Theory." *Du Bois Review* 6, no. 2 (2009): 375–395.

Kallen, Horace M. *Culture and Democracy in the United States.* New Brunswick, NJ: Transaction Publishers, 1998.

Kamp, David. "Rethinking the American Dream." *Vanity Fair,* March 5, 2009. www.vanityfair.com/culture/2009/04/american-dream200904.

Kanstroom, Daniel. *Deportation Nation: Outsiders in American History.* Cambridge, MA: Harvard University Press, 2007.

Kasana, Mehreen. "Who Is Marco Gutierrez? The Latinos for Trump Founder Will Speak at MOAR." Bustle, September 16, 2017. www.bustle.com/p/who-is-marco-gutierrez-the-latinos-for-trump-founder-will-speak-at-moar-2366790.

Kasinitz, Philip. *Caribbean New York: Black Immigrants and the Politics of Race.* Ithaca, NY: Cornell University Press, 1992.

Katz, Michael B. *The Undeserving Poor: America's Enduring Confrontation with Poverty.* New York: Oxford University Press, 2013.

Kazal, Russell A. "Revisiting Assimilation: The Rise, Fall, and Reappraisal of a Concept in American Ethnic History." *American Historical Review* 100, no. 2 (1995): 437–471.

Kearney, Michael. "The Effects of Transnational Culture, Economy, and Migration on Mixtec Identity in Oaxacalifornia." In *The Bubbling Cauldron: Race, Ethnicity, and the Urban Crisis,* edited by Michael Peter Smith and Joe R. Feagin, 226–243. Minneapolis: University of Minnesota Press, 1995.

Kessler, Glenn. "The 'Very Fine People' at Charlottesville: Who Were They?" *Washington Post,* May 8, 2020. www.washingtonpost.com/politics/2020/05/08/very-fine-people-charlottesville-who-were-they-2/.

Kim, Daniel Y. "Once More, with Feeling: Cold War Masculinity and the Sentiment of Patriotism in John Okada's *No-No Boy.*" *Criticism* 47, no. 1 (2005): 65–83.

Kingsley, Patrick. "Kos: The Greek Island Where Refugees and Tourists Share the Same Beaches." *Guardian,* September 5, 2015. www.theguardian.com/world/2015/sep/05/refugees-and-holidaymakers-in-kos-patrick-kingsley.

Kivisto, Peter. "What Is the Canonical Theory of Assimilation?" *Journal of the History of the Behavioral Sciences* 40, no. 2 (2004): 149–163.

Kristeva, Julia. *Powers of Horror: An Essay on Abjection.* New York: Columbia University Press, 1982.

Lanard, Noah. "Cuccinelli's Family Tree Suggests His New Immigration Rule Might Have Blocked His Ancestors." *Mother Jones,* August 14, 2019.

www.motherjones.com/politics/2019/08/cuccinellis-family-tree-suggests
-his-new-immigration-rule-might-have-blocked-his-ancestors/.

Latinos Who Lunch. Episode 43: Julio Salgado. October 19, 2017. www.latinoswho
lunch.com/episodes/2017/10/19/julio-salgado.

Ledesma, Alberto. *Diary of a Reluctant Dreamer: Undocumented Vignettes from a Pre-American Life.* Columbus, OH: Mad Creek Books, 2017.

———. "Illustrating My Immigrant Experience." TEDx Ohlone College Newark, May 23, 2018. www.youtube.com/watch?v=B_5pounNiTo.

Lee, David, and Charles Roberts. "The Market at Tlacolula." *Focus on Geography* 47, no. 4 (2004): 29–33.

Lee, Erika. *At America's Gates: Chinese Immigration during the Exclusion Era, 1882–1943.* Chapel Hill: University of North Carolina Press, 2003.

"Lenguas indígenas en México y hablantes (de 3 años y más) al 2015." http://cuentame.inegi.org.mx/hipertexto/todas_lenguas.htm.

Lewis, Oscar. "The Culture of Poverty." *Scientific American* 215, no. 4 (1966): 19–25.

———. *Five Families: Mexican Case Studies in the Culture of Poverty.* New York: Basic Books, 1959.

———. *La Vida: A Puerto Rican Family in the Culture of Poverty—San Juan and New York.* New York: Random House, 1965.

Limerick, Patty. "The Myth of the Vanishing Indian." *Denver Post*, October 16, 2015. www.denverpost.com/2015/10/16/limerick-the-myth-of-the-vanishing
-indian/.

Lindsey, Donald F. *Indians at Hampton Institute, 1877–1923.* Urbana: University of Illinois Press, 1995.

Ling, Jinqi. "Race, Power, and Cultural Politics in John Okada's *No-No Boy.*" *American Literature* 67, no. 2 (1995): 359–381.

Lipsitz, George. *The Possessive Investment in Whiteness: How White People Profit from Identity Politics.* Philadelphia: Temple University Press, 1998.

Liptak, Adam. "Supreme Court Allows Trump's Wealth Test for Green Cards." *New York Times,* January 27, 2020. www.nytimes.com/2020/01/27/us
/supreme-court-trump-green-cards.html.

Lomawaima, K. Tsianina, and T. Tsianina Lomawaima. "Estelle Reel, Superintendent of Indian Schools, 1898-1910: Politics, Curriculum, and Land." *Journal of American Indian Education* 35, no. 3 (1996): 5–31.

Lopez, Mark Hugo, and Ana Gonzalez-Barrera. "If They Could, How Many Unauthorized Immigrants Would Become U.S. Citizens?" Pew Research Center Fact-tank, June 27, 2013. www.pewresearch.org/fact-tank/2013/06/27/if-they
-could-how-many-unauthorized-immigrants-would-become-u-s-citizens/.

Lopez, Mark Hugo, Ana Gonzalez-Barrera, and Gustavo López. "Hispanic Identity Fades across Generations as Immigrant Connections Fall Away." Pew Research Center, December 20, 2017. www.pewhispanic.org/2017/12/20 /hispanic-identity-fades-across-generations-as-immigrant-connections -fall-away/.

Los Angeles Public Library. "Painted Decoration: Goodhue Building." n.d. www.lapl.org/branches/central-library/art-architecture/painting.

———. "Visualizing Language: Oaxaca in L.A." n.d. www.lapl.org/whats-on /exhibits/oaxaca.

Ludlow, Helen. *Ten Years' Work for Indians at the Hampton Normal and Agricultural Institute at Hampton, Virginia, 1878-1888.* Hampton, VA: Hampton Normal and Agricultural Institute, 1888.

Ludlow, Helen W. "Hampton's Indian Students at Home." In *Hampton Institute, 1868 to 1885: Its Work for Two Races,* edited by M. F. Armstrong, Helen W. Ludlow, and Elaine Goodale, 15–19. Hampton, VA: Normal School Press Print, 1885.

Luibhéid, Eithne. "Sexuality, Migration, and the Shifting Line between Legal and Illegal Status." *GLQ* 14, nos. 2–3 (2008): 289–315.

Lukens, Patrick D. *A Quiet Victory for Latino Rights: FDR and the Controversy over "Whiteness."* Tucson: University of Arizona Press, 2012.

Lund, John M. "Boundaries of Restriction: The Dillingham Commission." *University of Vermont History Review* 6 (1994). www.uvm.edu/~hag/histreview /vol6/lund.html.

Lyman, Stanford M. "Robert E. Park Reconsidered: The Early Writings." *American Sociologist* 21, no. 4 (1990): 342–351.

Malloy, Robert. "'Cast Down Your Bucket Where You Are': Black Americans on Immigration." Center for Immigration Studies. June 1, 1996. https://cis .org/Report/Cast-Down-Your-Bucket-Where-You-Are-Black-Americans -Immigration?&utm_source=email&utm_medium=social-media&utm _campaign=addtoany.

Martinez, Larissa. "America Can Be Great Again without the Construction of a Wall Built on Hatred and Prejudice, McKinney-Boyd High School—2016." June 8, 2016. https://speakola.com/grad/larissa-martinez -mckinney-boyd-high-2016.

Marx, Karl, and Frederick Engels. *Manifesto of the Communist Party.* February 1848. www.marxists.org/archive/marx/works/download/pdf/Manifesto.pdf.

Mauro, Hayes Peter. *The Art of Americanization at the Carlisle Indian School.* Albuquerque: University of New Mexico Press, 2011.

Mayo-Smith, Richmond. "Assimilation of Nationalities in the United States, I." *Political Science Quarterly* 9, no. 3 (1894): 426–444.

Mazza, Ed. "Laura Ingraham Targets Even Legal Immigrants in Off-the-Rails Rant." *Huffpost*, August 9, 2018. www.huffingtonpost.com/entry/laura-ingraham-immigration-rant_us_5b6bbfd7e4b0bddo620646fa.

McCall, Leslie. "The Complexity of Intersectionality." *Signs* 30, no. 3 (2005): 1771–1800.

McClain, Charles J. "Tortuous Path, Elusive Goal: The Asian Quest for American Citizenship." *Asian Law Journal* 2, no. 3 (1995): 33–60.

McDonnell, Janet A. *The Dispossession of the American Indian, 1887–1934.* Bloomington: Indiana University Press, 1991.

McNeill, William. *Polyethnicity and National Unity in World History.* Toronto: University of Toronto, 1986.

McWilliams, Carey. *Southern California Country: An Island on the Land.* New York: Duell, Sloane & Pearce, 1946.

Menjívar, Cecilia. "Liminal Legality: Salvadoran and Guatemalan Immigrants' Lives in the United States." *American Journal of Sociology* 111, no. 4 (2006): 999–1037.

Mezzadra, Sandro, Brett Neilson, Lisa Riedner, Stephan Scheel, Glenda Garelli, Martina Tazzioli, and Federico Rahola. "Differential Inclusion/Exclusion." In "New Keywords: Migration and Borders," edited by Nicholas De Genova, Sandro Mezzadra, and John Pickles. Special issue, *Cultural Studies* 29, no. 1 (2015): 25–26.

Mieder, Wolfgang. "'The Only Good Indian Is a Dead Indian': History and Meaning of a Proverbial Stereotype." *Journal of American Folklore* 106, no. 419 (1993): 38–60.

Mignolo, Walter. *The Darker Side of Western Modernity: Global Futures, Decolonial Options.* Durham, NC: Duke University Press, 2011.

Mink, Gwendolyn. *The Wages of Motherhood: Inequality in the Welfare State, 1917–1942.* Ithaca, NY: Cornell University Press, 1995.

Mlk best. "Immigrant from South Korea Interrupt [*sic*] Obama's Speech." Published December 20, 2013. www.youtube.com/watch?v=YBw4Su5XCm8.

Molina, Natalia. "Examining Chicana/o History through a Relational Lens." *Pacific Historical Review* 82, no. 4 (2013): 520–541.

———. "'In a Race All Their Own': The Quest to Make Mexicans Ineligible for U.S. Citizenship." *Pacific Historical Review* 79, no. 2 (2010): 167–201.

————. "The Power of Racial Scripts: What the History of Mexican Immigration to the United States Teaches Us about Relational Notions of Race." *Latino Studies* 8, no. 2 (2010): 156–175.

Montellaro, Zach. "Latinos for Trump Founder Warns of 'Taco Trucks on Every Corner.'" *Politico*, September 1, 2016. www.politico.com/story/2016/09/latinos-for-trump-founder-taco-trucks-marco-gutierrez-227667.

Moreton-Robinson, Aileen. "I Still Call Australia Home: Indigenous Belonging and Place in a White Postcolonizing Society." In *Uprootings/Regroundings: Questions of Home and Migration*, edited by Sara Ahmed, Claudia Castañeda, Anne-Marie Fortier, and Mimi Sheller, 23–40. Oxford: Berg, 2003.

Morris, Aldon. *The Scholar Denied: W.E.B. Du Bois and the Birth of Modern Sociology*. Berkeley: University of California Press, 2015.

Morrison, Toni. "On the Backs of Blacks," *Time* 142, no. 21 (December 2, 1993): 57.

Moynihan, Daniel Patrick. "The Negro Family: The Case for National Action." Office of Planning and Research, United States Department of Labor. March 1965. https://web.stanford.edu/~mrosenfe/Moynihan's%20The%20Negro%20Family.pdf.

Mullen, Harryette. "Optic White: Blackness and the Production of Whiteness." *Diacritics* 24, nos. 2/3 (1994): 71–89.

Muñoz, José Esteban. *Cruising Utopia: The Then and There of Queer Futurity*. New York: New York University Press, 2009.

Nail, Thomas. *The Figure of the Migrant*. Stanford, CA: Stanford University Press, 2015.

Nájera, Lourdes Gutiérrez, M. Bianet Castellanos, and Arturo J. Aldama. "Introduction: Hemispheric *Encuentros* and Re-memberings." In *Comparative Indigeneities of the Américas: Toward a Hemispheric Approach*, edited by M. Bianet Castellanos, Lourdes Gutiérrez Nájera, and Arturo J. Aldama, 1–19. Tucson: University of Arizona Press, 2012.

Nájera, Lourdes Gutiérrez, and Korinta Maldonado. "Transnational Settler Colonial Formations and Global Capital: A Consideration of Indigenous Mexican Migrants." *American Quarterly* 69, no. 4 (2017): 809–821.

Napolitano, Regina. "Julio Salgado's 'Queer Butterfly' Featured in CAC's Art Series." *Daily Bruin*, January 8, 2014. https://dailybruin.com/2014/01/08/julio-salgados-queer-butterfly-featured-in-cacs-art-series/.

Navarro, José-Manuel. *Creating Tropical Yankees: Social Science Textbooks and Ideological Control in Puerto Rico, 1898–1908*. New York: Routledge, 2002.

Navarro-Rivera, Pablo. "Acculturation under Duress: The Puerto Rican Experience at the Carlisle Indian Industrial School, 1898–1918." *Centro Journal* XVIII, no. 1 (2006): 222–259.

———. "The Imperial Enterprise and Educational Policies in Colonial Puerto Rico." In *Colonial Crucible: Empire in the Making of the Modern American State*, edited by Alfred W. McCoy and Francisco A. Scarano, 163–174. Madison: University of Wisconsin Press, 2009.

Navi. "Undocuqueer Artist Julio Salgado on Creating to Counter Crisis." Into, January 17, 2018. www.intomore.com/culture/undocuqueer-artist -julio-salgado-on-creating-to-counter-crisis/5e5563fb49f74a5e.

Nayeri, Dina. *The Ungrateful Refugee: What Immigrants Never Tell You*. New York: Catapult, 2019.

NBC Bay Area. "President Obama Talks Immigration, Fundraises in San Francisco, Los Angeles." November 25, 2013. www.nbcbayarea.com/news/local /President-Obama-to-Talk-Immigration-Fundraise-in-San-Francisco-Los -Angeles-233329131.html.

NBC News. "One Year Later, Obama's Immigration Heckler Feels Vindicated." www.nbcnews.com/news/asian-america/one-year-later-obamas -immigration-heckler-feels-vindicated-n258951.

Neiwert, David. "When White Nationalists Chant Weird Slogans, What Do They Mean?" Southern Poverty Law Center Hatewatch, October 10, 2017. www.splcenter.org/hatewatch/2017/10/10/when-white-nationalists-chant -their-weird-slogans-what-do-they-mean.

Nelson, Alondra. "Introduction: Future Texts." *Social Text* 20, no. 2 (2002): 1–15.

New York Times. "The Rush at Castle Garden." May 15, 1880, 4. www.nytimes .com/1880/05/15/archives/the-rush-at-castle-garden.html.

New York Times. "U.S. Immigration Commission Back." September 7, 1907, 11.

Ngai, Mae M. "Birthright Citizenship and the Alien Citizen." *Fordham Law Review* 75, no. 5 (2007): 2521–2530.

———. *Impossible Subjects: Illegal Aliens and the Making of Modern America*. Princeton, NJ: Princeton University Press, 2005.

———. "'An Ironic Testimony to the Value of American Democracy': Assimilationism and the World War II Internment of Japanese Americans." In *Contested Democracy: Freedom, Race, and Power in American History*, edited by Manisha Sinha and Penny Von Eschen, 237–257. New York: Columbia University Press, 2007.

Nguyen, Viet Thanh. *Race and Resistance: Literature and Politics in Asian America*. New York: Oxford University Press, 2002.

Nicholls, Walter J. *The DREAMers: How the Undocumented Youth Movement Transformed the Immigrant Rights Debate.* Stanford, CA: Stanford University Press, 2013.

Nicholls, Walter J., and Tara Fiorito. "Dreamers Unbound: Immigrant Youth Mobilizing." *New Labor Forum* 21, no. 1 (2014): 86–92.

Novoa, Mónica. "Julio Salgado: Creating Undocu-Love and Undocu-Queer Art." *Colorlines*, March 15, 2012. www.colorlines.com/content/julio-salgado -creating-undocu-love-and-undocu-queer-art.

O'Brien, Matt. "San Francisco Shout Helped Set the Stage for Obama Immigration Action." *San Jose Mercury News*, November 20, 2014. www .mercurynews.com/2014/11/20/san-francisco-shout-helped-set-stage-for -obama-immigration-action-2/.

———. "SF State Student Who Shouted at Obama Has History of Gutsy Protests." *San Jose Mercury News*, November 25, 2013. www.mercurynews.com /2013/11/25/s-f-state-student-who-shouted-at-obama-has-history-of-gutsy -protests/.

O'Connor, Alice. *Poverty Knowledge: Social Science, Social Policy, and the Poor in Twentieth-Century U.S. History.* Princeton, NJ: Princeton University Press, 2001.

Oh, Anna, dir. *Halmoni.* [2017]. https://vimeo.com/213793631.

Okada, John. *No-No Boy.* Seattle: University of Washington Press, 1976.

Okihiro, Gary Y., and David Drummond. "The Concentration Camps and Japanese Economic Losses in California Agriculture, 1900–1942." In *Japanese Americans: From Relocation to Redress*, edited by Roger Daniels, Sandra C. Taylor, and Harry H. L. Kitano, 168–75. Seattle: University of Washington Press, 1991.

Omi, Michael, and Howard Winant. *Racial Formation in the United States, Third Edition.* New York: Routledge, 2014.

Ong, Aihwa. "Cultural Citizenship as Subject-Making: Immigrants Negotiate Racial and Cultural Boundaries in the United States." *Current Anthropology* 37, no. 5 (1996): 737–762.

Organized Communities against Deportations. "National Come Out of the Shadows Day!" February 17, 2010. http://organizedcommunities.org /national-coming-out-of-the-shadows-day/.

Osajima, Keith. "Asian Americans as the Model Minority: An Analysis of the Popular Press Image in the 1960s and 1980s." In *A Companion to Asian American Studies*, edited by Kent A. Ono, 215–25. Malden, MA: Blackwell Publishing, 2005.

Osuna, Juan José. "An Indian in Spite of Myself." *Summer School Review* 10, no. 5 (1932): 2–4.

Paret, Marcel. "Precarious Class Formations in the United States and South Africa." *International Labor and Working-Class History* 89 (2016): 84–106.

Park, Lisa Sun-Hee. "Assimilation." In *Keywords for Asian American Studies*, edited by Cathy J. Schlund-Vials, K. Scott Wong, and Linda Trinh Vo, 14–17. New York: New York University Press, 2015.

———. "Continuing Significance of the Model Minority Myth: The Second Generation," *Social Justice* 35, no. 2 (2008): 134–144.

Park, Robert E. "Assimilation, Social." In *Encyclopaedia of the Social Sciences*, vol. 2, edited by Edwin R. A. Seligman, 281–283. New York: Macmillan Company, 1930.

———. "Racial Assimilation in Secondary Groups with Particular Reference to the Negro." *American Journal of Sociology* 19, no. 5 (1914): 606–623.

Park, Robert E., and Ernest W. Burgess. *Introduction to the Science of Sociology*. Chicago: University of Chicago Press, 1924.

Park, Robert Ezra. "An Autobiographical Note." In *Race and Culture: The Collected Papers of Robert Ezra Park*, vol. 1, edited by Everett Cherrington Hughes et al., v–ix. Glencoe, IL: Free Press, 1950.

———. "Politics and 'The Man Farthest Down.'" In *The Collected Papers of Robert Ezra Park*, Volumes 1, 2 and 3 edited by Everett Cherington Hughes et al., 166–176. New York: Arno Press, 1974.

———. *Race and Culture.* New York: Free Press, 1950.

Petersen, William. "Success Story: Japanese-American Style." *New York Times Magazine*, January 9, 1966, 20–21, 33, 36, 38, 40–41, 43.

Pilkington, Ed. "Black Americans Dying of Covid-19 at Three Times the Rate of White People." *Guardian*, May 20, 2020. www.theguardian.com/world /2020/may/20/black-americans-death-rate-covid-19-coronavirus.

Politico. "2016 Texas Presidential Election Results." www.politico.com/2016 -election/results/map/president/texas/.

Portes, Alejandro, and Joseph Böröcz. "Contemporary Immigration: Theoretical Perspectives on Its Determinants and Modes of Incorporation." *International Migration Review* 23, no. 3 (1989): 606–630.

Portes, Alejandro, and Rubén G. Rumbaut. *Immigrant America: A Portrait.* Berkeley: University of California Press, 1990.

———. *Legacies: The Story of the Immigrant Second Generation.* Berkeley: University of California Press; New York: Russell Sage Foundation, 2001.

Portes, Alejandro, and Min Zhou. "The New Second Generation: Segmented Assimilation and Its Variants." *Annals of the American Academy of Political and Social Science* 530, no. 1 (1993): 74–96.

Potter, David M. *The People of Plenty: Economic Abundance and the American Character.* Chicago: University of Chicago Press, 1954.

Pratt, Richard Henry. "The Advantages of Mingling Indians with Whites." In *Americanizing the American Indians: Writings by the "Friends of the Indian," 1880–1900,* edited by Francis Paul Prucha, 260–271. Cambridge, MA: Harvard University Press, 1973.

———. *Battlefield and Classroom: Four Decades with the American Indian, 1867–1904.* New Haven, CT: Yale University Press, 1964.

Prucha, Francis Paul. *American Indian Policy in the Formative Years: The Indian Trade and Intercourse Acts, 1790–1834.* Cambridge, MA: Harvard University Press, 1962.

———, ed. *Americanizing the American Indians: Writings by the "Friends of the Indian," 1880–1900.* Cambridge, MA: Harvard University Press, 1973.

———, ed. *Documents of United States Indian Policy (Third Edition).* Lincoln: University of Nebraska Press, 2000.

Quadango, Jill. *The Color of Welfare: How Racism Undermined the War on Poverty.* New York: Oxford University Press, 1994.

Rahulb. "Interview Highlights: Dreamers Adrift and the 'I Exist' Collection." MIT Center for Civic Media, April 8, 2012. https://civic.mit.edu/2012/4/8/interview-highlights-dreamers-adrift-and-the-i-exist-collection/.

Ramirez, Renya. *Native Hubs: Culture, Community, and Belonging in Silicon Valley and Beyond.* Durham, NC: Duke University Press, 2007.

Rasmussen, Cecilia. "Shaman and Freedom-Fighter Led Indians' Mission Revolt." *Los Angeles Times,* June 10, 2001. http://articles.latimes.com/2001/jun/10/local/me-8853.

Ratner, Sidney. "Horace M. Kallen and Cultural Pluralism." *Modern Judaism* 4, no. 2 (1984): 185–200.

Raushenbush, Winifred. *Robert E. Park: Biography of a Sociologist.* Durham, NC: Duke University Press, 1979.

Ravani, Sarah, and Trisha Thadani. "For Immigrant Trump Voter, Tensions Reach Boiling Point at Home." *San Francisco Chronicle,* March 26, 2017. www.sfchronicle.com/bayarea/article/For-immigrant-Trump-voters-tensions-reach-11029064.php.

Richman, Josh. "Obama's Immigration Speech in Deep-Blue San Francisco Interrupted by Anti-deportation Hecklers." *San Jose Mercury News,* November

25, 2013. www.mercurynews.com/2013/11/25/obamas-immigration-speech-in
-deep-blue-san-francisco-interrupted-by-anti-deportation-hecklers/.

Rivera, Luis Muñoz. "Una visita a Indian School." *Puerto Rico Herald* September 14, 1901, n.p.

Rivera de Tudó, Angela. *Idioms and Other Expressions in English and Spanish, and Their Use with a University Supplement, and about 500 Proverbs in English and Spanish, and a List of Homophonous Words.* San Juan, PR: Casa Baldrich, 1940.

Roediger, David R. *The Wages of Whiteness: Race and the Making of the American Working Class.* London: Verso, 1999.

———. *Working toward Whiteness: How America's Immigrants Became White.* New York: Basic Books, 2005.

Rogin, Michael Paul. *Blackface, White Noise: Jewish Immigrants in the Hollywood Melting Pot.* Berkeley: University of California Press, 1996.

Roosevelt, Theodore. "Address before the National Congress of Mothers, Washington, D.C., March 13, 1905." In *Presidential Addresses and State Papers of Theodore Roosevelt,* 3:282–291. New York: Kauss Reprint, 1970.

Rosa, Sonia Migdalia. "Puerto Ricans at Carlisle Indian School." In *The Praeger Handbook of Latino Education in the U.S.,* vol. 2, edited by Lourdes Diaz Soto, 387–88. Westport, CT: Praeger, 2007.

Rumbaut, Ruben G. "Assimilation of Immigrants." In *International Encyclopedia of the Social and Behavioral Sciences,* vol. 2, edited by Neil J. Smelser and Paul B. Baltes, 81–87. New York: Elsevier, 2001.

Rumbaut, Rubén G., and Alejandro Portes. *Ethnicities: Children of Immigrants in America.* Berkeley: University of California Press; New York: Russell Sage Foundation, 2001.

Rupert, Evelyn. "Clinton: A Taco Truck on Every Corner Sounds Delicious." The Hill, September 15, 2016. https://thehill.com/blogs/blog-briefing-room /news/296251-clinton-a-taco-truck-on-every-corner-sounds-delicious.

Rural New-Yorker. Advertisement, 57 (November 5, 1898), 761. https://books .google.com/books?id=YqBIAQAAMAAJ&lpg=PA761&ots=RxVFp MoaTD&dq=J.%20Fenimore%20Cooper%20Dr%20Pierce%20Golden %20Medical%20discovery&pg=PA760#v=onepage&q=J.%20Fenimore %20Cooper%20Dr%20Pierce%20Golden%20Medical%20discovery&f= false.

Sakuma, Amanda. "Undocumented Immigrants Tell Trump They Are #Here-ToStay." NBC News, November 9, 2016. www.nbcnews.com/storyline/2016 -election-day/undocumented-immigrants-tell-trump-they-re-heretostay -n681206.

Saldaña-Portillo, María Josefina. "Critical Latinx Indigeneities: A Paradigm Drift." *Latino Studies* 15, no. 2 (2017): 138–155.

Salgado, Julio. "Emory Douglas on SB1070." CultureStrike, July 19, 2012. http:// archive.culturestrike.org/emory-douglas-on-sb1070/.

———. "I Am Undocuqueer." n.d. http://juliosalgadoart.com/post/15803758188 /i-am-undocuqueer-is-an-art-project-in.

———. "Queer, Undocumented and Unafraid." *Huffpost*, October 13, 2011. www.huffingtonpost.com/julio-salgado/queer-undocumented_b_1007869 .html.

Salgado, Julio, and Favianna Rodriguez. "A Conversation with DREAMer Julio Salgado." CultureStrike, August 21, 2012. http://archive.culturestrike .org/julio-salgado-and-favianna-rodriguez-at-la-pena/.

Sánchez, Erika L. "The UndocuQueer Movement Rises to Push for a Dream Act." NBC Latino, November 2, 2012. http://nbclatino.com/2012/11/02/the -undocuqueer-movement-rises-to-push-for-a-dream-act/#s:quip-7.

Sanders, Sam. "#Meme of the Week: Taco Trucks on Every Corner." NPR, September 2, 2016. www.npr.org/2016/09/02/492390405/-memeoftheweek -taco-trucks-on-every-corner.

Sato, Gayle K. Fujita. "Momotaro's Exile: John Okada's *No-No Boy*." In *Reading the Literatures of Asian America*, edited by Shirley Geok-lin Lim and Amy Ling, 239–258. Philadelphia: Temple University Press, 1992.

Schreiber, Rebecca. *The Undocumented Everyday: Migrant Lives and the Politics of Visibility*. Minneapolis: University of Minnesota Press, 2018.

Schuyler, George S. *Black No More: Being an Account of the Strange and Wonderful Workings of Science in the Land of the Free, A.D. 1933–1940*. Boston: Northeastern University Press, 1989.

Schwartz, Ian. "Jeff Sessions: 'What Good Does It Do to Bring in Somebody Who Is Illiterate in Their Own Country?'" www.realclearpolitics.com /video/2018/01/16/jeff_sessions_what_good_does_it_do_to_bring_in _somebody_who_is_illiterate_in_their_own_country.html.

Scott, Eugene. "Trump's Most Insulting—and Violent—Language Is Often Reserved for Immigrants." *Washington Post*, October 2, 2019. www.washington post.com/politics/2019/10/02/trumps-most-insulting-violent-language-is -often-reserved-immigrants/.

Seif, Hinda. "'Layers of Humanity': Interview with Undocuqueer Artivist Julio Salgado." *Latino Studies* 12, no. 2 (2014): 300–309.

Shah, Nayan, *Contagious Divides: Epidemics and Race in San Francisco's Chinatown*. Berkeley: University of California Press, 2001.

Shapiro, Rebecca. "Tom Brokaw: 'Hispanics Should Work Harder at Assimilation.'" *Huffpost*, January 27, 2019. www.huffingtonpost.com/entry/tom-brokaw -hispanics-should-work-harder-at-assimilation_us_5c4e2ed3e4b0287e5 b8bd250.

Sheller, Mimi, and John Urry. "The New Mobilities Paradigm." *Environment and Planning* 38 (2006): 207–226.

Shibutani, Tamotsu, and Kian M. Kwan. *Ethnic Stratification: A Comparative Approach.* New York: Macmillan, 1965.

Shiller, Robert J. "The Transformation of the 'American Dream.'" *New York Times*, August 4, 2017. www.nytimes.com/2017/08/04/upshot/the-transformation-of -the-american-dream.html.

Shook, David, ed. *Visualizando el lenguaje: Oaxaca en L.A./Visualizing Language: Oaxaca in L.A.* Los Angeles: Library Foundation of Los Angeles and Phoneme Media, 2017.

Simons, Sarah E. "Social Assimilation, I." *American Journal of Sociology* 6, no. 6 (May 1901): 790–822.

"Sold, Damaged, Stolen, Gone: Japanese American Property Loss during World War II." *Densho Blog*, April 4, 2017. https://densho.org/sold-damaged -stolen-gone-japanese-american-property-loss-wwii/.

Southern Poverty Law Center, Center for Immigration Studies. n.d. www.spl center.org/fighting-hate/extremist-files/group/center-immigration-studies.

Standing, Guy. *The Precariat: The New Dangerous Class.* London: Bloomsbury Academic, 2011.

———. *A Precariat Charter: From Denizens to Citizens.* London: Bloomsbury Academic, 2014.

Steinman, Louise, and Maureen Moore. "Telling Another Story: A Conversation between Louise Steinman and Maureen Moore." In *Visualizando el lenguaje: Oaxaca en L.A./Visualizing Language; Oaxaca in L.A.*, edited by David Shook, 71–75. Los Angeles: Library Foundation of Los Angeles and Phoneme Media, 2017.

Stephen, Lynn. *Transborder Lives: Indigenous Oaxacans in Mexico, California, and Oregon.* Durham, NC: Duke University Press, 2007.

Stepick, Alex. *Pride against Prejudice: Haitians in the United States.* Boston: Allyn and Bacon, 1998.

Streib, Jessi, Saunjuhi Verma, Whitney Welsh, and Linda M. Burton. "Life, Death, and Resurrections: The Culture of Poverty Perspective." In *The Oxford Handbook of the Social Science of Poverty*, edited by David Brady and Linda M. Burton, 247–269. New York: Oxford University Press, 2016.

Stribley, Robert. "The Way We Speak about Unauthorized Immigrants Matters." *Huffpost*, October 19, 2016. www.huffingtonpost.com/entry/the-language-of-illegal-immigration_us_58076b62e4b00483d3b5cdba.

Strochlic, Nina. "'We're Hurting, We're Hurting'—Grief and Outrage Converge in Minneapolis." *National Geographic*, May 30, 2020. www.national geographic.com/photography/2020/05/were-hurting-were-hurting-grief-and-outrage-converge-in-minneapolis/#close.

Suárez-Orozco, Carola, Hirokazu Yoshikawa, Robert T. Teranishi, and Marcelo M. Suárez-Orozco. "Growing Up in the Shadows: The Developmental Implications of Unauthorized Status." *Harvard Educational Review* 81, no. 3 (2011): 438–472.

Sumida, Stephen H. "Japanese American Moral Dilemmas in John Okada's *No-No Boy* and Milton Murayama's *All I Asking for Is My Body*." In *Frontiers of Asian American Studies: Writing, Research, and Commentary*, edited by Gail M. Nomura, Russell Endo, Stephen H. Sumida, and Russell C. Leong, 222–233. Pullman: Washington State University Press, 1989.

Takaki, Ronald T. *Strangers from a Different Shore: A History of Asian Americans*. Boston: Little, Brown, 1989.

Talbot, Edith Armstrong. *Samuel Chapman Armstrong: A Biographical Study*. New York: Negro Universities Press, 1969.

Taxin, Amy. "U.S. Launches Bid to Find Citizenship Cheaters." Associated Press, June 11, 2018. https://apnews.com/1da389a535684a5f9d0da74081c242f3.

Taylor, Sandra C. "Evacuation and Economic Loss: Questions and Perspectives." In *Japanese Americans: From Relocation to Redress*, edited by Roger Daniels, Sandra C. Taylor, and Harry H. L. Kitano, 163–67. Seattle: University of Washington Press, 1991.

Telles, Edward, and Vilma Ortiz. *Generations of Exclusion: Mexican Americans, Assimilation, and Race*. New York: Russell Sage Foundation, 2008.

Thomas, Isaac, and Florian Znaniecki. *The Polish Peasant in Europe and America: Monograph of an Immigrant Group*. Chicago: University of Chicago Press, 1919.

Totten, Gary. "Southernizing Travel in the Black Atlantic: Booker T. Washington's 'The Man Farthest Down.'" *MELUS* 32, no. 2 (2007): 107–131.

Transcript of Chinese Exclusion Act (1882). www.ourdocuments.gov/doc.php ?flash=false&doc=47&page=transcript.

Transcript of the Burke Act (1906). https://public.csusm.edu/nadp/a1906.htm.

Transcript of the Dawes Act (1887). www.ourdocuments.gov/print_friendly .php?flash=false&page=transcript&doc=50&title=Transcript+of+Dawes +Act+%281887%29.

Transcript of the Indian Citizenship Act of 1924, http://legisworks.org /congress/68/publaw-175.pdf.

Trask, Haunani-Kay. "Settlers of Color and 'Immigrant' Hegemony: 'Locals' in Hawai'i." In *Asian Settler Colonialism: From Local Governance to the Habits of Everyday Life in Hawai'i*, edited by Jonathan Y. Okamura and Candace Fujikane, 45–65. Honolulu: University of Hawaii Press, 2008.

Treglia, Gabriella. "Using Citizenship to Retain Identity: The Native American Dance Bans of the Later Assimilation Era, 1900–1930." *Journal of American Studies* 47, no. 3 (2012): 777–800.

Tudó, Angela Rivera. "Los 'Indios' de Puerto Rico." *La Correspondencia de Puerto Rico*, January 3, 1931, 4.

Türken, Salman, Hilde Eileen Nafstad, Rolv Mikkel Blakar, and Katrina Roen. "Making Sense of Neoliberal Subjectivity: A Discourse Analysis of Media Language on Self-Development." *Globalizations* 13, no. 1 (2016): 32–46.

Turner, Frederick Jackson. *The Frontier in American History*. New York: Henry Holt, 1921.

Tyler, Imogen, and Katarzyna Marciniak. "Immigrant Protest: An Introduction." *Citizenship Studies* 17, no. 2 (2013): 143–156.

UC Berkeley Newscenter. "Ju Hong, UC Berkeley Undocumented Student." Published December 10, 2012. www.youtube.com/watch?v=UktXJIeBıtg.

UN High Commissioner for Human Rights. "International Convention on the Protection of the Rights of All Migrant Workers and Members of Their Families." December 18, 1990. www.ohchr.org/en/professionalinterest/pages /cmw.aspx.

United Nations. "Universal Declaration of Human Rights, Article 13." [December 10, 1948]. www.un.org/en/universal-declaration-human-rights/.

United Nations High Commissioner for Refugees. "Master Glossary of Terms." June 2006. www.refworld.org/docid/42ce7d444.html.

———. "What Is a Refugee?" n.d. www.unrefugees.org/refugee-facts/what-is -a-refugee/.

US Citizenship and Immigration Services. I-821, "Application for Temporary Protected Status." www.uscis.gov/i-821.

———. I-821D, "Consideration of Deferred Action for Childhood Arrivals." www.uscis.gov/i-821d.

———. "Nonimmigrant." n.d. www.uscis.gov/tools/glossary/nonimmigrant.

———. "Public Charge." n.d. www.uscis.gov/greencard/public-charge.

———. "Public Charge Fact Sheet." n.d. www.uscis.gov/news/fact-sheets /public-charge-fact-sheet.

———. "Temporary Protected Status Designated Country: El Salvador." n.d. www.uscis.gov/humanitarian/temporary-protected-status/temporary-protected-status-designated-country-el-salvador.

———. "Temporary Protected Status Designated Country: Haiti." n.d. www.uscis.gov/humanitarian/temporary-protected-status/temporary-protected-status-designated-country-haiti.

———. "Temporary Protected Status Designated Country: Nicaragua." n.d. www.uscis.gov/humanitarian/temporary-protected-status/temporary-protected-status-designated-country-nicaragua.

US Department of Homeland Security. "Memorandum on Identification of Essential Critical Infrastructure Workers During COVID-19 Response." March 19, 2020. www.cisa.gov/sites/default/files/publications/CISA-Guidance-on-Essential-Critical-Infrastructure-Workers-1-20-508c.pdf.

US Department of Justice. "Attorney General Jeff Sessions Issues Statement on DACA." September 5, 2017. www.justice.gov/opa/speech/attorney-general-sessions-delivers-remarks-daca.

US Department of State. Bureau of Consular Affairs. "Directory of Visa Categories." n.d. https://travel.state.gov/content/travel/en/us-visas/visa-information-resources/all-visa-categories.html.

US News & World Report. "Success Story of One Minority in the U.S." December 26, 1966, 73–78.

Vankin, Deborah. "Oaxacalifornia Dreaming: L.A. Library Mural Project Looks at a Visual Language That Transcends Borders." *Los Angeles Times*, September 20, 2017. www.latimes.com/entertainment/arts/la-ca-cm-oaxacan-murals-central-library-20170920-htmlstory.html.

———. "Oaxacan Muralists' L.A. Works Give Voice to Indigenous Peoples—But the Artists Cannot Travel to the U.S. to View Them." *Los Angeles Times*, August 29, 2018. www.latimes.com/entertainment/arts/la-et-cm-tlacolulokos-visa-revoked-20180829-story.html.

Vargas, Alicia. "The Voice of Indigenous Resistance in Oaxaca." *Telesur*, September 17, 2017. www.telesurtv.net/english/opinion/The-Voice-of-Indigenous-Resistance-in-Oaxacalifornia-20170914-0023.html.

Vargas, Jose Antonio. *Dear America: Notes of an Undocumented Citizen*. New York: Dey Street Books, 2018.

———, dir. *Documented: A Film by an Undocumented American*. New York: Apo Anak Productions, 2013.

————. "Not Legal, Not Leaving," *Time* 179, no. 25 (June 25, 2012): 34–44.

Villarrubia-Mendoza, Jacqueline, and Roberto Vélez-Vélez. "Iconoclastic Dreams: Interpreting Art in the DREAMers Movement." *Sociological Quarterly* 58, no. 3 (2017): 350–372.

Vizenor, Gerald. "Aesthetics of Survivance: Literary Theory and Practice." In *Survivance: Narratives of Native Presence*, edited by Gerald Vizenor, 1–24. Lincoln: University of Nebraska Press, 2008.

Waldinger, Roger. "The Bounded Community: Turning Foreigners into Americans in Twenty-First Century L.A." *Ethnic and Racial Studies* 30, no. 3 (2007): 341–374.

————. "Transforming Foreigners into Americans." In *The New Americans: A Guide to Immigration since 1965*, edited by Mary C. Waters and Reed Ueda, 137–148. Cambridge, MA: Harvard University Press, 2007.

Walker, Neil. "Denizenship and the Deterritorialization in the EU." *EUI Working Paper LAW*, no. 2008/8 (2008): 1–12.

Warner, W. Lloyd, and Leo Srole. *The Social Systems of American Ethnic Groups.* New Haven, CT: Yale University Press, 1945.

Washington, Booker T., and Robert E. Park. *The Man Farthest Down: A Record of Observation and Study in Europe.* Garden City, NY: Doubleday, Page & Company, 1912.

Waters, Mary C. *Black Identities: West Indian Immigrant Dreams and American Realities.* New York: Russell Sage Foundation, 1999.

————. *Ethnic Options: Choosing Identities in America.* Berkeley: University of California Press, 1990.

Waters, Mary C., and Tomás R. Jiménez. "Assessing Immigrant Assimilation: New Empirical and Theoretical Challenges." *Annual Review of Sociology* 31 (2005): 105–125.

Wattenberg, Ben, and Richard Scammon. *The Real Majority: An Extraordinary Examination of the American Electorate.* New York: Coward-McCann, 1970.

Weglyn, Michi. *Years of Infamy: The Untold Story of America's Concentration Camps.* New York: William Morrow, 1976.

Weill, Kelly. "The Jewish Group Taking on ICE—and the 'Concentration Camp' Taboo." *Daily Beast,* July 13, 2019. www.thedailybeast.com/never-again-action-takes-on-ice-and-the-concentration-camp-taboo?source=email&via=desktop.

Weisell, Kristin. "At Graduation McKinney Boyd Valedictorian Reveals Undocumented Immigrant Status." 11/21 CBS DFW, June 9, 2016. https://

dfw.cbslocal.com/2016/06/09/at-graduation-mckinney-boyd-valedictorian
-reveals-undocumented-immigrant-status/.

Wheeler-Howard Act. June 18, 1934. http://aghca.org/wp-content/uploads
/2012/07/indianreorganizationact.pdf.

White, Melissa Autumn. "Documenting the Undocumented: Toward a Queer
Politics of No Borders." *Sexualities* 17, no. 8 (2014): 976–997.

"White Nationalists Chant 'You Will Not Replace Us.'" BBC News, August 12,
2017. www.bbc.com/news/av/world-asia-40911744/white-us-nationalists
-chant-you-will-not-replace-us.

Wiener, Jon. "'Call Me a Refugee, Not an Immigrant': Viet Thanh Nguyen."
Nation, June 11, 2018. www.thenation.com/article/call-refugee-not
-immigrant-viet-thanh-nguyen/.

Williams, Raymond. *Keywords: A Vocabulary of Culture and Society, Revised Edition.*
New York: Oxford University Press, 1983.

Wilson, William Julius. *The Truly Disadvantaged: The Inner City, the Underclass,
and Public Policy.* Chicago: University of Chicago Press, 1987.

Witmer, Linda F. *The Indian Industrial School, Carlisle, Pennsylvania, 1879–1918.*
Carlisle, PA: Cumberland County Historical Society, 1993.

Wolfe, Patrick. "Land, Labor, and Difference: Elementary Structures of Race."
American Historical Review 106, no. 3 (2001): 866–905.

———. "Settler Colonialism and the Elimination of the Native." *Journal of
Genocide Research* 8, no. 4 (2006): 387–409.

Wong, Jade Snow. *Fifth Chinese Daughter.* New York: Harper & Row, 1950.

Worldometer. COVID-19 Coronavirus Pandemic, May 31, 2020. www
.worldometers.info/coronavirus/.

Wray, Matt. *Not Quite White: White Trash and the Boundaries of Whiteness.* Durham,
NC: Duke University Press, 2006.

Wu, Ellen D. *The Color of Success: Asian Americans and the Origins of the Model
Minority.* Princeton, NJ: Princeton University Press, 2013.

Wu, Frank H. *Yellow: Race in America beyond Black and White.* New York: Basic
Books, 2002.

Wu, Harrick. "'Undocu-Queer' Artist Julio Salgado on Creative Resistance."
KQED Arts, July 5, 2018. www.kqed.org/arts/13836333/undocu-queer-artist
-julio-salgado-on-creative-resistance.

Yamashita, Karen Tei. "John Okada's *No-No Boy* Is a Test of American Character." *Atlantic*, May 21, 2019. www.theatlantic.com/entertainment/archive
/2019/05/karen-tei-yamashita-john-okadas-no-no-boy/588466/.

Yogi, Stan. "'You Had to Be One or the Other': Oppositions and Reconciliation in John Okada's *No-No Boy*." *MELUS* 21, no. 2 (1996): 63–77.

Zeidler, Jeanne. Foreword. *To Lead and to Serve: American Indian Education at Hampton Institute, 1878–1923*, edited by Mary Lou Hultgren and Paulette Fairbanks Molin, 6–7. Virginia Beach: Virginia Foundation for the Humanities and Public Policy, 1989.

Zéphir, Flore. *Haitian Immigrants in Black America: A Sociological and Sociolinguistic Portrait*. Westport, CT: Bergin & Garvey, 1996.

Zhou, Min. "Segmented Assimilation: Issues, Controversies, and Recent Research on the New Second Generation." *International Migration Review* 31, no. 4 (1997): 975–1008.

Zolberg, Aristide R., and Long Litt Woon. "Why Islam Is Like Spanish: Cultural Incorporation in Europe and the United States." *Politics & Society* 27, no. 5 (1999): 5–38.

INDEX

acculturation, 5, 11, 41, 58, 144
A donde quiera que vayas/Wherever You May Go (Tlacolulokos), 136–38, 137fig.
Affluent Society, The (Galbraith), 87
African Americans, 3–4, 8, 9, 13, 14, 89; co-education of with Native Americans at Hampton Normal and Agricultural Institute, 42–44; contrasted with Japanese Americans, 92; as denizens, 24, 59, 72–73; exclusion of from theories of assimilation, 58–59, 154n39; fear of immigrants, 63; isolation of from white communities, 67–68; role of in assimilation, 56–57; schemes to deport African Americans (colonization), 56; vital role of in the understanding of assimilation in the United States, 56–57
Africans, 13
Afrofuturism, 57, 73, 169n17
Aid to Families with Dependent Children, 89
Alba, Richard, 9
allotment and assimilation era, 4, 18, 34, 38

Alvarez, Jorge Garcia, 86
Amaya, Hector, 85
American Colonization Society, 56
American dream, the, 12, 22, 30, 71, 86, 97, 99, 100, 110; definitions of, 84–85
Americanization, 5, 75
Americanness, 12, 24, 59, 75, 76, 83, 91, 99, 100; and material wealth, 84–87, 88, 110–11; as whiteness and a form of property, 72
Anderson, Bridget, 88, 128
Anglo-conformity, 5–6
anti-Semitism, 6
Arce Pagán, Emilio de, 46
Armstrong, Samuel Chapman, 40–41, 51
arrivant, 114
Asian Pacific Americans, 91, 92
Asian Students Promoting Immigrant Rights through Education (ASPIRE), 115, 118, 119–22
Asiatic Barred Zone Act (Literacy and Immigration Act [1917]), 17, 18–19, 55
Assimilation: as acculturation, 5, 11, 41, 58, 144; as Americanization, 5, 75; as Anglo-conformity, 5–6; assimilation theory, 5–11; association of

Immigration Act (1965), 10
Immigration and Nationality Act
(Johnson-Reed Act [1924]), 6, 17, 19,
55, 72
Immigration Reform and Control Act
(IRCA [1986]), 104
imperialism, 114, 144; "new imperial-
ism," 18
Inadmissibility on Public Charge
Grounds (IPCG), 110
incorporation, 5, 15, 24, 31, 53, 59, 73, 143;
mode of, 10, 145
Indian Citizenship Act (Snyder Act
[1924]), 4–5, 51
Indian New Deal, 34, 162n12
"Indian question," the, 49–50
"Indian in Spite of Myself, An"
(Osuna), 47–48
Indigenous Environmental
movement, 53
indigenous migrant, 21, 23, 130, 139
Ingraham, Laura, 55
integration, 5, 7, 11, 17, 62
internment, 13, 78, 80, 82, 85, 90, 95, 96

Japanese Americans, 13, 14, 16, 147; as
the first US model minority, 67, 83;
as internees, 79–84; not-blackness
of, 90–91; property loss of during
the Second World War, 85–86;
success of, 91–92
Jefferson, Thomas, 56, 57, 72
Jim Crow era, 18, 42, 57, 64, 65, 78,
165n49; exclusion of blacks man-
dated by, 51; racial hierarchy
during, 59
Johnson, James Weldon, 70
Johnson, Lyndon B., 67
Johnson-Reed Act. *See* Immigration
and Nationality Act (Johnson-Reed
Act [1924])
Jones-Shafroth Act (1917), 19, 51
Ju Hong Interrupts President Obama
(Ledesma), 187n31
Jung, Moon-Kie, 9–10, 154n39

Kallen, Horace M., 6
Katz, Michael B., 86–87
Kearney, Michael, 190n72
Kristeva, Julia, 15
Ku Klux Klan, 65
kuleana, 139

Lange, Dorothea, 107
Larsen, Nella, 70
Latinos for Trump, 1, 27
Latinxs, 83, 89, 145; and assimilation,
74–75
*La Vida: A Puerto Rican Family in the
Culture of Poverty—San Juan and
New York* (Lewis), 89
Ledesma, Alberto, 84, 100–108, 141,
187n31
Leupp, Francis, 49
Lewis, Oscar, 88, 89
Liang, May, 120
Lipsitz, George, 72

Magnuson Act (Chinese Exclusion
Repeal Act [1943]), 18
M Is For Machine (Ledesma), 105–6, 106*fig.*
"Make America Great Again"
(MAGA), 77–78
Maldonado, Korinta, 139–40
*Man Farthest Down, The: A Record of
Observation and Study in Europe*
(Washington and Park), 57–58,
58–59, 62, 63–68, 75, 77; on the Afri-
can American adoption of Christi-
anity, 64; as an argument against an
anti-black present and a post-black
future, 63–64; criticism of, 66; rosy
appraisal of black life in, 65–66; on
African Americans in the South
and European peasants, 64; on
the threat presented by European
immigrants, 64–65
Márquez, Gabriel García, 127
Martinez, Larissa, 80–81
Martinez, Providencia, 46
Marxism, 9

Mayo-Smith, Richmond, 3
McCarren-Walter Act (1952), 91
McNeill, William, 31
McWilliams, Carey, 134
Medicaid, 110
melting pot, 6, 7
Menjívar, Cecilia, 14
meritocracy, 22, 24, 83, 85, 86, 92, 99,
 100, 107, 114, 147
Mexican-American War (1846–48), 20
Mexican(s), 19, 20, 27–28, 77, 81, 83, 89,
 103, 105, 134, 136, 138, 139, 140, 144; as
 "illegal aliens," 20
migrant: as "the global poor," 114; as an
 ostensibly broad and neutral term,
 114; as "poor, 'unskilled,'" 22
Migrant Mother, Nipomo, California
 (Lange), 107, 109*fig.*
mimesis, 70, 71
minorities: model minorities, 16, 67, 83,
 90–93; racial minorities, 8
mobility, 70, 71
Molina, Natalia, 15, 157–58n67
moral economy of deservingness, 25,
 82, 84, 110, 111
Morrison, Toni, 63
Moynihan, Daniel Patrick, 89–90
Moynihan Report, 89, 90, 91
multiculturalism, 6, 11, 26, 74, 139; logic
 of, 25, 116, 141; proto-multiculturalism, 136
Muñoz, José, Esteban, 116, 141
Muslims, and assimilation, 74–75

National Association for the Advance-
 ment of Colored People (NAACP),
 69, 174n90
Nail, Thomas, 113
Nájera, Lourdes Gutiérrez, 139–40
Native Americans, 3–5, 13, 18, 32, 51;
 allotment and assimilation era
 (1887–1943) of, 34; co-education with
 African Americans at Hampton
 Normal and Agricultural Insti-

tute, 42–44; nineteenth-century
 increase in reservation schools, 38;
 and US citizenship, 4–5; views of
 the assimilation and education of as
 failures, 49–50
Native Son (Wright), 93
nativism, the "new nativism," 18, 159n81
naturalization, 4, 5, 18, 19, 72, 91, 94;
 racial naturalization, 48
Naturalization Act (1790), 4, 72
Nayeri, Dina, 105
Nee, Victor, 9
neoliberalism, 83, 105, 132
Ngai, Mae M., 13, 17, 20, 116
Nguyen, Viet Thanh, 97, 112–13, 114
Nicholls, Walter J., 84, 117–18
Nieves, Delores, 46
"Nisei Discover a Larger America,
 The," 79
*No Longer Interested in Convincing You of
 My Humanity* (Salgado), 125, 126
nonimmigrant, 11, 21, 114
No-No Boy (Okada), 84, 93–99, 111
Notes on Virginia (Jefferson), 56, 57

Oaxaca, 130–32, 137, 138
Oaxacalifornia, 190n72
Oaxcalifornix, 115, 116, 129–41 *passim*
Obama, Barack, 75, 82, 130; speech of at
 the Betty Ong Recreation Center,
 25, 115, 118–20, 121–22
Okada, John, 84, 93–94
Okamura, Sono, 79
Okubo, Miné, 79–80
Omi, Michael, 7, 17
"Open Letter to the People of Great
 Britain and Europe" (Du Bois), 66
Osuna, Juan José, 47–48, 48–49, 52–53;
 education of, 50; as a farm laborer, 50
*Other America, The: Poverty in the United
 States* (Harrington), 87

Pacific Standard Time: L.A./L.A., 130
Page Act (1875), 17, 18

AMERICAN CROSSROADS

Edited by Earl Lewis, George Lipsitz, George Sánchez, Dana Takagi, Laura Briggs, and Nikhil Pal Singh

Founded in 1893,
UNIVERSITY OF CALIFORNIA PRESS
publishes bold, progressive books and journals
on topics in the arts, humanities, social sciences,
and natural sciences—with a focus on social
justice issues—that inspire thought and action
among readers worldwide.

The UC PRESS FOUNDATION
raises funds to uphold the press's vital role
as an independent, nonprofit publisher, and
receives philanthropic support from a wide
range of individuals and institutions—and from
committed readers like you. To learn more, visit
ucpress.edu/supportus.

www.ingramcontent.com/pod-product-compliance
Lightning Source LLC
Chambersburg PA
CBHW020852270326
41928CB00006B/666